DETAIL FROM VERMEER'S *THE ARTIST IN HIS STUDIO*, KUNSTHISTORISCHES MUSEUM, VIENNA.

THE STORY BEHIND THE PAINTING

Produced by the editors of LOOK

Text by LEO ROSTEN

Art direction by ALLEN HURLBURT

Published by COWLES MAGAZINES & BROADCASTING, INC., New York

Book trade distribution by DOUBLEDAY & COMPANY, INC.,
Garden City, New York

LOOK MAGAZINE

EDITOR: GARDNER COWLES

EDITORIAL DIRECTOR: DANIEL D. MICH

GENERAL MANAGER: MARVIN C. WHATMORE

Detail from St. Luke
*by Rogier van der Weyden, in the
Pinakothek Museum, Munich*

CONTENTS

INTRODUCTION

THE SERIES BEGAN in the spring of 1956. It began with an idea: to tell revealing and dramatic stories about some of the world's great painters—and to link each artist to a particular picture he had painted.

We did not, please note, set out to tell the story of a painter's life, however colorful or tragic or glorious. We did not intend to offer readers a course in art appreciation, nor even to uplift them with elegies to Art. We simply wanted to tell a series of significant stories about those remarkably gifted men we call artists and about specific pictures they had created. We wanted to find answers to questions that, strangely enough, are ordinarily not asked about painting: Why did the painter paint *this* picture? Who or what was the subject—this girl or prince, landscape or pageant? What love or longing, accident or design, led this artist to paint this subject? What impulse or conflict, what urge toward what catharsis, possessed him while painting — and perforce shaped a picture, with or without his intention? What technical devices did he use, or adapt, or invent—in the effort to say what?

We did not think that there was anything particularly novel about such questions. They are, after all, the kind of questions journalists customarily address to their subjects: Who? When? Where? Why? How? These are questions no less relevant to painters than to politicians or heroes or knaves. After all, an artist, however hallowed by distance or exalted by fame, lived as other men do—in a given time and place. A painter wants, tries, succeeds, fails; he fears, believes, doubts. He is governed by pride or avarice, ambition or contempt for fame. His work, no less than his life, lies at the mercy of prevailing taste and styles and taboos. He is acclaimed or ignored with that unawareness of enduring merit that is the crowning deficiency of contemporary judgments. He is always a child of history, and sometimes a pawn of politics.

In all these respects, an artist is like other men — perhaps more sensitive, certainly more vulnerable. But he is different in one respect, and that one marks him a member of a special species: He has been endowed with that rare gift of the gods called talent. To some, like Fra Angelico, this was a blessing; to others, like Cézanne or Modigliani, it was a curse; but to every artist who ever lived—whether painter or poet, musician or sculptor—his talent set him apart from his fellows.

The artist is driven by the demon of his talent—always, incessantly, often beyond his capacity to understand, much less control. He is driven by the need to express that talent and, through it, to express himself. He is enslaved by the compulsion to communicate, to say something, to make a personal statement, to share his feelings, his insight, his visions, his sense of revelation. Above all, he is beholden to the necessity of *creating* something (it may be beautiful, it may be horrifying), something that did not exist before. He can create it only out of his own inner and insistent universe. . . .

So we set out to find stories about painters. Each story, we resolved, must reveal a man—not the myth or the legend or the time-encrusted simulacrum. Each story should pin down his motivation, illuminate his problems, identify that peculiar slant or stance or skill that made him unique. We wanted to make each painter "come to life," so that a reader might understand what an artist *is*, how he thinks, how he works, what lures him on, what gratifies him, what thwarts him, what lifts him to divinity or drives him to destruction.

We were determined to avoid the technical jargon in which so much writing about art, alas, is imbedded and through which so much of it, alas, becomes pompous and pretentious. We resolved never to inflate a man or a picture beyond the dimension of good sense. We would strive at all costs to be clear and direct; purple verbiage is a poor substitute for substance.

All we wanted for each artist, to begin with, was a story. How simple. A story. But a story is an extraordinarily complex creature. A story is not an episode; it is not an anecdote; it is not an arresting but unresolved

4

REMBRANDT AND HIS WIFE SASKIA, PIERPONT MORGAN LIBRARY, NEW YORK

The capacity of an artist to capture the nuances of character,
of temperament and mood and human suffering, was never better
realized than by Rembrandt—who communicated his own
unfailing compassion in whatever medium he used. Compare
this etching of himself with the remarkable self-portrait on page 19.

CHILD IN WHITE, SOLOMON R. GUGGENHEIM MUSEUM, N. Y.

This evocative treatment of the human form suggests the imagination and economy with which crayon and chalk can be used. Child in White was drawn by Georges Pierre-Seurat as a study for A Sunday Afternoon at the Grand Jatte.

slice of experience. A story can be structured only within its own unyielding architecture. A story is a narrative. It must have a point, a purpose, an interior momentum. A story, as the cliché has it, must have a beginning, a middle and an end. We soon found that good stories about many painters are not so easy to find.

We discarded some stories because they have been told so often that they have become hackneyed, and we did not want stories about paintings that have been reproduced so often that they have lost the priceless attribute of freshness. Where we simply could not avoid well-known paintings (with Botticelli, for instance, or El Greco), we tried to find something fresh—a fact, a clue, even a conjecture—from which a fresh tale might grow.

One final limitation bedeviled us beyond measure; we were committed to a striking layout design that lim-

ited each story to a maximum of 780 words. And 780 words, dear reader, is $2\frac{1}{3}$ pages of double-spaced typing. . . . It was astonishing how much we learned about how much can be said in how little space.

Our researchers launched into their explorations. Now "research" is a dull word and conveys the dreariest of overtones. But the research for *The Story Behind the Painting* took us down strange and surprising avenues. We seized upon a lead wherever we could find it: in a biography or an art book, a history or art journal or monograph; in an artist's notebooks or letters; by writing to scholars, historians, collectors, museum curators; by-plaguing the experts and ravaging the superb reference libraries with which New York is favored. We delved into French, Italian, German, Spanish sources. We read and read, and once we found a lead, pursued it—by telephone, by interview, by letters, through our representatives in Paris and California, by cables to London, Rome, Vienna, Tokyo, São Paulo, Istanbul, Madrid.

Unexpected windfalls came to us. A LOOK photographer on assignment in Russia spent his spare time photographing paintings in the Hermitage Museum in Leningrad; among the hundreds of color transparencies he brought back was one of a Chagall we had seen in no book. We had not seen it because it had never been photographed. Through our Paris representative, we communicated with Chagall and showed him a photograph of the painting in Leningrad. Reminiscence poured out of him; he had painted the picture (page 125), which he had all but forgotten, 43 years earlier.

Behind a bedroom door in the house in Farmington, Conn., now called the Hill-Stead Museum, we found the exquisite pastel you will find on page 65. We traced a long-neglected Velázquez to a castle in Salisbury, and obtained permission from the Earl of Radnor to photograph it (page 117).

We ran down a magnificent Rouault, which was for sale in a small gallery, five blocks from our offices. It had never been reproduced; and the day before Rouault died,

it happened, he answered our inquiries, through his daughter, and told us that this painting (page 37) was one of 40 he had made of the identical subject, and one he considered perhaps the loveliest.

A woman told our Art Director of certain paintings she had seen in Picasso's villa in the south of France, pictures that had never been seen by any but Picasso's friends. She was about to visit her friend, Jacqueline Roque (now Mme. Picasso), in the Picasso villa. We drew up a list of questions for her to ask both Picasso and Jacqueline—all of which ended with the story about the painting that hangs in her bedroom (page 51).

We interviewed Matisse's son Pierre, the noted art dealer, who remembered a childhood episode that had taken place just before Matisse painted a certain picture some 52 years before. We found the painting (page 85) in a private collection in Ascona, Switzerland.

We heard that Gabrielle Renard, the servant-governess who had been Renoir's favorite model for 21 years, was still alive; she was now Gabrielle Slade, was over 80 years old and lived in California, not far from Renoir's son Jean, the distinguished movie director. You will find her and Jean Renoir on page 11—and her portrait on page 69.

All these are moderns, of course. What of the painters long since dead? What of the men who painted very few pictures? What of those about whom very little is known at all? What story could we possibly unearth about the immortal but shadowy Vermeer; the fantastic but virtually unknown Hieronymus Bosch; the father of painting as we know it today, Giotto; the wonderful Persian master, Bihzad? What tale could we possibly tell about Leonardo, Michelangelo, Bruegel, Titian, Holbein, Rubens, Goya that had not been told a hundred times?

In the case of Leonardo, our investigation assumed the quality of a detective story—some 450 years after the event. We did not want to reproduce the *Mona Lisa*, which has surely been seen enough, or retell one or another of the insubstantial stories about why La Gioconda was smiling that way. (A physician interested in art made many front pages by announcing that Mona Lisa's smile was clearly the expression of a woman who was pregnant.) We came upon a clue in a most roundabout fashion. After looking once more at the pictures Leonardo painted, we were struck by a curious thought: the Mona Lisa smile, that subtle, evanescent, dreamlike smile, is not limited to the *Mona Lisa*. It appears long *before* he painted La Gioconda. It appears on the faces of his angels and cherubs, madonnas and holy infants. It appears on the lips of men (John the Baptist) no less than women. Sigmund Freud, in an incomparable psychological reconstruction, traced the smile back to Leonardo's memory of the mother he adored, and from whose spell he never freed himself after he was taken away from her (he was illegitimate) at the age of five. But was there more than this? Was there perhaps a story in some model of Leonardo's other than La Gioconda?

One day, a researcher came in with the text of the fragment of a letter that had been found among Leonardo's effects after his death in 1519. The letter was addressed to "*Magnifica Cecilia*" and contained the phrase "*amantissima mia diva*" (my beloved goddess). This "Cecilia" was one Cecilia Gallerani, an Italian girl whose portrait Leonardo had painted when she was only 17. But that portrait, we learned to our chagrin, has long since disappeared. Leonardo painted Cecilia Gallerani several times, the historical data showed—or suggested. The face of Cecilia recurs in his work, certain authorities said—or implied. She was the model for the angel in *The Madonna of the Rocks*.

The intensely personal way in which an artist "sees" a scene
is illustrated by the sketches on these two pages.
Cézanne sought to imprison the essence of Quais de la Seine *(left)*
in watercolors, which demonstrate his unique use
of small blocks and planes of color. The meticulous pen-and-ink
drawing below, called Tree Man, *is Hieronymus Bosch's*
fascinating sketch for the much more fully
elaborated detail in the extraordinary painting on page 45.

TREE MAN, ALBERTINA MUSEUM, VIENNA

Botticelli's archaic grace and flowing line pervade Abundance, *the pen and wash above. The same unmistakable touch sings out to us, in Botticelli's strange, cool colors, in his masterwork on page 89. Renoir's tender impression (opposite) of his maid and son,* Gabrielle and Jean, *offers a striking contrast to Botticelli, in mood, technique and purpose. Compare this crayon sketch with Renoir's oil of the same woman,* Gabrielle With Roses, *on page 69.*

Who was this Cecilia Gallerani? What was Leonardo's relationship to her? We launched an investigation much as though we were a Missing Persons Bureau trying to learn anything we could about a girl who had vanished—450 years or so ago.

We learned that Cecilia Gallerani had been the mistress of Ludovico Sforza. We learned that she was a poetess in her own right and that her beauty was extolled by contemporary Italian poets. (We ran down her poems and the poems about her.) And in reading a weighty tome about the Renaissance, we ran across a footnote that electrified us. The footnote contained an excerpt from a book, written early in the 16th century by one Agnolo Firenzuola—a book entitled *A Treatise on the Feminine Graces.* The excerpt was nothing less than a description of how a well-brought-up young lady, seeking to enhance her attractiveness to young men of breeding, might improve her coquetry. . . . The reader may see for himself how our story (page 32) ended. To us, at least, it offers a new explanation for the Mona Lisa smile that has tantalized men down the centuries.

BUT AS WE LOOK BACK UPON this series, we find our thoughts revolving not around the romance or drama with which the lives of many of our painters were charged; we find ourselves marveling once more over the limitless range of that beauty which is captured on canvas or paper or wood, with pigments or pencil or chalks. We find ourselves impressed by the endless richness of art, the miraculous singularity of an artist's vision, the astounding variety of ways there are of seeing the world around us. Most of all, we marvel at what painters have created out of their own unconscious universe—to make it a new part of ours.

The simple but startling fact is that painters *see* differently from the rest of us. This process we call "seeing," which we all take for granted, is unbelievably complicated. For we see not what is "there," but what we have been taught to see there. We see not what is "real" (a phantom seems real enough to one terrified by it), but what we have been conditioned to think of as "real." The human eye is a lens, to be sure, but that lens only receives images; and these images are referred back to the brain, where they must be patterned and given meaning. And meaning is a convention that stems from our education and our expectations.

Constable once said that seeing is itself an art and that even seeing nature is an art that must be learned. Degas, that irascible genius, declared: "Drawing is not what one sees, but what others have to be made to see."

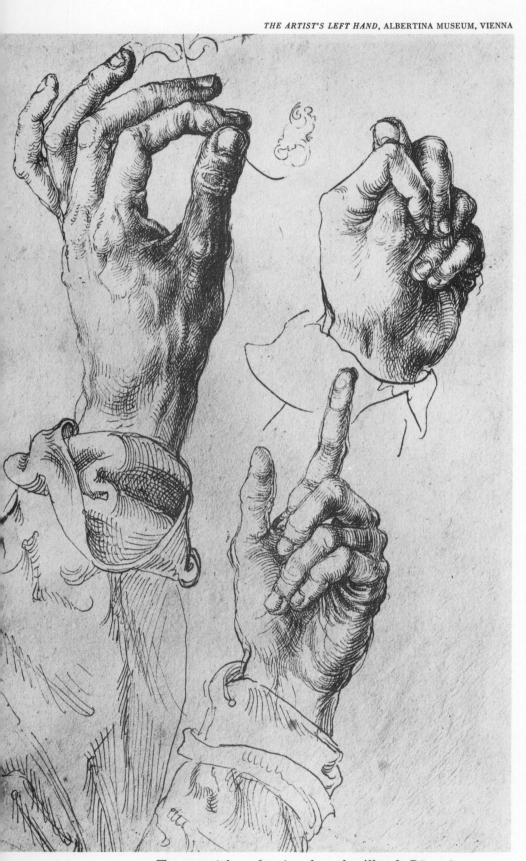

The masterful pen drawing above, by Albrecht Dürer, is entitled The Artist's Left Hand. *The very "personality" of these hands, compared to those drawn by van Gogh (opposite page), offers a striking insight into the differences in temperament between two great artists.*

Does this idea seem preposterous? The brilliant art authority E. H. Gombrich reminds us that ancient artists used to draw eyelashes on the lower lids of horses. There are no lashes on the lower eyelids of horses. Still, the artists "saw" them there—because they were so accustomed to seeing lashes on men's lower lids. A great painter, as skillful a recorder of "reality" as you could ask for, made certain mistakes in drawing the heart, from cadavers opened for examination, because he had been reading Galen—and Galen was wrong. Even so impeccable a draftsman as Dürer made certain errors in drawing the human eye because his own vision was skewed by the fallacious stereotypes of his day.

Chinese artists were instructed to record not what they "see"—but what they feel about what they see. They use a brush as Western poets use words—to express emotions, not record literal images. When the Impressionists began to use color to express feelings, when they put the green of envy or the red of anger into the human face, when they put color into shadows (as children have been doing for centuries), they shocked eyes that had, since the Renaissance, been taught to see a different constellation of visibilities.

What we call "reality" is not much more than those perceptions that pass through the filters of our conditioning. And reality changes for us as we free ourselves from the crippling restrictions of the preconceived. We all live, in part, within the conceptual prisons of the past. "We see things as *we* are, not as *they* are." It is the great, revolutionary role of the artist to liberate us from the straitjackets of the too-familiar.

Does all this seem unreal to you? Do you believe in a realness, an absoluteness of things which are visible to anyone and everyone alike? Perhaps you do. Perhaps you are thinking, "All this is intellectual quibbling. Reality is simple enough. Just set a camera down and press the trigger—and *that* will record exactly what is 'there'!"

Well, let us test that out. Suppose you take a camera and set out to photograph, say, a house. Any house. You want "just a picture of a house." Now consider the decisions you will have to make — consciously or unconsciously, intuitively or by default. From what distance

The strength, even the poverty, of peasants is conveyed by van Gogh's blunt, powerfully drawn crayon Study of Three Hands With Fork, *a sketch for his painting,* The Potato Eaters.

STUDY OF THREE HANDS WITH FORK, STEDELIJK MUSEUM, AMSTERDAM

shall the house be photographed? From far away? From near? From the "middle"? Then at what angle? How high? How low? All these depend, of course, on what kind of picture you want—indeed, what kind of house you want to portray. And that depends on what impression or mood or atmosphere or detail you want to present. If the house is seen from a low angle, that will emphasize its height. If seen from a hill looking down, it will look different. "Just straight on," you say? Very well. Is the sycamore to the left to be included? The azalea on the right? The ridge beyond? Will you include the rail fence there, the rock here, the curving path? You will soon notice that each position, each view changes the total field of vision—and each contains its own cluster of characteristics.

Don't get impatient; this is but the beginning. Consider the light now. Shall it come from the left, the right, overhead, from behind? And how much light do you want? You can choose the time of day in which to shoot; you can use reflectors to diminish shadows, or floodlights, flashbulbs to light up what is dark or highlight a feature you want to stress. You can also manipulate light by varying the opening of your lens; you can even create an il-

lusion of dawn or dusk. And by changing the opening of your lens, you create new *contexts*, because groups of details can be made to come into focus, or be thrown out of it.

"Enough!" you cry? But you have much more to decide. Do you want to make this house crisp-clear in all its details—shutters, windows, shingles? That will also make sharp a mass of unpretty and distracting objects around. Do you want the scene made pastoral, scary, sad? Shall the sky be ignored or brought forward? A filter can make the clouds leap toward the eye. Even moonlight need not be the prerogative of the moon alone; infrared film can transform the sun into its sister.

And by the way, what kind of film will you use? "Just black and white!" you protest? Ah, but there is no such thing as "just black and white." Different films give different effects, different modulations of light and shade, different hues of gray, different textures and grains.

Well, suppose you take your picture, whatever it is. You are in the darkroom now. You have your negative. You are about to print your picture. And now a new army of possibilities marches before you. You can print any *part* of the picture. You can "crop" out the top, the bot-

HEAD OF THE VIRGIN, METROPOLITAN MUSEUM OF ART, NEW YORK, PURCHASE, 1951, DICK FUND

tom, either side or both. You can magnify a detail to achieve a quite unexpected effect. (You might notice how the details of a painting take on new meaning when they are isolated from the whole, as has been done with some pictures in the pages which follow.) You can darken or lighten the overall light. You can even manipulate the very lines and planes, to get calculated distortions, by tilting your paper. You can convert the projection lens into a sort of microscope or telescope. You can soften your original focus. You can take that innocuous house you recorded on film and endow it with shadows or highlights, make it saccharine or sinister. You can change the visual impact by selecting different papers on which to print your image. You can—but perhaps this is enough.

Now everything we have said about photographing a house is, of course, equally (or more) true of photographing a face or a flower, a landscape or a still life; recording a skyline, a boy biting into a hot dog, a girl blowing on a trumpet; trying to capture raindrops on a rose, or gulls in the air, or ants on a blade of grass.

No two photographers take precisely the same picture of the identical subject—even if they try to, because there are different emotions and mentalities behind the different lenses. The difference between a photograph taken by an amateur and one taken by a master is as great as the difference between a jingle and a sonata.

If what we have said here is true of photography, consider now how much more powerfully it applies to painting. Any camera, lens, film or filter contains certain mechanical limitations—none of which confines the

painter. An artist can draw what no camera can photograph. No camera can record the images in a man's mind. No camera contains the flexibility and resourcefulness of the human hand, to say nothing of the immense imaginative possibilities of the human brain.

It is the multitudinous differences—in vision and visual sensitivity; in the sensing of arrangement and accident; in the apprehension of line, light, color, form, mass, space; in recognizing unsuspected attributes of beauty, power, grace; in opening new windows of perception to surprise—it is the wonderful variations in these, to say nothing of differences in sheer skill, which distinguish the creative artist from his fellow men.

As Leonardo put it: "If the painter wishes to see beauties to fall in love with, it is in his power to bring them forth, and if he wants to see monstrous things that frighten or are foolish or laughable or indeed to be pitied, he is their Lord and God."

THE ARTIST, we have said, frees us from the bonds of tradition. He gives us new eyes, eyes with which we can see "reality" anew and, more importantly, with which we can see aspects of reality we did not dream were there. They were not, in fact, there—until he created them out of his vision, his active transformation of reality, his creating something to be seen for the first time. A Japanese master was once asked, "What is the most difficult part of a picture?" He answered, "The part that is to be left out."

We see a hillside or a bowl of fruit differently from

CHU TA (c. 1625-1705), *KINGFISHER AND LOTUS*, LEAF
FROM ALBUM. FREER GALLERY OF ART, WASHINGTON

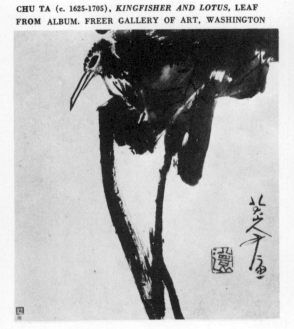

An artist breaks away from the literal through the singularity of his vision.
The bold, black blot on the left becomes a bird and a leaf and a stem after our mind
organizes the surprise that our eyes first experience. The Chinese artist
Chu Ta created this "abstract" impression over 250 years ago. To the right is
Miró's chalk-drawing arrangement of symbols into which, like his subterranean
fantasy on page 111, we may read our own meanings or memories.

the way our ancestors did, because Cézanne showed us how they look to him, and in doing so taught us a wholly new way of seeing them. We see a meadow, a cathedral, a river in cascades of light and color that our predecessors did not perceive because Monet liberated our eyes, not theirs. Each artist imparts his vision—to alter ours.

Was ever a woman's face as mysterious, as cool and lovely, as Botticelli painted it (page 87)?

Where, in any garden on earth, are there flowers so close to visual music as those from Redon's hand and heart (page 101)?

Was the stamp of psychotic doom ever seen with as terrible clarity as van Gogh put into his last, tragic self-portrait (page 131)?

Is deformity ever as final and as harsh as that which Bruegel assigned his *The Beggars* (page 59)?

Can the terror of wind and sea in storm be communicated with more power and subtlety than Turner achieved through his restless whirl of light and line (page 63)?

Is old age as bleak and desolate as Hals portrayed

it (page 97)? Or as mellow as Rembrandt transformed it into (page 19)?

Where, outside paradise itself, are water and light and lilies on a pond caught in such a miracle of iridescence as Monet wrought on canvas (pages 23-25)?

We have all been taught, through the eyes and minds and artistry of such men, to extract meaning from the confusing, unstructured plenitude of objects, details, impressions, distractions that clamor all around us. We have all been led to find beauty where previous generations did not dream it lay concealed—or uncreated. There is a penetrating truth, no less than mischief, in Oscar Wilde's aphorism: "Nature imitates art."

The moral to all this is perhaps best found, as it so often is, in an anecdote. A woman who "knew what she liked in art" was visiting Matisse's studio. She studied the painting on his easel for a while, then said, "You have made the arm on that girl much too *long*." To which Matisse made this shattering rejoinder: "Madame, that is not a girl; it is a picture."

—LEO ROSTEN

COLOR PLATES

Rembrandt

THE LAUGHING PHILOSOPHER

HE WAS 62 YEARS old now. His hand and brain had poured out an astonishing torrent of creation—600 paintings, 2,000 drawings, 200 etchings. He was 62 — and alone. Death had taken those whom he loved: his mother; his wife Saskia; their first three children, who had died in infancy; his beloved Hendrickje, who had borne him a daughter out of wedlock and had been excommunicated by the Church; and now his son Titus, recently married and about to become a father himself.

He was living in a poor quarter of Amsterdam, where the faces of the common people—the wise, sad, foolish, proud, world-weary faces—never ceased to intrigue him. His wealth, his popularity, his immense success were behind him. The glossier style of his students, or the flattering elegances of a Van Dyck, were now in favor with the rich and the wellborn.

He had long since been declared bankrupt, his great house sold, all his possessions auctioned. He had lost to creditors the remarkable collection on which he had spent so much with such extravagance: paintings (including two Raphaels), sculpture (including a bust by Michelangelo), oils, drawings, woodcuts, engravings by Italian and Flemish masters, Greek statues, Roman busts and a fantastic armory — helmets, shields, turbans, swords, velvets, gorgets, maces which he used to costume the figures he loved to envelop in a golden glow of pageantry.

He had painted himself more than a hundred times, in different moods and moments, in a lifelong search for "the soul," the inner self behind the visible features. He was driven by a passion to find insight with brushes, to reveal character on canvas.

And now, in the year 1668, with an intensity of concentration which had made him turn princes away from his door while working, Rembrandt Harmens van Rijn set forth once more to explore the human mystery. The subject he chose was well known to artists: Heraclitus and Democritus, "the Dark Philosopher" and "the Laughing Philosopher." Heraclitus he fixed in a half-profile, losing him in shadows at the left. Democritus, who maintained 400 years before Christ that reality consists of atoms and void, and (anticipating modern physics) that matter is indestructible—Democritus would be Rembrandt himself. For the Laughing Philosopher had preached what Rembrandt now knew: that the greatest good is tranquility.

He put the pigment on the canvas thickly, with his thumb or palette knife, in juxtaposed gobs of color, building up layer upon layer, scratching through the paint with his nail or brush handle to let the color beneath break through, covering pigment with glaze and scratching through and putting pigment on again, creating images the critics would deride as "wild smears" — until, 200 years later, some French geniuses would smash the bounds of the literal, just as he dared to do, to bring the breathtaking new visions of Impressionism into the universe of art.

"Don't stand close to the picture," Rembrandt warned visitors to his studio. "The smell of the colors will bother you." This was nonsense, and a ruse: He wanted his painting to be viewed from a distance — so that the eye of the beholder would fuse the separated flashes of color, so that the viewer's mind would participate in the making of the magic illusion, so that light and shadow could move and float and play out their drama. He lured the eye into the canvas, seizing its attention with highlights, teasing it with adumbrations of the half-caught, the half-hidden, the half-revealed. He used color with unparalleled richness and splendor. He used shadows like music, somehow enlisting senses other than the visual. He used light like the blast of a trumpet.

No painter before had so directly confronted emotion, or entered so deeply into it. No artist captures *our* feelings with such immediacy. In this haunting self-portrait, the roughhewn features of this untidy, arrogant, introspective man move out to us in an expression that symbolizes triumph over suffering.

One year later, Rembrandt was dead.

Self-Portrait, a masterpiece of characterization (32½" x 25"), today hangs in the Wallraf-Richartz Museum in Cologne.

Fra Filippo Lippi

THE MONK AND THE MADONNA

FIVE HUNDRED YEARS ago, in 1456, Fra Filippo Lippi, a friar of the Carmelite Order, was appointed chaplain to the good nuns of the convent of Santa Margherita in the little town of Prato, Italy. This Fra "Lippo" Lippi was a vigorous, good-humored man of 50 who lived with gusto and painted like an angel. He was often in trouble, generally in debt, but always managed to get absolved. He had been an abbot in Florence, where, accused of fraud and forgery, he was tortured on the rack and "confessed." Now, appointed the nuns' chaplain, he moved into a little house near the convent and attended to his duties.

Fra Lippo Lippi was already famed as the first Italian to use real men and women in paintings of the Virgin and the Child and the Holy Family. He painted the religious mysteries without awe or abnegation, with a rare sense of intimacy, as if less concerned with theology than art. His astonishing skill had won him the patronage and the friendship of the great Cosimo de'Medici.

The abbess of Santa Margherita asked Lippi to paint a Madonna for the altar of the chapel. Lippi suggested that one of the sisters pose for him —particularly a lovely, slender, pensive girl he had noticed in the convent. What better model for the Virgin than this chaste and exquisite child? The abbess consented, and Sister Lucrezia, a Florentine from the scholarly Buti family, was permitted to put off her habit and pose in worldly clothes.

Fra Lippo Lippi painted his Madonna for the altar, then painted another—with Sister Lucrezia his model again. And this, alas, was not simply because of the delicacy of her features or the purity of her expression. The fact was that the monk and his Madonna were madly in love.

On May 1, 1456, during a holy procession for the Madonna of the Cintola, Sister Lucrezia broke away from the other nuns, ran to Lippi's house and refused to return to the convent.

The enchanting *Madonna and Child With Two Angels,* the third picture for which Lucrezia Buti posed, was painted in tempera for Giovanni de'Medici—with Lippi's marvelous delicacy and sweetness, his subdued colors and fairy-tale mood. The light falls not on the canvas but seems to emanate from the people themselves. The gentle contours, the draped folds are rendered so beautifully that they were copied by other painters. The detail, so harmonious, so precise, brought home to the Renaissance that things could be included in religious paintings simply because they were pleasing to the eye; that the theological could be fused to the human; that piety could respect the secular.

In 1458, Lucrezia returned to the convent in contrition and renewed her vows. But three years later, she fled once more—to live with Lippi. And now a frightful scandal broke out. An anonymous letter revealed that the girl had long since presented a son to Fra Lippo Lippi—probably the very Infant in this picture. It was said that Lippi had first seen Lucrezia when she was only 16, and had gotten himself appointed chaplain to the convent because he wanted to be near her. Prato was in an uproar. The turmoil reached Florence and echoed in Rome.

Lippi appealed to his great friend and protector, Cosimo de'Medici, who talked to the Pope. And, in a special decree, Pope Pius II released the friar and the convent girl from their vows. They were married. And Lippi painted Lucrezia Buti as his Madonna again and again, till the day he died. He was buried in a tomb Lorenzo the Magnificent erected for him, with this epitaph: "So rare was his grace in painting that scarcely any other artist comes near him in our time."

They all achieved immortality: the friar, for a genius greater than his sins; the nun, as the first Madonna to look like a maiden; the child, as Filippino Lippi, an artist ranked among the masters in his own right—and a second child of the monk and his Madonna, a daughter named Alessandra, as the haunting and unforgettable Goddess of Love in Botticelli's masterpiece, *Birth of Venus.*

Madonna and Child With Two Angels *b
Fra Filippo Lippi (35½" x 24"). This exquisit
tempera hangs in the Uffizi Gallery, Florenc*

Monet

THE MIRACLE OF THE WATER LILIES

NO ONE HAD EVER heard of a studio 70 feet long, 40 feet wide, 50 feet high. But he built it. Then he ordered 50 canvases, each 7 by 15 feet, and constructed immense easels, on rollers—so he could wheel his work around under huge skylights to get exactly the light he desired. In 1916, aged 76, his eyesight failing, Claude Monet started the most ambitious project of his life.

Some 26 years earlier, Monet had diverted a stream to make a large pond in his garden at Giverny, near Paris. He spanned the water with a wooden bridge from which, hours on end, he studied the reflection of sky and clouds—at different hours and seasons, on bright or overcast days, when the wind was still or scudded the clouds. "I have undertaken things impossible to execute," he wrote. "One can go crazy trying to paint them." A month later: "It is endless torture. I have destroyed the little I was able to do. . . ."

He began painting the water lilies in his pond, crying, "They have become an obsession with me. It is beyond the strength of an old man. I have destroyed many [canvases], and begin all over. . . ." In 1914, he decided to paint the entire lily pond, in 50, perhaps more, gigantic pictures—and it was for this that he built the vast studio. The day after the Armistice in 1918, Premier Georges Clemenceau came to this studio. At his urging, Monet offered *Les Nymphéas* (water lilies) to France, to commemorate victory—if they would be housed in a building of his design, and if he were allowed to revise them as often as he wanted.

For four more years, Monet kept changing his water lilies. He often wanted to burn them; only Clemenceau's eloquence prevented it. In 1922, after an eye operation, he resumed the endless repainting. And at the age of 82, he took Clemenceau by the hand and led him into his studio. "You were afraid I would spoil them, weren't you?" he asked. "So was I. But somehow, in spite of the mist over my eyes, I saw—so clearly—what needed to be done. Now, look." Clemenceau was staggered by the loveliness of what he beheld.

Les Nymphéas crowned a career of such frustration as few men could have endured. For years, after a few early successes, the salons of Paris had refused to show Monet's pictures. The critics called him a charlatan and a madman. His paintings were seized and sold in lots of 50 to pay off his debts—at 30 francs a lot! Renoir brought him bread. Once, Monet tried to commit suicide.

By 1874, he was the leader of one of the greatest revolutions in the history of art—Impressionism, a name coined by a mocking critic from Monet's painting *Impression: Sunrise*. An exhibition of the work of Monet, Renoir, Degas and Berthe Morisot was denounced as "outrageous . . . vulgar . . . disgraceful." Spectators openly laughed or jeered. The heartsick Monet even overheard the celebrated Daumier, standing before one of his paintings, ask the owner of the gallery, "Who is forcing you to handle such horrors?"

What provoked such virulence? It was Monet's rendition of the shimmering, formless play of light itself, light that diffused outlines and entirely altered the appearance of objects from what we "know" them to be. He saw no absolute colors in nature. He did not mix a green, say, but set down streaks of pure blue and yellow—to let the viewer's eye fuse them into greenness. He wrapped railroads, cathedrals, haystacks in a luminous mist. Seen close up, his pictures were a preposterous hodgepodge of colored dabs and dashes; viewed from a distance, they trembled with life and iridescence.

He painted the same scene a hundred times, under ever-changing light, even in wind and rain—when he wore high boots and a hooded slicker, and weighted his easel down with stones. The wind sometimes tore the palette out of his hands. He was so jealous of time that he made the local barber come to the open fields to cut his hair while he painted. He was so intrigued with prismatic hues that one day, "at the deathbed of a woman I dearly loved, I looked at her temples and said, 'There is a kind of violet there. What is there in it of blue? of red? of yellow?' "

He died in 1926, aged 86. Some 20 immense *Nymphéas*, reaching almost 300 feet in length, were placed in the Musée de l'Orangerie in Paris. They are a monument to a genius so stubborn, yet so lyrical, that it could transform a pond into a timeless mirage.

Monet painted 50 to 100 Nymphéas.
This detail is from the one in
the collection of the Department of Fine Arts,
Carnegie Institute, Pittsburgh

*These magnificent water lilies were painted by Monet
sometime between 1920 and 1926. They are part of the
immense series, Les Nymphéas, gigantic pictures
of Monet's pond in his garden at Giverny, near
Paris. The Orangerie Museum, in Paris, houses some
20 great canvases, which reach almost 300 feet in length.
The scene above is 79″ high and 236″ long. It was in the
Walter P. Chrysler Collection in New York when we
photographed it; today, it adorns the Department of
Fine Arts of the Carnegie Institute, Pittsburgh.*

Clouet

LADY OF THE ICE-COLD BATH

THE LADY whom nature so admirably endowed is taking a bath—at least she is seated in the kind of tub French noblewomen used in the 16th century. She is Diane de Poitiers, Duchess of Valentinois, for 25 years the mistress of King Henry II. The children are not hers, but (it is believed) the sons of Henry and Catherine de'Medici. The boy became Francis II; the baby, Charles IX. The *ménage à trois* that existed between Diane and the King and Catherine de'Medici ranks among the more novel libidinal arrangements in history.

François Clouet, the court painter, produced this crisp portrait around 1550. Diane was then 51. She attributed her beauty to her habit of rising at 6 o'clock each morning to take an ice-cold bath; she followed this arctic rite with a furious three-hour ride on horseback before breakfast. She never used makeup and always braided her hair. She was tall, graceful, vivacious, and the historian Brantôme observed: "She always displayed her beautiful bosom; she was not one of those widow-hypocrites and homebodies who bury themselves with the dead."

At 15, Diane de Poitiers married Louis de Brézé, the Grand Seneschal of Normandy, to whom she bore two daughters. Her husband died in 1531, and she forever after wore black and white—in formal, if somewhat nominal mourning. At 35, she seduced (or vice versa) the 15-year-old Duke of Orleans (son of Francis I), who then married the 14-year-old Catherine de'Medici.

Diane knew where her future and her fortune lay. She remained Orleans' faithful paramour, virtually adopted the Medici girl and acted as her confidante and protector at court. For ten years, the union of Orleans and Catherine remained unblessed by progeny. For ten years, Diane urged Catherine to keep trying. Confidence bore fruit, and Catherine bore children—ten in all, of whom seven survived. To them, Diane de Poitiers became a most affectionate grandmother.

In 1547, Orleans came to the throne as Henry II. Diane remained his precious doxy. He showered her with gifts—cash, the Duchy of Valentinois and the fabulous castle of Chenonceaux. One day, Henry gave her the crown jewels. Another day, in a gesture unmatched by even the more exuberant monarchs, he endowed her with all of the vacant land in France. It came to a tidy fourth of the total realm.

Not even court gossips hinted at the shadow of a feud between the Queen and Diane de Poitiers. This is all the more remarkable if we remember that Diane eclipsed the Queen in power and that Catherine was a ruthless, superstitious woman who engineered the infamous St. Bartholomew's Day Massacre, hearkened to the advice of astrologers and accepted the admonitions of horoscopes.

Henry, a foolish and pliant man, poured out his love to Diane with unflagging ardor, once writing: "I thank you humbly that you have sent me news of yourself. . . . I cannot live without you. . . . I beg you to remember the one who has always known only one God and one mistress."

Diane's love for Henry was fine and true, though garnished by a keen appreciation of francs, sous, jewels and real estate. She diverted taxes to her own coffers, sold public offices and even asked ransom in her own name from Spain for Spanish noblemen captured in battle by the French Army.

This talented, pious, ambitious and crafty woman died in 1566. Her will decreed that she be buried next to the husband who had preceded her into heavenly rest by 35 years. In 1795, Diane de Poitiers was exhumed. The bodies of two girls, about five and seven, were found in the coffin with her. They were said to be Henry's children.

If little has been said of the artist whose painting is here celebrated, it is because the painter is less interesting than the painted. François Clouet was the son of the master Jean Clouet, and replaced him as "*peintre du Rois*" in 1545. He signed himself Janet in honor of Jean. He was intelligent, successful, never married and, true to the elastic morality of his time, fathered at least two children.

Clouet's pictures are not lyrical. But they are superb for the impact of their drawing, the clarity of their light, the hard, bright luster of their finish, the flawless rendering of silk draperies, the exquisite treatment of fruit and flowers. He broke trail for the school of *genre* painters and put his mark on technique with a reach into depth so decisive that it could link the distant servant girl with her jug to the unperturbed and unforgettable Jezebel in the bath.

*Diane de Poitiers, by François Clouet (c. 1505-1572) is one of
the gems in the priceless Samuel H. Kress Collection in the National Gallery of
Art in Washington. (Oil on wood, 32″ x 36″.)*

Hokusai

"MAN MAD WITH DRAWING"

THE PATRIARCH RAPT IN WONDER before the waterfall of Lo-Shan (and kept from falling off the precipice by two boys delightfully entwined in his robe) is Ri Haku, a famous Chinese poet. The waterfall was itself celebrated in verse:

> The wind-blown snow speeds the waters—
> A great white rainbow in the dark.
> Can it be that the river of Heaven
>   has fallen from the sky
> Through banks of clouds?
> I raise my eyes in wonder, Oh
>   mighty force!
> How immortal the creation of the Gods!

The man who created this color print, Katsushika Hokusai, was crazy about waterfalls. He once devoted an entire book to *Waters in Their Thousand Aspects.* He was also crazy about people, costumes, gestures, flowers, birds, horses, grasses—anything and everything that caught his eye. He was a slave to the observable.

Proud, restless, cantankerous, Hokusai used 30 different names, inhabited 93 different houses, illustrated 437 separate volumes and enriched the art of Japan with no less than 30,000 pictures, drawings and sketches. He illustrated novels, poems, calendars, greeting cards, *kibyoshi* (comic books). Hokusai's woodcuts were printed in massive quantities to make him the favorite of tradesmen, workers and peasants; only the connoisseurs scorned both his talent and his prodigality.

Once the mighty Shogun held a competition, challenging artists to create a masterpiece before his eyes. Annoyed, Hokusai pulled a palace door from its hinges, demanded a rooster, dipped the claws of the rooster in red paint, set the rooster scuttling across the door, added a few marvelously free lines, then rose to name the painting: *The River Tatsuta in Autumn, with Maple Leaves Floating Downstream.* Another time, he used a broom and buckets of Chinese ink to draw a figure 50 feet high. And once he painted two flying sparrows—on a grain of rice.

Hokusai's delight in the life around him may seem natural to us, but we must remember that he was born in 1760, in Edo (now Tokyo), into a world in which art, like life itself, was straitjacketed by ancient and exacting conventions. The aesthetic ideal was calligraphy—line used with the utmost purity in the service of design, not meaning. Art was an exercise in the exquisite, a stylized extension of that love of ornamentation which led the Japanese to decorate anything they used. In such a world, Hokusai was a radical.

He depicted life as he saw it and without bowing to tradition. He drew the natural with directness, humor and a mania for the particular. He once complained, "I paint birds and insects so vividly it seems they could fly right off the paper. It is the engraver's fault they don't."

The turning point in his career came when, through some European sea captains, he saw some copperplate engravings by French and Dutch artists. He was astounded by the realism, the colors, the mastery of perspective. He began to use light and shade to model forms and features; he set the brilliant colors of the West for the first time against the muted hues of the Orient.

The prints of this "Man Mad With Drawing," as he sometimes signed himself, were so lightly valued that they were used as wrapping paper for Japanese exports. And it may have been in the tea shops of Paris that the French Impressionists—searching for new transformations of the literal—first saw the work of Hokusai. He became a near-cult to Manet, Degas, Toulouse-Lautrec, Gauguin, Van Gogh. Hokusai's obliterations of the unessential, his marvelous sketches of the unposed and the casual, broke trail for the fragmented moments of the candid camera. It is ironic that, influenced by the West, Hokusai in turn influenced Europe far more than the Orient—where he remained a towering but solitary figure.

In his epilogue to *A Hundred Views of Fuji,* this man, an apostate to the ancients, who saw the purpose of art as art itself, said: "I have been in love with painting ever since I was six. . . . I will really master the secrets of art at 90. When I reach 100, my work will be truly sublime. My final goal will be attained around the age of 110, when every line and dot will be life itself."

The man who could paint a waterfall with such superb boldness—as a striated column of blue-and-white—died at 89 (counted as 90 in Japan, where a child is considered one year old at birth). In his last years, he signed himself "Gakyo-rojin." It means "The Art-Crazy Old Man."

Hokusai created this color print around 1830, along with many others, for The Imagery of the Poets of China and Japan. *It is in the British Museum, London.*

Seurat

"A TECHNIQUE OF FATAL INTRICACY..."

NOTHING IN HIS LIFE was dramatic, nothing remarkable, nothing romantic. Night after night, lost to the world, he stubbornly dabbed thousands upon thousands of tiny particles of pigment on canvas, in clusters from which color and form strangely emerged—rarely using a conventional line or stroke.

He was accustomed to having his work rejected and, when exhibited, laughed at. What must have hurt him most were the sneers of painters he admired: Gauguin mocked his style, which became famed as "*Pointillism*," by calling him "the dot-and-carry-one" artist; and after he spent two years on his immense *Sunday Afternoon on the Isle of the Grand Jatte*, building its majestic rhythms out of almost a quarter of a million pindots of color, and offered it to the great 1886 exhibition of the Impressionists, men no less important than Monet, Sisley and Renoir withdrew—refusing to allow his painting to be hung in the same room with theirs.

So Georges-Pierre Seurat shunned human contact, working alone, speaking to almost no one, spurning even the few avant-garde painters who wanted to be his disciples. He took a studio in Montmartre and each night roamed the streets of Paris, intrigued by the nocturnal mood, the shifting mystery of artificial light, the street carnivals, the sidewalk jugglers and acrobats and musicians who traveled about in odd side shows that tickled the fancy of Parisians. In *La Parade* (opposite page), he strove to capture the melancholy radiance of things seen by gaslight, a fantasy half real, half dreamed. He froze these stiff and curious silhouettes into a grave tableau, like an Egyptian frieze; he set strange grays next to stranger violets, put orange halos around his blues, touched dusty rose with gold. His whole enigmatic procession— so odd, so stilted, so wistful and archaic—seems transfixed in a closed-in, closed-off world.

This remarkable painting was one of the first he undertook after reading the monograph of a scientist, Charles Henry, on the psychological effects of color. Seurat became obsessed by the idea that the secrets of painting could be reduced to scientific formulas; he delved into optics and chemistry; he devoured a treatise entitled *Harmony and Simultaneous Contrast of Colors* and adopted a line from Charles Blanc as his goal and his credo: "Color can be reduced to definite rules and can be taught, like music."

All around him, the Impressionists were seizing on "the spontaneous moment," making light sing, defying all that our eyes identify as real and true, ignoring verisimilitude, transforming the familiar by breaking it up into images of light and color in which outlines, forms, shapes disappear— until blended back, in the viewer's own eyes, into freshly seen impressions more vivid and lyrical than naturalistic art can offer.

All this Seurat admired and accepted, but he wanted to take another bold step; he wanted to restore form, weight, volume to the subjective and the impressionistic. He broke the smallest shadings of color into tiny galaxies from which varied nuances of tone would glow—and assume form. He wanted to recapture the real with the very instruments of technique which had fragmented and transformed the visible. It was obsessive; it was fantastic; but it was original.

He even wrote an elaborate "code" on painting technique: "Sadness of *tone* is achieved by the dominance of dark; sadness of *color*, by the dominance of cool colors; sadness of *line*, by downward direction. . . . Gaiety of tone is gained by the dominance of light; gaiety of color, by the dominance of warm hues; gaiety of line, by lines above the horizontal." He believed in the innate psychological effect of pure line and tried to formulate the differing impact of the vertical, the horizontal, the line placed high, the line dropped low.

As an art student, Seurat had dutifully studied and copied the masters: Raphael, Holbein, Ingres. For a while, he had even worked entirely in pencil or charcoal, seeking to wrest characterization and mood solely from the austere contrast of black and white. Then he discovered Delacroix—that brilliant

omantic who painted like a dramatist—and
plunged into a preoccupation with color that con-
umed the rest of his life.

When Seurat died, only 31 years old, he left
housands of exquisite drawings, scores of studies
n oil—but only six major paintings. Yet he suc-
eeded in achieving what is given to few men: an
xpression of his identity so distinctive that it
eems to owe nothing to either his predecessors or
is contemporaries.

"They pretend to see poetry in my work," he
nce said, "but they are wrong. I simply apply my
ystem." It was he, not "they," who was wrong.
'or the paradox of Seurat is that his elaborate
system" and intricate theories are dead; what
ves is the lovely, stately harmony of his art. It
as technique, not inspiration, which hobbled
is work. In Thomas Craven's incisive phrase, it
as "a technique of fatal intricacy."

*The extraordinary "dot-by-dot"
technique invented by Seurat may
be seen clearly in the ringmaster's face,
reproduced in its exact size
at left. Form and meaning emerge
when the painting is viewed
from a museum visitor's distance
(above). The haunting* La Parade
*(39½" x 59¼", 1888) is in
the Metropolitan Museum
of Art, bequest of
Stephen C. Clark, 1960.*

31

Leonardo

THE TANTALIZING SMILE

WHO HAS NOT BEEN bewitched by the Leonardo smile, that enticing and elusive smile, "more divine than human," that seems to move before our eyes? For almost 500 years, men have tried to solve the riddle of that luminous, dreamlike smile —from Raphael, who imitated it, to Dr. Freud, who traced it back to Leonardo's memory of the mother he was forbidden to see after he was five. (Leonardo was illegitimate; when he was five, his father took him away from his mother and into the da Vinci household.)

Whose smile cast such a spell on Leonardo? Who was this tantalizing angel (opposite) from *The Madonna of the Rocks*, which he painted 20 years before *Mona Lisa?*

In 1482, the 30-year-old Leonardo wrote a letter to Lodovico Sforza, Duke of Milan, recommending himself "with the utmost humility" as an architect, engineer, inventor, expert on irrigation, designer of military equipment and strategist of sieges, climaxing this astounding catalogue of talents with these words: "I can carry out sculpture in marble, bronze and clay, and also can do in painting whatever may be done as well as any other, be he who he may."

None of this was extravagant. Leonardo da Vinci was the most gifted man the human race has yet produced. His intelligence was enriched by insight and exceeded only by curiosity. He accompanied condemned criminals to their execution, to study the expressions on their faces, and dissected 30 cadavers, to perfect his knowledge of anatomy.

He explored the laws of motion and light and magnetic waves. He designed portable bridges and artificial birds which flew through the air. He invented ingenious gears and deadly catapults, described tanks and submarines. He analyzed the flow of rivers and the structure of mountains. Before Copernicus, he wrote, *"Il sole non si move"* ("The sun does not move"), and before Galileo, "The earth is a star, like the moon. . . ." And, as if the gods had not blessed one man enough, he was so handsome that the art historian Vasari wrote, "His personal beauty could not be exaggerated, his every movement was grace itself."

Lodovico Sforza invited Leonardo to Milan and commissioned him to paint a portrait of Cecilia Gallerani, celebrated for her beauty, 17 years old — and Lodovico's mistress.

No one knows where Leonardo's portrait of Cecilia Gallerani is. Leonardo painted her again, it is said, as *The Lady with an Ermine.* Then he painted *The Madonna of the Rocks*, which today hangs in the Louvre. He seems to have loved this painting so much that he kept it for himself and painted another, which is now in London (see following pages). In both masterpieces, the same alluring angel commands our attention with a sublime and seductive smile. Is she Cecilia Gallerani? Was Leonardo, as some imply, in love with her?

The evidence is as odd as the theory. Leonardo died in 1519, and among his effects was found a fragment of a letter addressed to *"Magnifica Cecilia"* and containing the phrase "my beloved goddess" *("amantissima mia diva").* But, unfortunately for those who spin romances, the letter is not in Leonardo's handwriting. Could he have dictated it? Possibly. Does this mean he loved the fair Cecilia? Not at all. Renaissance artists often found it politic to flatter their patron's courtesans. The overriding evidence is that da Vinci was never intimate with any woman; he surrounded himself with handsome young men and even chose apprentices for their beauty rather than their talent.

And the "Gioconda smile"? Ah . . . Painters before Leonardo outlined their figures, so that they stood away from the backgrounds in stiff, immobile poses. They did not know how to force viability from flat surfaces. It was Leonardo who invented what the Italians call *sfumato:* He deliberately omitted outlines, deliberately blurred and softened the corners of the eyes and mouth, blending light into shadow, teasing our eye to find where the one ends and the other begins.

One final fact: During the Renaissance, well-born maidens were carefully schooled in the components of charm. In one primer on the feminine graces, Agnolo Firenzuola advised the ladies: "From time to time, close the mouth at the right corner with a suave movement, and open it at the left, as if you were smiling secretly. . . ."

A thousand Giocondas smiled this way in the *palazzi* of Rome and Florence and Milan; only Leonardo had the genius to capture the transient and knowing delight which is its secret.

The Madonna of the Rocks *(detail, right)*
today is in the Louvre, Paris.

After Leonardo painted The Madonna of the Rocks, *probably between 1483 and 1490, he kept it—instead of turning it over to the Duke of Milan, who had commissioned it—and produced a copy (opposite page). A triumph of composition and lighting, this canvas (198" x 123") is one of the most priceless pictures in the Louvre.*

This version of The Madonna of the Rocks *(189″ x 120″)* scarcely compares—in style, subtlety, coloring—with the original on the preceding page. It may have been copied by students, with distinctive touches by Leonardo. Note that in this copy (now in the National Gallery, in London), "Cecilia Gallerani" is represented as an angel with wings.

Rouault

"I BELIEVE IN SUFFERING..."

A MEDIEVAL LEGEND tells of a girl who, with her veil, wiped the sweat from the face of Jesus as he carried His cross to Calvary. And on the veil was imprinted a perfect image of His features. The girl became St. Veronica (perhaps from *vera icon*, "true likeness"), and the miracle of Veronica's veil has come down the centuries.

On February 12, 1958, the day before he died, Georges Rouault, the moody, mystical "conscience" of modern art, said that he had painted 40 versions of *Veronica's Veil*—and that the painting on the opposite page (reproduced for the first time) was one of the loveliest.

Rouault was rarely so contented with his work; he sometimes held a picture for 25 years, changing it innumerable times. A month before he died, the 86-year-old recluse awakened in the middle of the night, padded silently to his studio, took a painting off the wall and, without a shred of remorse, threw the picture (for which a museum would have paid $60,000) into the fireplace.

It was not the first time this stubborn, secretive genius had burned his work. Forty years ago, Rouault made a strange compact with the art dealer Ambroise Vollard: He lived and worked in an apartment in Vollard's mansion, and for 15 years gave Vollard exclusive rights to his work. After Vollard's death, Rouault sued his heirs, demanding the return of eight hundred lithographs and canvases, insisting that it is for the artist alone to decide which of his works shall be seen. After many years, Rouault won the case; then, before representatives of the court, he calmly burned

313 precious works of art in a factory furnace.

Rouault was born in 1871. At 14, he was apprenticed to an artisan in stained glass. When sent on errands, he would pocket the carfare and run alongside the horse-drawn vehicles, so as not to cheat his employer. "I do not feel as if I belong to modern life," he once said. "My real life is back in the age of the cathedrals." Lost in religious preoccupation, and influenced by Léon Bloy, a Catholic writer with a savage pen, Rouault would prowl through Paris at night, studying the dockers and streetwalkers, the poor and the worldweary. His paintings became a mordant chronicle of human evil: judges with corrupt faces, prostitutes bloated with venery, clowns in tragic meditation. "I believe in suffering," he exclaimed. "It is not feigned in me."

Rouault wanted to create paintings with the splendor of stained glass. He wanted to make light pour *out* from his pigments. He used radiant hues in mysterious juxtapositions, placing daubs of fiery red within brooding blues and strange sea greens. He outlined eyes, cheeks, noses, breasts with coarse, ominous blacks until they resembled leaded panes. Above all, he painted with a sense of the terrible.

The critics called him "a chimney sweeper, not a painter," a clod who used "coal tar, caviar paste and shoe polish." And Rouault himself lamented, "It is terrible what I have done." He always deplored the "emptiness" of modern art, and once said, "For me, painting is a way to forget life. It is a cry in the night, a strangled laugh."

Converted to Catholicism, he considered becoming a monk. Later, he suffered a nervous breakdown and was taken to Switzerland.

He lived in fanatical secretiveness. "I do not want to be known," he announced. For years, no one knew his exact address. He lived with his wife and four children in an apartment on a noisy square opposite one of the busiest railway depots in Paris. No one was ever allowed inside his studio. He always wore an immaculate white surgeon's cap and gown when he worked, and no one ever saw him paint. Yet he was a gay, sprightly, energetic little man who loved to talk, hours on end, and roared with laughter over childish jokes. "I have been happy painting," he said, "obsessed with painting. The critics did not recognize the joy because my subject matter was serious. But is joy only in the subject?"

This incredible, incorruptible, truly original artist once confessed: "My only ambition is to paint a Christ so moving that those who see Him will be converted." The great *Holy Face* (opposite) asks only that you look at it long and with patience; for you must permit its hidden harmonies to communicate that sense of the human tragedy, that mystic mood of tenderness and anguish and nobility, with which Georges Rouault achieved immortality.

The Holy Face (30" x 24") was painted in 1928 with
oils on paper, then mounted on canvas.
It is in the Gallery Umeda, Osaka, Japan

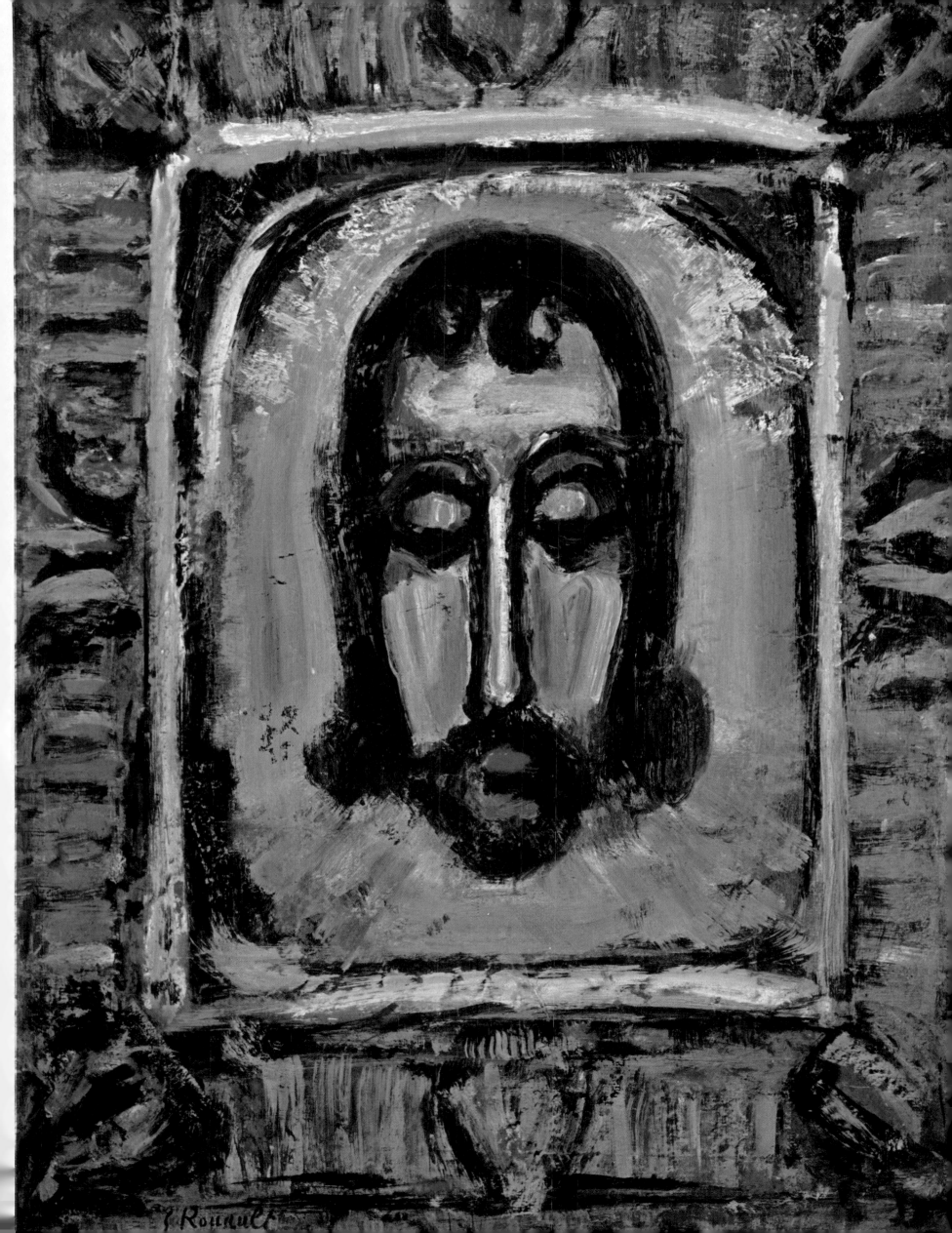

Hogarth

A MAN'S PAINTER

IN THOSE DAYS, campaigns for Parliament were conducted like circuses, in "a frenzy of bacchanalian merriment." Polling places, said one observer, were "offuscated with clouds of tobacco, obstructed by casks of ale and polluted by the presence of loose women." And victory was celebrated by "chairing" the new M.P.—carrying him aloft in triumph to his home.

This was the scene William Hogarth painted with such gusto in 1754. He substituted for the face of the winner (of an election in Oxford) the vapid features of a notorious London politician named Doddington and, in a neatly sarcastic touch, highlighted a fat white hog—inviting comparison between politicians and pigs.

Chairing the Member was the fourth painting in Hogarth's *Election Series*, in which he undertook political satire after immense successes with seriocomic engravings that chronicled the customs of his time. Not a fashion or foible or folly escaped his scorn. "He never looks at anything," said William Hazlitt, "without finding a moral or a ludicrous effect."

Hogarth used art both to record and to lampoon the society in which he lived. He had a malicious sense of caricature and an antiseptic instinct for quackery. He once said, "My picture is my stage, and men and women are my players." He populated his canvases with a rollicking pageant of types from every social stratum: lords, ladies, lunatics, beggars, boozers, fops, rakes, harpies, chimney sweeps. He once remarked that so long as his eyes were open, he was working. Too impatient to carry a sketchbook ("It interferes with my pleasures"), he could fix the decisive aspect of an expression, a gesture or a scene in his mind. Sometimes, he used his thumbnail as a sketchpad.

He was "a strutting little man," pert, bright-eyed, just over five feet tall and something of a dandy. He bought a sword as soon as he could afford one, and wore it cockily wherever he went. He was vain, opinionated and contentious, but the brilliance of his drawing and the surgery of his wit won him the respect of Swift, Fielding, Boswell and Dr. Johnson.

Hogarth served his apprenticeship by etching family crests on household silver, then went into business as an engraver and publisher of his own prints. He was in love with London, steeped in its sights and sounds, and left the great city only twice in all his 67 years.

He carried on bitter feuds with the dilettantes and the Brahmins of art. Yet all his life, paradoxically, he yearned to be exactly the kind of artist he never was: a grand painter of epic themes. He greatly admired Sir James Thornhill, whose academic frescoes in the cathedral of St. Paul's he vastly overrated. He also admired Sir James's daughter, whom he married.

Hogarth was unrivaled as a portraitist; he painted gentle character studies of his servants and beguiling portraits of children. But his paintings were never greatly prized. It was the engravings he made *from* his paintings and sold by the hundreds of thousands that brought him fame and wealth: illustrations for John Gay's *The Beggar's Opera*; a wicked series called *The Harlot's Progress*; *The Rake's Progress*, which traced the adventures of a wastrel-gigolo who died, with exaggerated sadness, in the asylum known as Bedlam. The critics resented Hogarth; they dismissed his style as "colloquial" and his content as "vulgar"; but the public chortled over his mocking fables of rectitude and iniquity.

Hogarth used his art to tell a story; he unfolded his tales scene by scene, with a wealth of delicious detail and irreverent insight. He infused his social documents with tongue-in-cheek moralism: Reprobates are shameful, to be sure; evil corrodes the soul; sin is always foredoomed—but how fascinating they are to observe!

He was a man's painter if ever there was one, the first Englishman to cut away completely from the Italian masters and the classical tradition. His style was altogether unique: brisk characterizations, robust colors and (as in the tumultuous *Chairing the Member*) impertinent humor that punctured whatever was smug or hypocritical. His work is a panorama of characters as original as those Dickens created with words a hundred years later. And, like Dickens, says Peter Quennell, he was "a special correspondent for posterity."

Hogarth never became the elegant painter he dreamed of being. He disparaged his best work as "of little consequence." But in the judgment of many, he remains the most interesting painter England ever produced.

Detail from Chairing the Member *(oil, 52″ x 3*
Reproduced by courtesy o
trustees of the Sir John Soane's Museum, Lon

Veronese

LIGHT AND COLOR

When the Inquisition took offense, Veronese changed the title of his The Last Sup

ON JULY 28, 1573, the fashionable painter Paolo Caliari (known as "Il Veronese" because he came from Verona) was summoned before the dread Inquisition in Venice on charges of sacrilege. Veronese's immense painting of *The Last Supper*, for the refectory of the monastery of St. John and St. Paul, contained such "sacrilegious" details as a dwarf, blackamoors, a servant with a nosebleed and German soldiers with pikestaffs. (The Vatican abhorred Germans, for had not the archheretic Luther snorted: "What have we Germans to do with St. Peter!"?)

The text of Veronese's cross-examination has come down to us; and if we rearrange the Inquisitors' questions and the painter's answers for dramatic effect, we read:

Q. "Is it fitting that, at the Lord's last supper, there should be buffoons, drunkards, Germans, dwarfs and such other scurrilous creatures?" *A.* "No, Sir."

Q. "Why then did you paint them?" *A.* "For ornament, Reverend Sir. If there is an empty space in a picture, I fill it with figures."

Q. "Do you not know that, in Germany and other places infected with heresy, they use paintings full of scurrility to deride, vituperate and flout the teachings of the Holy Catholic Church?" *A.* "Indeed, Sir, it is wrong; but I am obliged to follow what my masters did."

Q. "Did *they* then do such things?" *A.* "Michelangelo, in the Pontifical Chapel in Rome, painted our Lord Jesus Christ and His mother and the heavenly host . . . with little reverence, all naked, from the Virgin Mary down."

Q. "In the Last Judgment . . . it is not necessary to depict clothing. But there are no jesters or dogs or arms. . . . Do you protest that this picture is suitably done?" *A.* "Reverend Sir, we painters take liberties, the way poets and lunatics do."

The Inquisitors ordered Veronese to change *The Last Supper*. The chastened artist replaced the servant with a nosebleed—but could not go on. . . .

Veronese was just not interested in theology. He was a good-natured, gregarious man, happily married, who led so exemplary a life that, even in the gossip-loving and amoral Renaissance, not a breath of scandal was ever attached to his name. He dressed luxuriously, in fine silks and brocades, and thrived on the sumptuous life of Venice. He had painted 20 massive Biblical "feasts"—but always as spectacles, not religious subjects, as pag-

Feast in the House of Levi. *The gigantic oil (42' x 18') hangs in the Academy of Fine Arts in Venice.*

eants, not moral legends. Veronese used Scripture as no more than an excuse for the painting of romantic figures in gorgeous costumes and settings that bore not the slightest resemblance to humble Jerusalem. He had an irresistible love of grandeur, a flair for the heroic that perfectly served his time's adoration of imperial Rome. He could make color quiver; he knew the magical secrets of light; and he had so mastered the geometry of composition that he could arrange innumerable figures with supreme felicity in stunning thrusts and counterthrusts of movement.

Now, commanded by the Inquisition to emasculate his masterpiece, Veronese dolefully sought the advice of a friend who was well versed in canonical law. And that genius sardonically suggested that Veronese change not the painting, but the title! He could outwit the Inquisitors simply by pretending he had taken his text from Luke: "And

Levi made Him a great feast in his house; and there was a large company of tax collectors and others. . . ." Veronese leaped at this stratagem, blithely changed the title of his picture to *Feast in the House of Levi*, and let all else remain—including his dashing self-portrait, in luminous greens, standing with outflung hand at the head of the stairway that leads down to the left.

Three centuries later, Renoir returned again and again to study the rippling sheen of Veronese's colors. And of the man from Verona who so enjoyed his plentitude of gifts, no less an authority than Cézanne exclaimed: "Here is painting! An immense composition magnificently bathed in the same clear and warm light. The miracle is there —the world changed to painting. Veronese is a painter—not a poet or a philosopher. His psychology lies in the relationship of his colors. That is where his emotions lie too."

Breton Village Under Snow *(25½" x 35¼", oil on canvas), now in the Louvre, was once sold upside down as* Niagara Falls.

Gauguin

TORMENT IN PARADISE

HE WAS A BIG, dark, hawk-nosed man who liked to boast that he was descended from the Borgias of Aragon, rulers of Peru, and had savage blood in his veins. He had been born in Paris in 1848 and lived briefly in Peru, where his great-uncle had served as viceroy. He entered a Jesuit seminary in France, left in misery, and at 17 went to sea as an apprentice. He served in the merchant marine. Then, Paul Gauguin got a job with a Paris stockbroker, and in 1873 married a Danish girl, by whom he eventually had five children.

Gauguin became a well-to-do stock speculator, a respected and respectable bourgeois. One Sunday, solely for his own pleasure, he began to paint. . . . Who could have known that it would lead him down one of the most stormy and tragic roads known even to art, which is not unfamiliar with genius dredged out of suffering?

One day, without warning, at age of 35, Gauguin resigned from the stockbroker's office. He wanted to spend his life doing nothing but painting. It had become his passion, his obsession. He moved to Rouen, then Copenhagen, with his wife and children. His first exhibition there was a fiasco that closed in five days. He went back into business for a year, quit in disgust, left his family in Copenhagen, and returned to Paris with one son. He took a job pasting billboards in railway stations, so that he could paint. He ended up in a hospital. Then, he moved to Brittany, where living was less costly, and painted the peaceful villages, the devout Bretons, the gentle hills.

Whether it was because his money was running out, or because he yearned to see tropical skies and exotic foliage, Gauguin shipped out for Martinique. In Panama, he earned money for his passage by working on the great Canal.

His health broke under the climate of Martinique, and he worked his way back to France. He visited Van Gogh, who admired him, in Arles; but Van Gogh, in a fit of insanity, threatened to kill him, and Gauguin fled to Paris. Early in 1891, he auctioned all his pictures and sailed for Tahiti.

He knew not a word of the native language nor a soul in the South Seas. He built a hut in the wilderness and took as his "wife" a 13-year-old native girl, Tehura, who bore him a son. He was enthralled by the magnificence of the scenery, the beauty of the native girls, the primitive rites. "Here near my cabin," he once wrote, ". . . amid the intoxicating perfumes of nature, I dream of violent harmonies, a delight enhanced by I-know-not-what sacred horror I divine in the infinite."

But in 1894, Gauguin was back in Brittany—with a Javanese mistress, who deserted him. Sick and harassed by debt, he had returned home briefly to his wife and children in Copenhagen. "For nine years," he had written before his return, "I have been living without seeing my family, without home, often without eating. . . ." Finding no peace, he held a second auction of his works in Paris, and sailed back to Tahiti.

"My health falls off from day to day," he wrote a friend in Paris in 1896. He drank absinthe

steadily as he worked. He was spitting blood now, his body ravaged by excesses, his mind plagued by discontent.

Gauguin was plunged into terrible grief when a letter from Paris told him that his favorite daughter was dead. He went into the mountains and tried to commit suicide by drinking arsenic, but "even death did not want him."

A cyclone destroyed his house. In 1903, he was sentenced to three months in prison for a vitriolic letter to a local official. Before he could serve his sentence, he died.

But he left his mark on the 20th century: intensely original paintings, brilliant and mysterious, with colors splashed across broad areas and forms reduced to strong, simple outlines. The dark-skinned women he so loved (see opposite page) were a type of nude the West had not seen before—voluptuous, dignified, pagan Eves who had not learned the meaning of sin.

And in that hot, sun-drenched paradise, the picture they found on Gauguin's easel when he died, his last painting (see above), was of a village in Brittany, cool, hushed, gray in the snow. It was a cry for the past, and for a land more than 11,000 miles away. The picture brought seven francs. Today, it is in the Louvre.

Maternity (36¾" x 23½", oil on canvas) was painted in Tahiti. It is now in a private American collection.

Bosch

GEOGRAPHER OF HEAVEN AND HELL

WE KNOW VERY LITTLE about the remarkable man who created these remarkable paintings. We know that his name was Van Aeken, but he called himself Bosch—after the Flemish town of Hertogenbosch where, around 1450, he was born. We know that he was married, well-to-do, belonged to a religious brotherhood known as the Confraternity of Our Lady, and died in 1516.

Bosch's masterpiece was a triptych 7′2″ high, now in the great Prado Museum in Madrid, called *The Garden of Worldly Delights*. The left panel, *Earthly Paradise* (reproduced on this page), portrays an enchanting Garden of Eden; the central panel (see pages following) is a fabulous pageant of naked men and women frolicking among exotic animals, birds and fishes; the right panel is a shattering and apocalyptic vision of hell (reproduced in part on the opposite page).

For more than 400 years, experts have been intrigued by the meanings-within-meanings of Bosch's fantastic symbols. He was a devout Catholic, it is said, a medieval moralist who captured the mentality of the medieval world in diabolic visions, translating Biblical passages into pictures, painting even the metaphors, dramatizing sin and salvation, charting man's lusts and follies with dazzling ingenuity, foretelling the torments of purgatory.

But art historian Wilhelm Fränger (in *The Millennium of Hieronymus Bosch*) has advanced a startling theory: that Bosch belonged to a heretical Adamite sect called the Brothers and Sisters of the Free Spirit. They exalted nudity, held sexual congress a prayer in the sight of God and believed that Christ would set up paradise *on earth*. Bosch painted in riddles, not to baffle men, but to outwit the Inquisition. His pictures excoriated orthodox dogmas and attacked church corruption. He put monks in hell with savage caricature—as cackling creatures riding on the backs of the faithful, or with horns on their heads or with devils' tails under their habits. His "sinners" are not sinners at all, says Fränger; they are unashamed of their nakedness and delight in their pleasures.

Fränger deciphers the bizarre symbolism as if it were a medieval rebus: The huge key with the limp body in it (opposite page) symbolizes Jesus' attack on those Pharisees who seized the key of knowledge and kept it from the elect. Atop the disc on the head of the ashen-faced monster with the horrendous carcass, demons parade the damned around a bagpipe—which was the emblem of fools. Since this sect preached equality, Bosch placed knighthood in hell. The armored knight being devoured by monsters clutches a vessel of the Eucharist; but on his banner, Bosch mordantly placed the medieval sign of evil—a toad. And the two immense ears taunt those who have ears but hear not the truth.

Whatever Bosch's secret purpose, his artistry is miraculous: jeweled surfaces and glowing colors, superb drawing and unmatched imagination. He delineated horror with a curious serenity and balanced terror with charm. He used realism to invent surrealism. He explored the nightmare world of dreams and fears and fever. His influence stretches from Bruegel to Dali. Four centuries before Freud, this cartographer of paradise and purgatory apprehended man's unconscious.

This is the central panel of Hieronymus Bosch's huge
triptych, The Garden of Worldly Delights (oil on wood,
86⅝″ x 76¾″). It is flanked, left and right, by
the panels reproduced on the preceding pages. The
work was once referred to as The Strawberry Tree—and
strawberries, blueberries, cherries abound among the
fantastic details in this merry vision of the
earth after the creation of Eve. Bosch introduced
Negroes and Negresses in his cryptic celebration
of love, perhaps to suggest the equality of God's
creatures. The triptych is one of the glories of the
Prado Museum in Madrid, which contains the finest
Bosches in the world—because Philip II of Spain, then
ruler of the Netherlands, too, admired and collected them.

Giotto

THE FIRST "MODERN"

ONE DAY, over 750 years ago, Francesco di Bernardone, a strange, God-possessed young man (he had led a dissolute life until he heard a voice in a vision), appeared with his father before the Bishop of Assisi. Without a word, Francesco took off all his clothes, to symbolize his renunciation of this world and its rewards. The bishop wept, so moved was he, and covered Francesco with his own cloak. . . . Francesco worked among the lepers, founded the Franciscan order, and died in 1226. He was canonized two years later and is enshrined in men's hearts as Saint Francis of Assisi.

The dramatic scene with the bishop (opposite page) was painted in 1296. It is one of 28 great frescoes on wall spaces in the Upper Church of San Francesco at Assisi. (They are called frescoes because the plaster must be painted while *fresco*, meaning fresh, or wet.)

For centuries, scholars have argued over what paintings Giotto himself painted; some say only four of the Assisi frescoes are his; some dispute the old story that Giotto first worked in Assisi as a 14-year-old apprentice to the master, Cimabue. But none denies that Giotto walked the very streets Francis had walked, and so loved the saint that he gave his first-born son the name Francesco. And no one questions the immensity of the empire Giotto conquered—singlehanded—for art.

Giotto di Bondone founded painting as we know it today. For a thousand years, art had lain stifled, stilted, decadent and unchanged under the deadened style of the Byzantine. Roman and early Gothic painting involved little more than repetitive exercises in imitation—always expressionless faces on full-length figures in lifeless poses. Nothing was known of perspective, anatomy, foreshortening, contour. No one had learned to wrest the illusion of depth from a flat surface. It was Giotto who broke through the unexamined strait jacket in which painting was imprisoned.

He was the first European to paint people, not stereotypes. And he dared to let his people *feel*. He brought emotion into art, and presented man with the staggering idea that the sacred could be depicted through the human. He used pictures to tell a story. He even dared to "crop"—to paint only a head or part of a body to suit the needs of composition. He was the first Italian to paint a Madonna with a smile. Nearly seven hundred years ago, Giotto was a "modern."

This wonderful, pure, original talent was born near Florence in 1266 or 1267. The legend (written by Vasari and repeated by Leonardo da Vinci) says that Cimabue was walking through the fields and saw a shepherd boy drawing on a stone; he was so astounded by the draftsmanship that he took the 10-year-old Giotto into his studio and taught him the technical secrets of mosaics, tempera and fresco.

Giotto was no somber soul neurotically beset by demons. He was witty, earthy, happy, a superb raconteur who married while young—and sired at least six exceedingly unattractive children. Once Dante told him: "Master, throughout the world none equals you in art. I am amazed that while you make such beautiful figures for others, you make such ugly ones for yourself." To which Giotto replied, "I make my paintings by better light. . . ." When Giotto was court painter in Naples, the king, who liked to watch him work, one day said, "It is very hot. If I were you, I would stop painting." To which Giotto replied, "I would, too—if I were you."

Giotto was aware of his immortality, for his genius was extolled during his own lifetime by Dante, who named him in *The Divine Comedy*. Boccaccio also put him into *The Decameron*.

In this lambent, muted fresco of St. Francis before the bishop, we can see the magic hand (or influence) of the man who dared to paint men, not symbols, who learned how to render rounded limbs and bodies under flowing robes, who discovered the way to create the illusion of the third dimension. However quaint this picture seems to our eyes, accustomed to the accumulated craftsmanship of seven centuries, there are marvels of originality and insight beneath the soft, lovely colors and the simple, gentle surface.

Giotto — admired by the intellectuals and adored by the common people — died in 1337. Lorenzo the Magnificent later erected a marble statue in his honor in the Church of Santa Maria del Fiore, in Florence. The last lines of the Latin epitaph read:

"I am Giotto, that is all.

The name alone is a triumphal poem."

Giotto illustrated this morning scene in St. Francis Breaks With His Father *(12'2" x 10'5"),*
one of 28 frescoes painted in the Upper Church of San Francesco at Assisi over 650
years ago. It shows St. Francis as he was renouncing this world. He "removed all of his
clothes and gave them to his father," wrote St. Bonaventura. "The Bishop, weeping,
took him in his arms and took off his cloak and put it around him."

49

Picasso

ANARCHIST IN ART

THIS PAINTING has never been seen outside the home of that short, taut, burning-eyed force of nature known as Pablo Picasso. The story behind the painting is simply the story of the way this supreme talent, who has stamped his unique and passionate mark on the art of the Western world for over 50 years, went about painting it.

The subject is Jacqueline Roque (now Mme. Picasso), descendant of an old French family, a vivacious, cultivated woman with jet-black hair and green eyes, an excellent cook, delightful conversationalist and the devoted companion who cares for Picasso and protects him from the banalities of living. One of her friends tells the tale:

"One brilliant Mediterranean fall day in 1955, I was Jacqueline's guest at *La Californie*, the Edwardian villa at Cannes that Picasso bought a few years ago. Picasso did not come down until midday (he is not ruled by clocks), when he appeared, relaxed and innately elegant, in a new Italian shirt and a bright cowboy scarf. Our fourth at lunch was a poet. The discussion was very animated—poetry, Rimbaud, Balzac, religion, the nature of reality. Picasso disagreed with the poet. 'For me,' he cried, 'the truth is this table.'

"I remember that for dessert Jacqueline surprised him with some sweet Turkish *halvah*. He was as delighted as a child. He always searches for new tastes. As soon as the poet and I left, Jacqueline later told me, Picasso spontaneously asked her to pose for him. He had never before asked her to sit for a portrait—though he has made dozens of

her, all from memory. Now, he had her put on a Turkish costume of blue velvet and silver. 'Let us see what will come out,' he said.

"He began to work. 'When you draw, you must close your eyes and sing.' First, he drew her realistically. Then, he began to do what he calls 'destroying the sketch'—using her face, her limbs, her torso as though they were unrelated objects. He drew her in the classical manner, then as a succession of cubes, then in boldly simplified outlines—on and on; he did one variation after another, whenever a new idea struck him, incorporating different styles, always finding some new aspect, however small, to set him off on a new exploration. Jacqueline said it was like watching a magician. 'Even the taste of the *halvah* seemed to get into his sketches. . . .' When he put aside the drawings and began to lay paint on canvas, Jacqueline left him. He worked straight through until almost midnight. Then he showed the painting to her: 'This came today. We shall see what comes tomorrow.'

"During the following weeks, he worked on other paintings, drawings, lithographs. Then, one afternoon, he picked up this canvas impulsively and worked on it some more.

"Some friends saw the portrait and asked Picasso if it was finished. 'No,' he replied, 'a picture is never thought out, completed, beforehand. While I paint it, it changes—as my thoughts change. And when it is finished, it still changes—according to the state of mind of whoever observes it.' Even today, Picasso returns to the portrait."

At 75, Picasso, a dark, blunt, stormy Spaniard with magnetic eyes, bestrides the continents of art like a colossus. He has moved restlessly from school to school, from style to style (Impressionist, Cubist, Classical, Abstract, Surrealist), smashing precedents, defying conventions, transforming reality every time he picks up a brush. He cannot draw an apple or a jug without making it exciting. He finds the astonishing in the ordinary. He has liberated line from the prison of the familiar. He is in turn ironic, tragic, comic, bitter, but always fascinating. This great anarchist of art, utterly self-confident in his endless rebellions, has scored one of the greatest personal triumphs in the history of painting. His vast number of canvases and drawings (estimated by some in the tens of thousands) constitute one of the historic watersheds of art: It can never again be what it was before him.

In the elegant salon he has converted into a studio (and made a catchall for a conglomeration of letters, books, sketches, shells, utensils, paintings piled into a personal disorder no one must disturb), this prodigious and inexhaustible man turns his back to the Mediterranean sun when he works. "The light," he says, "comes from the sun in my belly."

Picasso's Portrait of Madame Z (36¼" x 28¾" hangs in the artist's home. This is the first time the picture has been reproduced courtesy of the artist

Cranach

THE IMPISH NUDE

SOMETIME AFTER 1537, Lucas Cranach painted *The Nymph of the Spring* (opposite page). He was over 65. He had ceased painting nudes almost 30 years before—because his first patron, Prince Frederick the Wise of Saxony, did not approve of "erotic" art. Frederick must have been as stubborn as he was wise, for in the 16th century, nudes were enormously popular among patrons of painting, and engravings of ladies unencumbered by clothing were circulated by the thousands to the populace. Even the illustration on the title page of Erasmus's *New Testament* (1519) included nudes. The Reformation was reforming more than theology.

The Renaissance had opened men's minds to the glory of humanism, and the Italians had opened their eyes to the beauty of the body. Yet most artists posed their models in the Greek manner—preserving their modesty with tresses or draperies or coy, if only part-concealing, hands. Then Cranach appeared on the scene.

His first nudes were stiff and dreamy, vaguely Botticellian. But he soon departed from tradition— the romantic mood of Raphael, the lush effects of Titian, the crisp brilliance of Van Eyck and Bellini —and began to paint the goddesses of mythology as no one before had ever dreamed or dared: with a merry and delicious impertinence.

He painted the classical heroines, not as lofty ideals, but as German maidens with narrow shoulders and small waists, tiny mouths and pointed chins, prominent abdomens and elongated limbs. To accent both their seductiveness and their earthiness, he added ribbons and necklaces to nature's garb, or flimsy veils and big, gay hats, rings and bracelets and gauzy scarves.

Cranach brought to the rendition of the female form two quite original qualities: forthrightness and humor. He expressed an unexpected wit in every line; he would separate the big toe from the others to wring character from a foot. He added sinuous curves to a modeling he held deliberately "shallow." Above all, he endowed his Teutonic charmers with impishness, giving them curious smiles that suggested some inner amusement with the revelation of their nakedness, and sidelong glances that made them quaintly sensual.

What emerged, in a manner altogether unique and diverting, were nudes who were naked but not carnal, beauties who were provocative but oddly chaste. Cranach placed them in pastoral settings, against foliage and meadows, castles and caves, and populated the countryside with amusing birds, beasts, lions and stags. He fused body to landscape with limpid colors and meticulous lucidity.

He was a delightful man, this Lucas Cranach the Elder (his son was also a painter). He was born in Kronach, Bavaria, in 1472, learned to draw from his father and married into one of the finest families in Gotha. He made a fortune in the service of the Cardinal of Brandenburg, the Duke of Brunswick, three electors of Saxony and King Christian II of Denmark. His skill as a portraitist made princes all over Europe clamor for his services.

Cranach was sent on diplomatic missions, held a lucrative monopoly on the sale of medicines, was even granted patent rights to the printing of the Bible and, for a time, retired from painting to manage his houses, his library, his investments and his apothecary's dispensary.

He was a close friend of Martin Luther, who had come to Wittenberg—where Cranach served as *Burgomeister* for seven years. Cranach painted many portraits of the great reformer, and for him created a remarkable set of woodcuts called *The Passion of Christ and Anti-Christ*, which helped launch the Protestant struggle against Rome. They contrasted the humble life of the Saviour with the worldly ambitions of the Pontiff. Yet Cranach never renounced his own Catholicism.

No artist in Germany ever approached Cranach for humor, charm and an instinct for the decorative. He was a master of painting, engraving, woodcuts, altarpieces. To the austere art of the North, he brought the fresh notes of the tender and the entertaining. His portraits are triumphs of technique and characterization. And his nudes, like *The Nymph of the Spring*, have endured down the centuries as the personal statements of a man with a delectable sense of the playful.

"I, the nymph of the sacred spring, am sleeping," reads the charming Latin inscription at the upper left. "Do not disturb." The bow and arrows on the tree are symbols of the goddess Diana. This little painting (18¾" x 28¾") by Lucas Cranach the Elder is in the National Gallery of Art, Washington, D. C. (gift of Clarence Y. Palitz).

Toulouse-Lautrec

NO SUN, NO SHADOWS

HE CAME FROM one of the noblest families in France. His father and mother, both of distinguished birth, were first cousins. And perhaps because of that, a congenital deficiency condemned Henri Marie Raymond de Toulouse-Lautrec-Monfa to a rare and tragic fate: His legs, which he broke when he was in his teens, never healed properly. He remained a grotesque midget, with a man's torso and stunted limbs, who could not walk without the help of a tiny cane.

He went through life witnessing the shock on people's faces when they saw him. "I went in to greet my guests," wrote *chanteuse* Yvette Guilbert, "and came to a dead stop in front of 'the little thing.' Imagine the immense head of a gargoyle stuck on the body of a dwarf: a dark, huge head, black beard, a nose big enough for two faces, flat, thick lips. . . . I was aghast, until I looked into Lautrec's eyes. They were astonishingly brilliant and luminous."

He settled in Paris in 1882, when he was 17, to study art. He kept a rowing machine in his studio and would exercise on it furiously for hours, vainly hoping to strengthen his feeble legs. Proud, morbid, sensitive, he discussed his deformity with irony, to ward off scorn, and adopted the mask of arrogance, to reject pity.

He dreaded being alone. Every night, he made the rounds of Montmartre's cabarets and music halls and brothels (where he sometimes maliciously received his family's patrician friends). He embraced the dissolute — fascinated by depravity, grateful to a moral underworld that accepted him as a man, not a freak.

He loved to entertain, often donning outlandish clothes and regaling his friends, for whom he poured fearsome cocktails, with bawdy stories.

His most constant and devoted companion was his cousin, Gabriel Tapié de Céleyran, a medical student. Lautrec's father and Gabriel's mother were brother and sister, as were Lautrec's mother and Gabriel's father. The "double cousins" showed a striking resemblance to each other (see small picture opposite). But Gabriel was very tall, thin, funereal; by his side, the mocking midget looked like "a horned owl." Night after night, they explored Bohemia together, Lautrec drawing, sketching, recording the ribald life. He immortalized the music-hall stars—Yvette Guilbert, Aristide Bruant, Jane Avril—in posters that were hung all over Paris. He made the poster a form of art.

Lautrec's genius lay in pitiless revelations of character. He neither condemned nor idealized. He saw only people, redeemed by talent or ravaged by corruption. He drew epigrammatically, with a bold, sharp, comic sense. And even when he painted Gabriel, in a rare formal portrait (opposite page), he emphasized the gawkiness, the pinched features, the family "nose big enough for two faces."

Lautrec joined no movement and advanced no theories of art. From Japanese prints, he learned to simplify his compositions and magnify his meaning. Degas's work, which he vastly admired, encouraged him to bypass tradition in the search for the candid and the decisive. To him, the dreary and the degraded were but vignettes in the drama of evil. He once said, "Ugliness has its beautiful aspects; it is thrilling to discover them where nobody else has."

He subordinated everything to impact. He perfected a flat, linear style that was surgical, sardonic, antisentimental. He mastered the absolute economy of the silhouette. The few colors he used were handled for psychological effect. Neither sun nor shadow ever entered the night world he illuminated with the deadly spotlight of insight.

Drink and dissipation took their inevitable toll: In 1899, Lautrec collapsed and was committed to a sanitarium. He begged his father, the Count of Toulouse, who wore D'Artagnan-like costumes while falconing, to get him out. "I am imprisoned," he wrote, "and everything that is imprisoned dies."

When he was released, his mother made a friend watch over him day and night to try to keep him from the madness of excess. But the scoffing dwarf outwitted his benevolent guard. In 1901, he had a stroke. They took him to his mother's home at Malrômé and summoned his gentle, adoring cousin, whom he loved to tease. Gabriel's face was one of the last the ugly little genius, "the Maupassant of painting," wanted to see before he died

The double portrait above is a
small detail in the background of
the great Au Moulin Rouge (47½″
x 55¼″), one of Lautrec's most
dramatic masterpieces, now in the
Art Institute of Chicago. It shows
the dwarflike Lautrec with his
tall, thin, gawky cousin, Dr.
Gabriel Tapié de Céleyran,
who fondly accompanied him
through the brassiest fleshpots of
Montmartre. It was painted in 1892.

The large portrait at the left
shows the artist's "double cousin"
in a corridor at the Comédie
Française. This pensive study (1894,
43¼″ x 22″) hangs in the
Musée Toulouse-Lautrec, Albi, France.

Uccello

A PASSION FOR PERSPECTIVE

NIGHT AFTER NIGHT, he would stand before the table, oblivious of weariness or time, drawing strange graphs and converging lines and polygons with 80 sides. Whenever his wife begged him to come to bed, he would reply abstractedly, *"Che dolce cosa è la perspettiva!"*—"Oh, what a delightful thing is perspective!"

He was consumed by a peculiar obsession—a single-minded, fanatical search for ways to create the optical illusion of a third dimension on a flat surface. No one before him had solved the mani-

fold puzzles of depth, or formulated the laws of perspective for painters and painting.

He was born Paolo di Dono, in 1397, and probably took Uccello as his name because he loved birds. (Uccelli means "of the birds.")

At the age of 10, he was apprenticed to the sculptor Ghiberti, who set him to work shining up the glorious golden doors of the Baptistry in Florence. At 28, he went to Venice to work at the Byzantine basilica of St. Mark's. His closest friends were the sculptor Donatello and the mathematician Giovanni Manetti; both nourished his preoccupation with perspective.

In 1436, Uccello was given a challenging commission—to paint a fresco in the cathedral of Florence, above the tomb of Sir John Hawkwood, the great mercenary captain, that would look so

The immense Battle of San Romano *(10′7″ x 6′), commissioned for a palace, is now in the Uffizi Gallery, Florence.*

much like a statue that it could serve as an economical substitute for the marble monument originally planned. Uccello produced such a remarkable illusion of a three-dimensional statue that he was acclaimed a master of visual deception.

Whenever an oddly shaped dome or vault, arch or cupola needed decorating, Uccello was called in. But he was so absorbed in his geometric puzzles that he never mixed his paints properly for the tricky requirements of fresco—which is painting on fresh, wet plaster. He had to repaint his work on the Hawkwood memorial because the colors were impermanent. Most of his other frescoes have disappeared with time.

His most celebrated work is *The Battle of San Romano*, commissioned by Cosimo de' Medici for a bedchamber in his palace. Uccello painted

three battle scenes on three huge wooden panels. He seized the chance to flaunt his virtuosity as a manipulator of distances. He placed lances and trumpets and crossbows in dazzling, slashing lines. He strewed men and horses and paraphernalia around at daring angles. In prodigious foreshortening, he painted a pink horse kicking his heels into the very face of the viewer. He froze the entire action in a deliberate exaltation of design over movement. And as if in a whimsical comment on chivalry itself, he made his knights toy knights and his horses hobbyhorses in a fairy-tale world.

Uccello sacrificed fame and success to his fascination with perspective. He transformed a picture of the Holy Family itself into an exercise in the rendition of depth. He once portrayed the Eucharist through an intricate web of receding

lines—with a tiny Christ at the far end. One work was so severely geometrical in emphasis that even Donatello protested: "Paolo, you are disclosing it when it should be covered up." These words so grieved Uccello that he went into seclusion and painted no more. He died, penniless, in 1475.

Today, almost 500 years later, some see in *The Battle of San Romano* an imaginative harbinger of modern art: colors that ignore nature; a breaking of motion into syncopated Cubist rhythms; a flat light that is neither day or night, but serves visual effect alone; an exquisite sense of the decorative. Not the least remarkable accomplishment of this stubborn, eccentric painter is that he could make so personal and poetic a statement whilst pursuing the mathematical goddess, perspective, with such passion.

Bruegel

AFFECTION AND IRONY

HE WAS CALLED "The Peasant Bruegel" or "Pieter the Droll," and, almost alone among artists of any rank in the 16th century, he was never commissioned to paint an altarpiece or a picture for a church or a palace. He was considered an illustrator, a chronicler of peasant life, a sort of pictorial journalist. He spent most of his creative years drawing the Biblical scenes and moralistic parables that were then popular with publishers of prints and engravings. Only in the last decade of his life, oddly enough, did Bruegel turn to oil paintings, for which he won no great acclaim—since his paintings were seen only by the guests of the few who bought them.

We know little about his life and can only deduce his character from his work. He was born between 1525 and 1530, in a village called Brueghel, from which the family name may have come. He spent his youth in Antwerp, was apprenticed to a painter-humanist, worked as staff artist in a shop called "The Sign of the Four Winds" and was admitted to the artists' Guild of St. Luke in 1551. He married the daughter of his teacher (he had carried her in his arms when she was a child), and their progeny became painters too; one son was known as "The Younger Bruegel," and another, Jan, as "Velvet Bruegel," because of the finish with which he painted flowers and landscapes.

It is a sign of the extraordinary independence of Bruegel's mind that he returned from a trip to Italy without making the slightest effort (as most of his Flemish contemporaries did) to imitate the elegance and romanticism of the great Italian artists. The Renaissance Latins painted idealized portraits, limning men as if they were heroes; Bruegel painted common people, recording the broad, lusty stream of the life around him in marvelous colors and breath-taking designs.

Bruegel associated with intellectuals and humanists in what was then one of the great cosmopolitan centers of Europe. Perhaps as an escape from the political troubles of Antwerp, which the Spaniards ruled with ferocity, he and a friend dressed themselves as peasants and wandered around the country. What he observed he put into his paintings, which became an unsurpassed documentary of the games, brawls, weddings and gluttonies of the countryside.

Two years before he painted the powerful, disturbing *The Beggars* (opposite page), an extraordinary event occurred in Antwerp: Several hundred patriots—noblemen and burghers—drew up a "petition of grievances" against the Spanish conquerors and against the tortures and executions of an Inquisition that was determined to crush the Protestant heresy. The patriots marched into the palace of the Spanish regent, the Duchess of Parma. When she blanched, one of her counselors was heard to remark, "What, Madame, is Your Highness afraid of these beggars?" The term of contempt became a slogan of honor. At a banquet of Netherlanders, the great hall resounded with cries of "Long live the beggars!" The patriots adopted the foxtail, the emblem of beggars, as their political symbol and began to put foxtails on their hats instead of feathers.

Some scholars deny that Bruegel meant to invest *The Beggars* with political meaning. But why, then, did he dress his beggars in white vestments, like penitential garments? Why did he place upon their heads the notched chimney-pot hats worn by victims of the Inquisition condemned to be burned at the stake? Bruegel could not have been so naïve as to ignore the likelihood that his symbols would be considered propaganda—especially since he was known as one of those the Church called "libertines" because they espoused religious freedom. Most important, before Bruegel died, he told his wife to burn his last works—lest she incur the wrath of the authorities.

Bruegel transformed the lowly peasant into a monumental symbol. He made the landscape a form in its own right, painting scenes that have never been surpassed for craftsmanship, originality and beauty. All of his work reveals the affection, tinged with irony, of a superior intelligence that reflected on the paradoxes of the human comedy, that refused to be swayed by sentimentalism, that accepted the truths of man's suffering and man's folly in this life on earth. His work became increasingly powerful, satirical and (as in *The Beggars*) bitter. It was as if he foresaw what our age calls mass behavior.

He never knew how great a painter he was, nor how high and distinguished a place he would hold among the immortals.

The Beggars *is one of the smallest paintings in the Louvre (7.2" x 8.6")*
and one of the most powerful. It did not seem as brutal to 16th-century eyes
as it does to ours. Deformity fascinated many painters; dwarfs
and cripples, often regarded with affection, were employed as court jesters.
Painted in 1568, the year before Bruegel died, this magnificently organized
work was probably intended to have political meaning.

Fra Angelico

THE PEOPLE MADE HIM A SAINT

HE NEVER TOOK up his brush without first offering a prayer to God. He never changed or retouched his work, lest it offend God's will. He could conceive of nothing but religious subjects, and most loved joyous themes—the Annunciation, the Ascension, the Virgin and Child. He could neither understand nor paint evil. When he painted a Crucifixion, wrote Vasari, the tears would stream down his cheeks. But he painted angels and saints of such beauty that even Michelangelo, who reserved his passion for sculpture and disparaged "flat decorations," cried, "Surely this good monk has visited paradise!"

No one knows how he came to be called Fra Angelico. He was born Guido di Pietro da Mugello in 1387, and at the age of 20 entered the austere monastery of the Observant Dominicans at Fiesole, in the hills above Florence, where he took the name Brother Giovanni. He was "a most holy, gentle and modest soul," who was never known to display anger or envy or discontent. He illuminated manuscripts, began to study painting, and around 1420 assembled a studio of monks, who worked under his direction. A Latin poem by a Dominican of his time called him "Angelicus Pictor"—which means "painter of angels" or "the angelical painter." Either is fitting praise for the quiet exaltation of his art.

When Cosimo de' Medici presented the Convent of San Marco in Florence to the Ob-

servant Dominicans, Fra Angelico spent six blissful years painting the refectory, the cloisters, the corridors, the monastic cells—some 50 of the loveliest works in art. "He bequeathed to the world," said Ruskin, "the most radiant consummation of the pure ideal of Christianity."

Pope Eugenius IV visited San Marco and, enraptured, is said to have offered Angelico the Archbishopric of Florence; but the good friar could not imagine himself exercising authority over others. He went to Rome, painted frescoes in the Vatican, and returned to the monastery in Fiesole where he had taken holy orders. He was over 62 now, and painted little.

One day, Piero de' Medici, son of Cosimo, commissioned Fra Angelico to decorate a large silver chest in a chapel. There were 36 cupboard panels in the chest, each only 15 inches square (one was a double panel). And for this silver chest, the inspired Brother Angelico — sometimes assisted by monks who followed his designs—painted glowing scenes from the life of Christ, of which *The Flight into Egypt* is reproduced opposite. It is thought to be entirely by the master's hand.

Here is art so artless, painting so pure, content so noble, feeling so unmarred by the saccharine that we forget that Fra Angelico was one of the great masters who liberated painting from its medieval bonds and presaged the era of the modern. He was the first to paint the Christ Child as an infant, not a short adult. He was the

first Italian to put an identifiable landscape into his pictures. He used arches, columns, tunneled depths in what, for his time, were little miracles of perspective. He was matchless in his use of color: "blues, pinks, sea-greens, snow-whites," wrote Wilhelm Hausenstein, a biographer, "... melt one into the other caressingly . . . while ultramarine and vermilion . . . hold the entire scheme in firm embrace." As other painters of old, Fra Angelico insisted on his panel's being completely coated with gold. "The figures are isles and continents within a static sea of gold."

Above all, he was the embodiment of sheer harmony and grace. "What in the whole world of art is more rejuvenating than Angelico?" asks Bernard Berenson, the great critic. "The happiness on the faces, the flowerlike line and color, the childlike simplicity . . . [here is] perfect certainty of purpose, utter devotion to his task, a sacramental earnestness."

The silver chest has long since been taken apart; the 35 marvelous little paintings are enshrined in the Museum of San Marco, Florence, itself one great memorial to the glory of Fra Angelico's art.

He died in 1455. He was never beatified by the Church, as many believe; but the legend of his virtue was so great that the faithful began to pray to him, or in his name. They were confident that Fra Angelico must indeed reside in that heaven which, in "paintings like sacred music," he placed before the eyes of men.

THE FLIGHT INTO EGYPT, BY FRA ANGELICO

(c. 15″ x 15″, after 1450) MUSEUM OF SAN MARCO, FLORENCE

Turner

POET WITH A BRUSH

WHEN *Steamboat off a Harbor's Mouth Making Signals in Shallow Water, and Going by the Lead* was exhibited at London's Royal Academy of Arts in 1842, the critics exploded: "A frantic puzzle!" "Absurd and affected!" "A mass of soapsuds and whitewash!" In reply, Joseph Mallord William Turner only muttered, "I wonder what they think the sea is like? I wish *they* had been in it."

This strange, obstinate man had indeed been "in it": He had boarded the small steamboat *Ariel* at Harwich during a snowstorm, because he wanted to experience—with the most direct intensity—what a storm at sea was like. And as the fury of the storm raged about him, he asked the sailors to lash him to the mast. "I was lashed there for four hours," he later said, "and I did not expect to escape . . . I felt bound to record it if I did."

He recorded the snowstorm in a remarkable, radical picture that marked a turning point in his career and revealed a new and impassioned purpose in his work. What possessed Turner was the desire to paint things that have no shape or form—wind, speed, moods, atmosphere. He wanted to record not what the eye sees, but how the mind and heart respond. He wanted to paint sensations—using the language of light and the syntax of color.

"Paint your impressions!" Turner admonished young artists, a good 40 years before Manet and Monet. The critics had showered him with praise for his conventional pictures, but they called his free, lyrical canvases "incomprehensible daubs," "coloring run mad," "a disgrace to the Society that permits him to disfigure their walls."

But a discerning few recognized the quality of genius in this man who refused to be beholden to the familiar. Constable, the great landscape painter, said, "Turner has golden visions, glorious and beautiful. . . . One could live and die with such pictures." Ruskin, whose judgment sometimes played second fiddle to his prose, called Turner "beyond all doubt . . . the greatest man of the age."

Turner was born in London in 1775. His father ran a barbershop on Maiden Lane. His mother, a woman of ungovernable temper, died in a hospital—insane. The boy displayed little aptitude for studies but an immense interest in art. He studied at the Royal Academy and worked briefly under Sir Joshua Reynolds.

Turner was always "odd," remote, indifferent to the social graces. An acquaintance said of him: "He was singular, very silent. He was not polite at table. He did not like plays or music. He had no faculty for friendship. He would talk of nothing but his drawings. He was difficult to understand."

He was difficult to understand because he was so deeply absorbed in his own world. He once remarked that a man with a "ruling enthusiasm for art" simply could not look at anything superficially: "Every glance is a glance for study. Every look at nature is a refinement upon art."

He was a spectacular success as a painter, and was admitted to the hallowed ranks of the Royal Academy at the age of 27. He became one of the richest artists who ever lived, but remained stingy, suspicious and shrewd. Sir Walter Scott wrote: "His palm is as itchy as his fingers are ingenious.

He will do nothing without cash and anything for it. He is almost the only man of genius who is sordid in these matters."

Untidy, blunt, cold in manner, Turner was admired for his talent and detested for his boorishness. Never married, he was utterly unconcerned by the gossip that linked his name with his housekeeper, then with a woman named Booth, into whose house in Chelsea Turner moved. He lived there for some time as "Mr. Booth."

This curious, stubborn man made one of the most exciting discoveries in art: that light is color, and color a form of light. He bathed objects in mist and fume and smoke—not to hide them, but to accentuate the mood they inspired. Turner's later paintings were so formless that he had to attach rings to the frames so galleries would know which way to hang them. He was a poet with a brush.

When Monet and Pissarro visited London some 20 years after Turner's death, they were thunderstruck by the light-drenched freedom of his paintings—his bursts of translucent light, his audacious cancellations of shape, his violent and romantic visions.

Turner left to the people of England a fantastic conglomeration of his work: 20,000 sketches, countless etchings, about 200 paintings. None is more remarkable than this historic painting (now commonly known as *Snowstorm*), which asks of us that we dare to feel with freshness, that we surmount the crippling inhibitions of the customary, that we free our imagination to enter a world that cannot be put into outline or contour—or words.

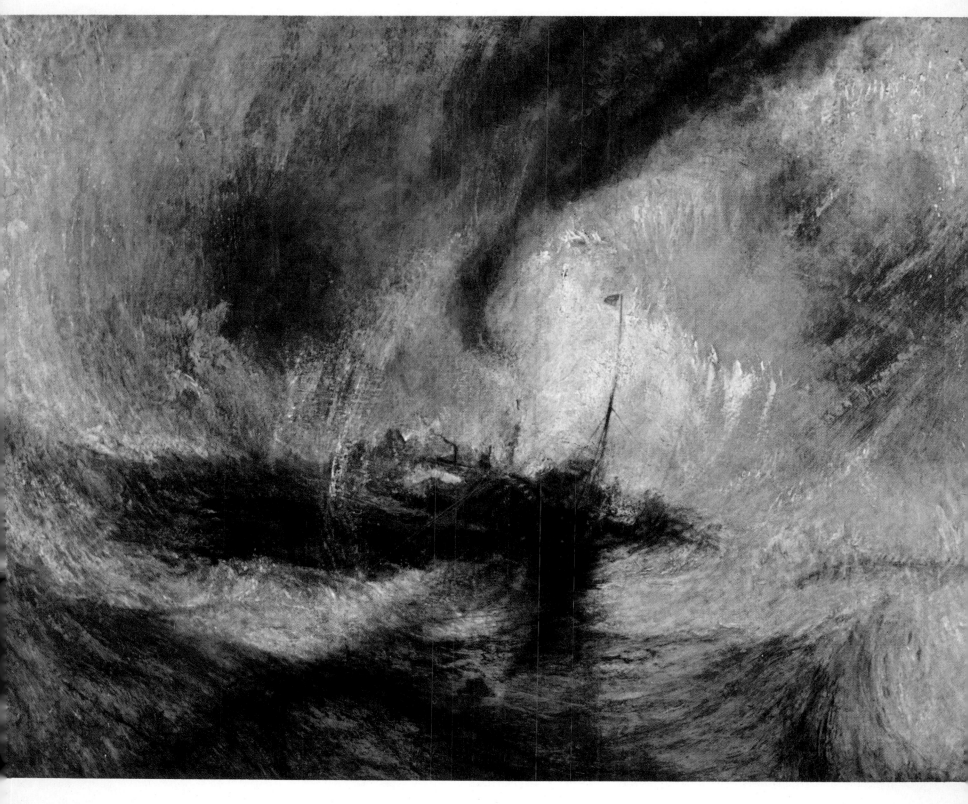

*This blurred, violent sweep of impressions, painted in 1842,
infuriated the critics, but opened a new frontier in art. Called*
Steamboat off a Harbor's Mouth Making Signals in Shallow Water,
and Going by the Lead, *Turner's daring painting (3′ x 4′) still
startles spectators. Courtesy of The Trustees, National Gallery, London.*

Degas

THE PAINTER WHO DESPISED WOMEN

In 1886, the Impressionists presented their eighth and final exhibition, among which was a startling group of pastels described by the artist as "a series of nude women, bathing, washing, drying, rubbing down, combing their hair...." The art world of Paris, so proud of its sophistication, was both astonished and scandalized.

Degas had brought the boudoir into the salon. This anonymous woman in *The Tub*, for instance: this was no recognizable woman, no familiar nude, carefully posed, reclining in grace and splendor; this was no ethereal goddess in female form, no voluptuous model for the mythology of Greece or Rome. This was not a woman; this was a body—arrested in natural movement, drawn without a face, apprehended in the unexpected grace of the ungraceful. This picture denied the aesthetic assumption of centuries: that the model is most beautiful when *posed*—and, in posing, presupposes an audience. This was art, the artist cynically confessed, "as if seen through a keyhole."

The critics fumed, calling the artist "a cruel observer," a man "morbid and neurotic." Even Emile Zola, the great and uncompromising apostle of realism, voiced displeasure with pictures that made women "vulgar," distorting their movements, trivializing their beauty.

To all of this, Edgar Hilaire Germain Degas responded with icy disdain. Elegant, scornful, a snob, this eldest son of a French banker and a Cre-ole mother from New Orleans held fast to his creed: "Drawing is not what one sees, but what others have to be made to see."

Behind the astonishing draftsmanship of *The Tub*, the tilted perspective (so reminiscent of the Japanese), the iridescent play of light on soft flesh, under which strong muscles rippled—behind all this lay one mordant strain of irony: Degas despised women. He portrayed them not because he thought them beautiful, but because he was fascinated by motion. He caught them off guard in moments of exertion—with a fresh and dispassionate vision that anticipated the candid camera. His nudes were oddly unsensual, unlike Rubens's Corybants, and most unluscious, unlike Titian's golden nymphs.

When one Parisian *grande-dame* asked indignantly why he showed women as ugly, Degas replied: "Because, madame, in general women *are* ugly." Once, he declared: "I show women deprived of their airs and affectations, reduced to the level of animals cleaning themselves."

His passion for cascading light and color and movement led Degas to haunt the cafés of Paris, the race track, the opera, the ballet he adored. But it was not the exquisite ballerinas he chose to paint; it was "the little rats" of the *corps*, the underfed dancers who worked for a few sous and yearned, with single-minded vulgarity, to catch a "rich gentleman friend." Women as ordinary as the one portrayed in *The Tub* came to his attic studio as models—shopgirls, dancers, laundresses, prostitutes—and he endowed them with a kind of accidental loveliness. He captured, with singular insight, the sad and lonely moments of their moods. Even his "brainless creatures" were suffused with reflectiveness. He painted with a compassion of which he was unaware.

Aloof, aristocratic, corroded by discontent, Degas's cavalier manners offended those who came to admire his work. He lived as a recluse. Invited to dinner, he would accept on peculiar terms: "No flowers on the table, please. Lock up your cat, and be sure no one brings a dog. If there are ladies, will they come without perfume? What horrors all those odors.... And very few lights—my eyes, my poor eyes."

He was terrified of going blind. His eyesight began to fail when he was 40, so that he had to work on tracing paper almost four feet high.

He created an atmosphere uniquely his own, poetic, thoughtful, marvelously patterned, rippling with movement, muted in color. He searched for the singing texture of an Oriental screen.

In his last years, he guarded his work jealously—refusing to exhibit, refusing to sell. He had no close friends. He never married. He wandered through the streets of Paris alone and in terror of the automobiles he detested. In 1917, 31 years after *The Tub*, Degas died. He was blind.

The painter: Edgar Hilaire Germain Degas (1834-1917). The model: unknown. Medium: pastel on paper.

This lovely and little-known work of art, executed

on an exact square 27½″ by 27½″, today hangs in the Hill-Stead Museum in Farmington, Conn.

Dürer

THE SECRET TREASURY OF THE HEART

ALBRECHT DÜRER was only 19 when he painted this faultless portrait of his father with a rosary. "My dear father," he wrote in his journal 34 years later, "a goldsmith, a pure and skillful man, passed his life in great toil and stern, hard labor. . . . He was a man patient of spirit, mild and peaceable to all, and very thankful toward God. . . ."

It is a mark of Dürer's fidelity to truth that even in this first portrait of the father he loved, he made not the slightest effort to flatter or exalt. He faithfully recorded every furrow, the pained eyes, the humble garb, the drawn lips of a man accustomed to adversity and resolute in faith. Dürer painted his father's portrait several times in the years ahead, and each time with the same reverent veracity. It was his special genius to combine such candor with such compassion.

He was born in Nürnberg in 1471, the third of 18 children. "My father took special pleasure in me," he wrote in his journal, "because he saw that I was diligent and striving to learn. So he sent me to school, and when I had learned to read and write, he took me away and taught me the goldsmith's craft. . . . But my liking drew me rather to painting . . . so I laid it before him. My father was not pleased . . . but he let it be as I wished, and in 1486 bound me apprentice to Michael Wolgemut, to serve him three years long. . . ."

Dürer became the greatest artist Germany has ever produced. He brought unerring taste and understanding to a portrait, a petal, a landscape (which he was among the first to paint). He seemed incapable of shallowness or irrelevance. His eye was so discerning, his talent so prodigious that he could make a masterpiece of an insect, a flower, hands in prayer. He once took a tuft of ordinary meadow and drew it with such insight that he transformed the plain grasses into a prefiguration of all the wonders of life that issue from the unimpressive sod.

He won acclaim for his voluminous paintings, drawings, water colors, engravings, woodcuts. He traveled widely and consorted with scholars, scientists, philosophers and princes. He studied languages and mathematics, read Euclid and Leonardo, wrote treatises on measurement, the fortification of towns and castles, the human body, the theory of art. He was befriended by Emperor Maximilian I, feted by the noblemen of Venice, pensioned by Charles V; and when he visited Antwerp in 1520, the artists of that thriving city gave him a great banquet and escorted him back to his quarters with a torchlight parade. "I thanked them," Dürer wrote dryly, "and went to bed."

Unhappily married, childless, he accepted his lot without complaint and lived with impeccable rectitude. He was very successful but not wealthy —because he often bartered his work for things that gratified his boundless curiosity: parrots, monkeys, coral, precious stones, buffalo horns from India. Occasionally, he gambled—but when he won, he would placate the pangs of conscience by drawing a portrait of the loser, gratis.

His father, a profoundly pious man, had raised his children in the teachings of the Roman Catholic Church. The times caught Albrecht Dürer in the terrible conflict between Luther and Rome. He became a giant of the Reformation. "If God helps me to see Dr. Martinus Luther," he wrote, "I will diligently make his portrait . . . as a lasting memory of the Christian who has helped me out of great anxieties." When a rumor swept Germany that Luther had been kidnaped, Dürer cried: "O God . . . who shall henceforth expound to us the Holy Gospels? . . . O all ye pious Christians, help me weep over this God-illumined man."

Dürer embraced Luther's principles, taking his place beside "those who stand in contempt and danger . . . and are sneered at as heretics." Yet he continued to work for his friend and patron, the Cardinal of Brandenburg, and continued to go to confession. He died in 1528.

His epitaph might well be the words he used when asked to explain his incomparable draftsmanship, his searching characterization, as in this moving, timeless study of his father: "I draw," said Dürer, "from the secret treasury of the heart."

Albrecht Dürer's Portrait of His Father (14½" x 16", oil on wood) hangs in the great Uffizi Gallery in Florence.

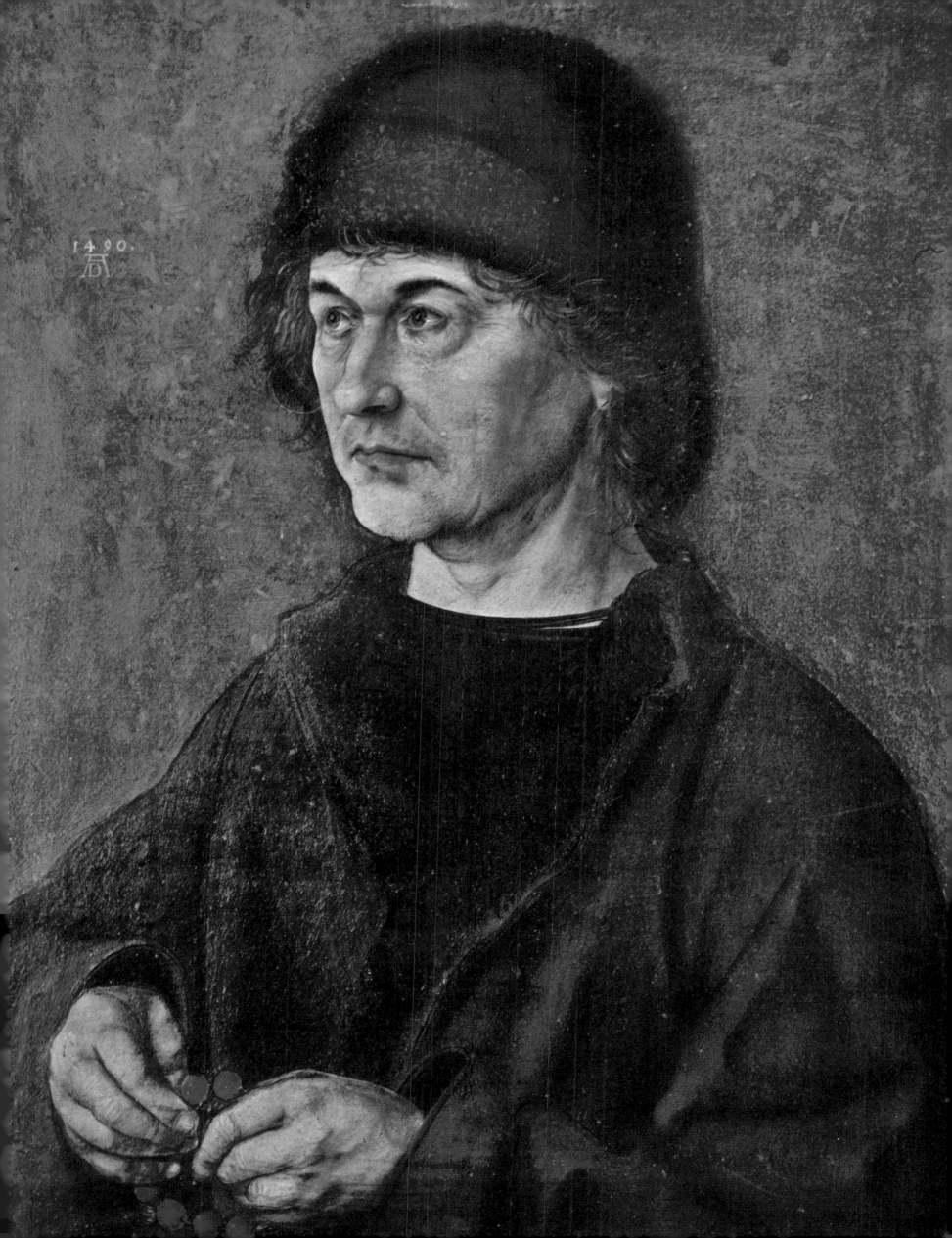

Renoir

THE SORCERY OF LIGHT

PARIS, 1893. The 15-year-old girl from the country smoothed her hair and knocked on the door. Her name was Gabrielle Renard. She had come to Paris because her cousin, Madame Renoir, was about to have a second child and needed a helper and nursemaid. The door opened. Gabrielle entered. She did not know she was entering posterity.

For she became Auguste Renoir's favorite model ("Her skin does not reject the light!" he cried), and some 300 portraits of her today adorn museums and collections throughout the world. One of the greatest, now in the Louvre, is *Gabrielle With a Rose* (opposite page, 21½″ x 18″).

Everyone in the Renoir ménage posed for the master: his wife, his son, the cook, the gardener, the maids. Luncheon guests might wait for hours because the cook was posing for their host. "But how can one *help* this?" Renoir would exclaim. "She has a complexion that takes the light!"

The household echoed with happy chatter. Whenever a servant was not singing or humming, Renoir would ask, "What's the matter with you? Why don't you *sing?*"

Renoir hummed while he painted; when he was quiet, Gabrielle knew he was preoccupied. He built a little glass studio under the olive trees, and because it was very tiny, Gabrielle had to pose in the garden outside; but Renoir was delighted with his studio because from it he could see the bustling life of the kitchen.

He was a supremely happy man who allowed nothing to interfere with his painting—four hours in the morning, four in the afternoon. He never stayed up late, lest it affect the next morning's work. After excruciating arthritis crippled his legs and gnarled his hands, the servants would carry him into the garden, set up his easel, place an umbrella over his head, and strap a brush to his hand so that he could paint.

He was enthralled by the sorcery of light. He never painted by artificial illumination. If he started a picture in the afternoon, he would work on another the next morning; when the afternoon light appeared, he would resume work on the first.

He kept his palette meticulously clean. He mixed his colors on the canvas itself, in small, deft dabs. He had made a success painting the society ladies of Paris—then painted them no more because he hated their pallid complexions.

"I like painting that is fat, juicy, supple," he said. "I want a red to be sonorous, to sound like a bell. . . . A picture should breathe joy which the painter felt while painting it. It should be a lovable thing, joyous and pretty—yes, pretty! . . . I *pet* a picture, stroke it with my hand."

Renoir was one of the Impressionists, then rebelled against their indifference to drawing, their disregard of form, their scattering of color. He went to Italy to see the Raphaels and never forgot their phenomenal drawing and modeling. "Unlike me," he wrote, "Raphael did not seek the impossible." He loved Titian, Rubens, Velázquez.

Renoir painted 4,000 pictures. He suffused his canvases with radiance and tenderness, in rippling cascades of color. He painted sunshine and flowers, mothers and children. Above all, he sang the glory and beauty of woman. Year after year, he plumbed the secrets of light—light on skin, on hair, on gowns, in dappled patterns through leaves—until he mastered the brilliant blaze of the summer sun itself and made his canvases quiver with sensuousness.

As his fame spread, young artists came to his door, unannounced, from all over the world. Renoir always invited them in. But he refused to teach them; he was too modest to think he could instruct anyone in the magic of art.

For 21 years, Gabrielle worked and modeled for Renoir. Then, one day, Conrad Slade, a young American from an old Boston family, appeared at Renoir's door. He and Gabrielle fell in love. They were married in 1914. At 80, she was living in California not far from Jean Renoir, the painter's son, whom she had cared for when he was a child and who became a brilliant movie director.

The last picture Renoir painted, at 78, was a water color—a bowl of anemones. He said it was his calling card "to introduce me to the great painters of heaven." The curé of Cagnes delivered the funeral oration over Renoir's grave in 1919. This was his peroration: ". . . the hour of light, that light without end, divinely radiant, on which we hope your eyes will rest forever open."

Renoir's Gabrielle With A Rose hangs in the Louvre, Paris.

El Greco

"THE LIGHT SHINING WITHIN ME..."

IT WAS THE DAY of martyrs and miracles. It was the time when piety went hand in hand with passion, and noblemen, no less than holy men, mortified the flesh and found strange ecstasies in that suffering through which they yearned to reach mystical union with God. It was the time the Holy Inquisition burned men for their "heresies," their doubts, or their faith. It was Spain—proud, cruel, violent—in the 16th century.

And no one caught its temper as well as a Greek painter who settled in Toledo in 1577, at 32. His name was Domenikos Theotokopoulos, but the Spaniards, unable to pronounce it, called him simply El Greco (the Greek). Born on the island of Crete, where he had mastered the Byzantine way of painting icons and miniatures, he sailed to Venice at 20 to study with the great Titian.

He was immensely talented, ambitious and tactless. In Rome, where he lived in Cardinal Farnese's *palazzo* by invitation, he brashly announced that if Michelangelo's *Last Judgment* vanished from the Sistine Chapel, "I could redo it in a way not inferior." He always signed his pictures in letters of the Greek alphabet and included the word "Greco" to emphasize his identity.

One beautiful spring day, a friend came to his quarters to find him seated in a room with the curtains tightly drawn. Invited to come out for a walk, the painter replied, "No, the sunlight would disturb the light that is shining within me."

He came to Spain to seek the patronage of Philip II, the most powerful monarch in Christendom, who finally asked him to paint an altarpiece.

But the King found it so disturbing—the figures so "grotesquely" elongated, the colors strange and upsetting, the entire mood too nervous, too intense—that he hired a third-rater to paint another. Crushed, the Greek retired to Toledo, living sumptuously on local commissions in an old castle.

His life contains many secrets, none more tantalizing than that of the beautiful woman who appears in his paintings so often: as Saint Veronica, as Mary Magdalene, as the Virgin (opposite page). Her name was Doña Jerónima de las Cuevas. She bore him a son, whom he adored and often painted, but there is no record that she and El Greco ever married.

In 1584, the Church of Santo Tomé authorized an extraordinary commission: to paint the burial of a man who had died over 200 years before. Back in 1312, the Count of Orgaz had commanded his subjects to contribute a given sum to Santo Tomé each year, plus "cattle, wine, firewood and 17 chickens" to the poor. When Orgaz died, it was said, Saints Stephen and Augustine descended from heaven to bury him with their own hands.

The villagers of Orgaz paid their annual tribute until 1570, then rebelled against so old and dubious an obligation—whereupon Church authorities held an ecclesiastical trial and solemnly redirected the citizens to pay up. El Greco's painting was intended to remind them, through the years, of an eternal obligation; he was explicitly instructed to show witnesses to the miracle, priests reading a Mass, "and above all this, there must appear Heaven opened up to glory."

It took him two years to complete the cumbersome assignment (and two more of legal wrangling to collect his fee). He called it "my sublime work." And what a work it was! He animated the complex composition with startling and ingenious rhythms: the flicker of hands and white ruffs, torch flames and imploring expressions, all cunningly designed to lead our eye up through bold, writhing patterns to the Saviour, from whom a supernatural radiance emanates. And the supposed witnesses of 1312, these gaunt saints and high-born pietists, these intense Spaniards with burning eyes and pale cheeks, these haughty yet consecrated grandees—they are all men from Toledo whom El Greco knew and used as models.

He died in 1614 and for centuries remained so obscure that art historians gave him but grudging notice, chiefly as an eccentric who "suffered from astigmatism." No museum in the world even presented an El Greco exhibition until 1902.

His audacious drawing, his deliberate disproportions (his vision was *not* faulty), his brilliant design and imaginative uses of color for psychological effect, his sheer expressiveness—all went far beyond the styles of his time. He took unheard-of license for something that was revolutionary in art: the purely personal statement.

No painter invested the faces of men with such tragic impulse, or so deeply understood the terrible ecstasy of faith and the sweet agony of devotion. His genius, as J. F. Matthews observed, sprang from neither madness nor miracles: "It is simply great painting."

The gigantic Burial of Count Orgaz *(15′ 11⅞″ x 11′ 9¾″), completed in 1586, is in the Church of Santo Tomé, Toledo, Spain.*

"MY SUBLIME WORK"
—EL GRECO

*(Opposite page) The astonishing profusion of
El Greco's details may be seen in the enlargement of part
of* The Burial of Count Orgaz. *The embroidered
robe on the far right is decorated with remarkable
portraits of saints. The pageboy at the lower left
is El Greco's son, Jorge Manuel; in his pocket is
a paper on which El Greco painted his son's
birth date. El Greco himself is the
gaunt face in the center staring directly
at us—just above the palm of the upturned hand.
(Top, left) This magnificently drawn angel is
transporting the soul of Count Orgaz—half child,
half cloud—from his dead body to the Redeemer above.
(Above) The model for the Madonna was Doña
Jerónima de las Cuevas, whom El Greco loved and
who bore his son. (Left) Here may be seen the details
that appear on the panel on Saint Stephen's robe (beside
El Greco's son)—a tour de force of color and draughtsmanship,
just one detail of this truly stupendous painting.*

Modigliani

THE RAGE TO PAINT

HER NAME WAS Jeanne Hébuterne. She was just 21, and she was expecting her second child by the painter Amedeo Modigliani. They had never married. Her parents had disowned her. She and Modigliani lived in the most abject poverty, in a barren studio which contained a few chairs, a table, a mattress on the floor.

He had come to Paris 13 years before, at the age of 22—a strikingly handsome young Italian with black hair, burning eyes and a charm so irresistible that, as a colleague once said, "he never lacked either models or mistresses." Then, driven by anguish, he plunged into a life so wild and debauched that, even among the Bohemians, he was known as "cursed."

He was possessed by a rage to paint; but he found beauty only in peculiar states of exaltation, which he induced by drink and drugs. "Then and only then," he said, "does one know the joy of creation which is at the same time a liberation."

He burned out his nights in orgies and drunkenness, reciting Dante at the top of his voice, reviling strangers, picking fights, attacking the gendarmes, charging down some secret path of self-destruction. "I need to be consumed by fire," he said. "My concierge or the butcher boy—they must preserve their precious lives. But as for me, my life is important only because of what I can put on canvas. What difference does it make if I give an instant of my life, if, in exchange, I can create a work that will perhaps last?"

He was phenomenally gifted; he drew with an astonishing purity of line, and with such sureness and speed that an artist friend remarked, "He is like a child who has been given a million dollars, but doesn't know what to do with it." He would finish a painting in two hours; he rarely worked on a portrait for more than two days. He haunted the cafés, sketching the people at the tables for a drink or a few francs.

He was fascinated by the human face and form; a landscape or a still life held no attraction for him. He began his portraits with a single feature—an eye, the mouth, an ear—and built the face around it. "My figures see even when I do not draw the pupils in the eyes," he said. "But like the figures of Cézanne, they do not want to express anything beyond a dumb acceptance of life."

He created his own dreamlike universe—a wistful world of languorous lines and beguiling colors, of oval faces and swanlike necks. All of his people seem lost in melancholy, absorbed in the many-faceted mood of solitude.

Now, in 1919, he looked back upon a career of bitter failure. His art was taken seriously by only a few. He got as little as 10 francs for a sitting. Thousands of his marvelous drawings were thrown away. The police had closed one of his shows because the nudes were too explicit and too carnal. He had tried to repay his debts with his paintings, but they were accepted at the value of the canvas alone. A street vendor used his drawings to wrap

up potato chips. One woman peeled the paint off a picture and used the canvas as a bedcover. Besotted with liquor, racked by tuberculosis, he lived between fever and defiance.

Soon after he finished this haunting, oddly chaste portrait of his beloved, with its Gothic grace and cool sadness, Modigliani was found wandering through the streets of Paris, chilled and delirious. He was taken to his squalid studio. He refused to let anyone call a doctor. In several days, he was taken to a charity hospital, where he died. Jeanne Hébuterne was brought to his bed and she fell upon the body, weeping, and covered the face with kisses.

His funeral was attended by almost 10,000 mourners — including Picasso, Braque, Cocteau, Utrillo, Vlaminck, Soutine.

It is said that art dealers scurried along the procession, offering to buy anything he had done. "A Modigliani that sold for 100 francs at the beginning of the funeral," according to one report, "brought 10,000 francs before it was over."

As the funeral wound through the streets, Jeanne Hébuterne returned to the home of her parents. What went on between them, no one can say. What is known is that the distraught girl went to the fifth floor of the building, opened the window and leaped to her death.

To some, there is tragic irony in the name Modigliani's mother had given him—Amedeo—which, in Italian, means "beloved of God."

*Jeanne Hébuterne
(oil, 51″ x 32″)
today hangs in the
home of Mr. and
Mrs. Sidney F. Brody,
Beverly Hills, Calif.*

Memling

"THE MAIDEN AND HER TRUE LOVE?"

FOR MANY YEARS, the demure maiden opposite has graced the Metropolitan Museum of Art in New York. And for many years, the painting of the two horses and the monkey has titillated the curiosity of viewers 4,000 miles away, in a museum in Rotterdam, the Netherlands.

Art experts had tried to locate the companion portrait to the Metropolitan's maiden, for the pink she is holding shows she was engaged, and in bygone days, young men of means often commissioned double portraits of their ladyloves and themselves, gazing fondly at each other, once they had pledged their troth.

The experts were no less convinced that the Rotterdam painting of the two horses must originally have been part of either a diptych (two panels) or a triptych (three panels, hinged, with the two sides folding over the center, as in an altarpiece).

Could anything seem more unlikely than that these two paintings *are*, in fact, companions? Or, even more improbable, that they are a double portrait of a betrothed couple? That the maiden's gallant swain is represented by the dark horse peering so moonily toward her? That the white horse represents a selfish suitor she rejected?

Yet this is precisely the theory advanced by the distinguished art historian Prof. Erwin Panofsky. Consider the evidence: Both pictures were painted by Hans Memling. Both are oils on wood, identical in size (16⅞" x 6¼"). They were both painted around 1470. They were framed alike. And just as a pink signified that a young lady

was engaged, so horses were often used—in medieval allegory, poetry and art—to symbolize lovers. Furthermore, it was customary for affianced damsels to appear on the left-hand panel, shown looking toward the right, and for their loyal fiancés to be portrayed on the right side, looking toward the left.

Now, consider the Rotterdam painting: The white steed gratifying his thirst in the stream, utterly oblivious of the lady, has plausible roots in Christian symbolism, where a white horse often stood for greed and faithlessness (*vide* the Book of Revelation). Consider the monkey, who rides the white quadruped: In medieval times, a monkey was used as an emblem of all that is base and selfish in human nature.

Nor is this all. Consider the striking similarity of details in both pictures: the arches, the position of the trees and bushes, the line of the lawn in the middle, the line of the sill in the foreground. If we bear in mind that the slight break in continuity of the lines across the paintings is accounted for by the space taken up by the two frames, the physical connection between the pictures becomes almost incontrovertible.

The man who painted these delightful companion pieces was born in northwest Germany in the third decade of the 15th century. His family originally spelled their name Memlinc (a version still favored by purists), probably after the town of Memmelinck in Holland. Hans Memlinc left Germany, after an apprenticeship in art, for Brussels, where he entered the workshop of the great

Flemish master Rogier van der Weyden. He ultimately settled in the prosperous and tidy city of Bruges, where, through his talent and personable manner, he became the town artist and one of its leading citizens. He amassed considerable wealth as a portraitist, was much honored by his fellows, married late in life and had three sons.

He lived in a world of political horrors and religious bloodletting: Flanders was overrun by conquerors, and savage wars, vicious persecution, pillage and atrocities darkened men's lives; yet nowhere is there the slightest trace of tragedy in Memling's work. His art is truly that "angelic retreat where," as Eugene Fromentin once wrote, "the passions are silenced and troubles cease . . . and sweet usages grow up like the lilies."

Only a spirit of pervading tenderness could transform whatever he touched with such purity and loveliness. A meticulous craftsman, steeped in the Gothic miniatures and illuminated manuscripts that Flemish artists admired, he worked on a modest scale, made no technical innovations, founded no stylistic school, left no corps of disciples. His was a personal vision, nurtured on the island of his own reticence.

His charming maidens and imperturbable Madonnas, with their high foreheads and narrowed eyes, their delicate brows, tiny waists and wistful mouths, form a quaint feminine type that was unknown to the painters who preceded him, and has long since vanished. Like the unknown *Lady with a Pink*, they are the unique offspring of an artist who was "in love with grace, nobility and beauty."

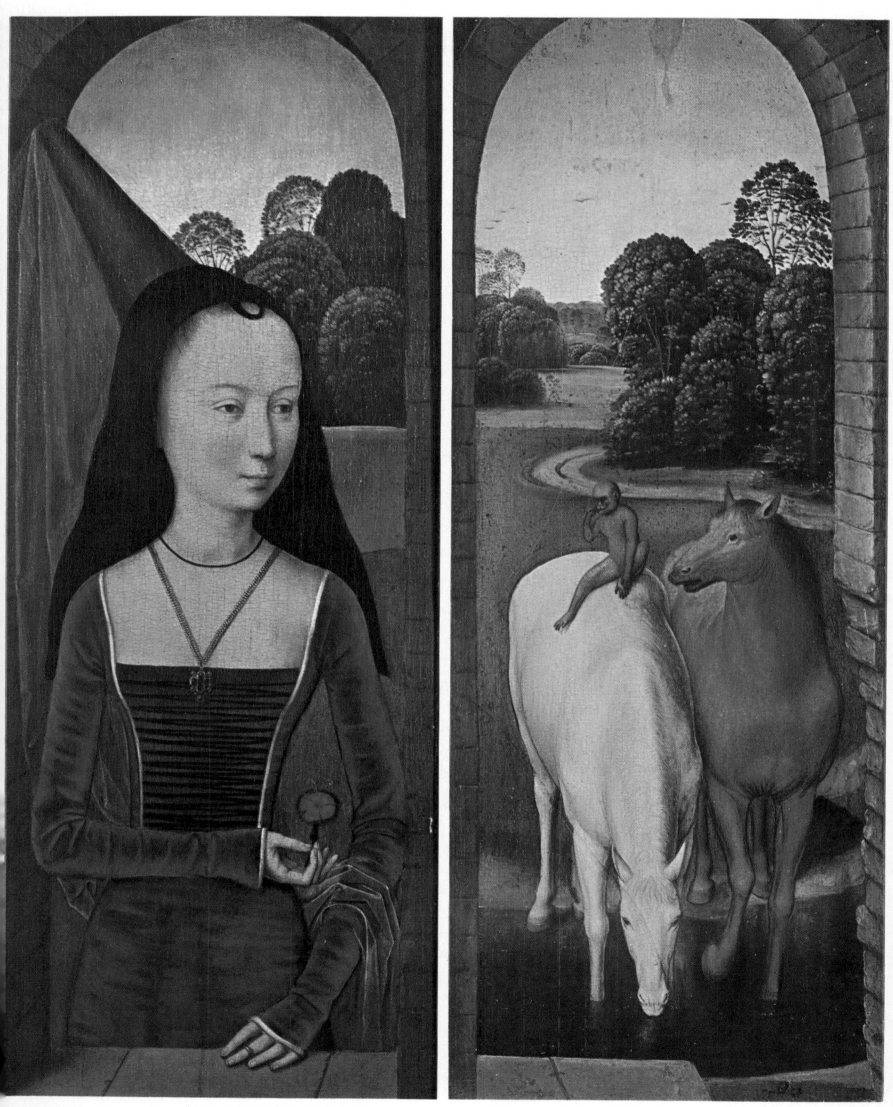

Memling's A Lady With a Pink *(left) is in the Metropolitan Museum of Art, Jules S. Bache Collection, 1949.* Two Horses *may be seen at the Museum Boymans/van Beuningen in Rotterdam.*

Cézanne

THE LONELY MAN

ONE DAY, he arranged some fruit, a glass, a bowl and a jug and began to paint the picture reproduced on the opposite page. He was obsessed by the idea that he could reveal the "inner character" of a pear or a napkin—for he saw them as living things, each with its own unique identity. And, as he had done in his paintings before, he reversed all the canons of perspective, thrusting his composition toward the front, not away, highlighting the foreground, leading the eye back and forth across the picture, not back deep into it. He wanted to wrest monumental power from fruit on a tablecloth. He applied his colors in small, slanting patches, "drawing with the brush."

When he had first shown his pictures, back in 1874, the critics had called him a butcher, "a Zulu," "a deluded madman who paints in fits of delirium tremens." Students at the École des Beaux Arts had marched one of his paintings around a hall, jeering and caterwauling. And the lonely, homely, stubborn Paul Cézanne, a balding man with boorish manners and an odd resemblance to Socrates, had left Paris in bitterness and defeat: "I am sick of the whole damn art racket."

Cézanne was morbidly sensitive and a hopeless perfectionist. He often got so disgusted with his work that he would throw canvases out of the window, or abandon them in open fields, or give them to his son to cut up for jigsaw puzzles. He always dreamed of painting a nude in the open air, but never dared to—because he was terrified of women. His angry outbursts embarrassed even his friends. He was difficult, dogmatic, argumentative. He lived like a hermit. He tried to please no one but his own unyielding demands. Art, he said, is a "priestly vocation." He pursued it with incredible patience and humility.

What he was trying to do was invent an entirely fresh way of handling space and form. He saw that the Impressionists would reach a dead end where all objects dissolved in a formless, shimmering haze. Cézanne, who revered the old masters, launched the Post-Impressionist search for form again.

He was not interested in beauty, but in technique. He saw a face or a landscape as only an arrangement of planes which absorb or reflect light. He knew that warm colors seem to move forward and cool colors seem to recede, and he set about using color itself to convey roundness or depth. "Treat nature by the cylinder, the sphere, the cone," he wrote dryly. He thought geometry the secret of art.

Cézanne saw that colors are never pure, but are formed by light that "breaks down" into infinitely modulated tones. To him, reds turn to orange, and yellows to green, in harmonies of singular freshness and delicacy. He would clean his brush after each of the thousands of strokes by which he worked, to get exact subtleties of shading and a thin, even layer of paint. He was actually reinventing the entire art of painting.

He detested sentiment and rejected "realism." Over and over, he told students: "Get to the bottom of what you find in front of you." He had the fanatical capacity of genius—to stay within the bounds of his own conviction.

He hated painting portraits because his sitters could not remain absolutely motionless, hour after hour, and because he demanded over a hundred sittings for a single picture. When a subject complained, he would snap, "Does an apple move?" He took over 115 sittings of Ambroise Vollard, then grunted only, "The front of the shirt is not bad." But he loved to paint still life (oranges and onions, like apples, "did not move"), and in it and the landscape he was a master. "Fruits and flowers opened their hearts to him."

He never completed the picture reproduced here. Many of his paintings look unfinished, though he never began one until he had "solved" it in his mind. "I am only a helpless pioneer on a lonely road," he cried. "The dream I have spent my life pursuing will never come true. . . . Life is horrifying." But when he died, in 1906, from a fever caught while painting stubbornly out in the rain, other artists seized upon his revelations—his endless experiments with color, his unique use of a kind of flattened space, his "nonobjective" vision —and transformed the familiar into the abstract. He had opened a new door in painting. He was the undisputed father of modernism in art. His signature is all around us.

Paul Cézanne's Still Life with Apples (oil on canvas,
26⅞″ x 36½″) was painted between 1890 and 1900, and
remained uncompleted. This stubborn, original painter
endowed ordinary objects with extraordinary power.
No other painter brought such intense observation
and conviction to landscape and still life. He
used innumerable contrasts of color to communicate
roundness and depth. "He painted a tablecloth as if it were
a mountain." This remarkable painting is in the Lillie P.
Bliss Collection in New York's Museum of Modern Art.

Michelangelo

MEN LIKE GODS

HE WAS 70—this chunky, bitter, intractable man whose art seemed to storm the gates of heaven. Popes and princes vied for his services. His genius ranged across sculpture, painting, poetry and architecture, and with so Olympian an imagination and so commanding an intelligence that some said he was not a man, but a miracle from some superhuman race of beings.

At 18, this broken-nosed Michelangelo Buonarroti was the greatest sculptor in the world. He worked in furies of intensity, attacking gigantic blocks of marble with mallet and chisel, shifting from right hand to left, "liberating" his figures from the stone in which, he said, he saw them "imprisoned." At 22, he went to Rome, where he was to work on and off for almost seven decades and for seven different Popes.

He had never married. Like the ancient Greeks, he admired a man—a handsome Roman named Tommaso dei Cavalieri, whom he drew in the only portrait he ever made. Later, he found a soul mate in a noblewoman named Vittoria Colonna, with whom he shared metaphysical journeys into poetry and religion, and to whom he opened his heart in Platonic devotion.

Men stood transfixed before his statues: the magnificent *David*, carved from an 18-foot slab of marble which had lain unused for years because no other sculptor thought it usable; the sublime *Pietà*, a heartbreaking Madonna with the body of her crucified Son on her lap; the haunting, brooding figures of *Night*, *Day*, *Dawn* and *Twilight* for the great tombs of the Medicis; the majestic *Moses*,

a masterpiece in grandeur. No one before had wrung such expressiveness from the human body.

Pope Julius II had hounded the proud, rebellious Michelangelo into an assignment he hated —painting the immense, curved and lunetted ceiling (over 10,000 square feet in area) of the Sistine Chapel. The irascible Florentine had spent four and a half years working on his back on a scaffold more than 60 feet above the ground, scarcely pausing to sleep or eat, rarely changing his clothes, the paint dripping into his face—to create, at last, his own divinities: prophets and sibyls and men like gods in scenes from Genesis rendered with frightening splendor. He had welded power to purity. He signed his masterpiece sardonically: "Michelangelo, *Sculptor*," for to him the noblest of the arts was always sculpture.

He was denounced in public for his "godlessness" in making all the figures in his *Last Judgment*, under the Sistine ceiling, nude. But his Creator, on that stupendous ceiling, gave Christendom what is still its image of God.

And now Pope Paul III asked him to paint a great fresco, in the Pauline Chapel of the Vatican, on the conversion of St. Paul. Michelangelo was preoccupied with religion at this time. As a youth in Florence, at the court of the Medicis, he had listened to the leading philosophers and humanists of the Renaissance. He had devoured his Dante and had heard the apocalyptic sermons of Savonarola. And now, sickened by the corruption of a sybaritic Rome, he was fascinated, some said, by the defiance which a German monk named

Martin Luther hurled at Catholicism.

So it was with some sense of personal involvement that this restless, sensuous, violent man, who often considered his matchless gifts a torment and a curse, began *Conversion of St. Paul* (opposite page). He took for inspiration the passage in Scriptures which describes Saul's vision: "Now as he journeyed he approached Damascus, and suddenly a light from heaven flashed about him. And he fell to the ground and heard a voice saying to him, 'Saul, Saul, why do you persecute me?'"

The 70-year-old giant crowded a tumult of Promethean figures—soaring, crouching, twisting, turning—into the 20-x-22-foot wall. Once more, his thick, muscular forms, caught in moments marvelously poised between tension and balance, seemed both terrible and divine. He made the massive arm of God reach down in a shaft of light that blinds the stricken Saul, on the ground, shielding his eyes from the awesome vision. And as the face of Saul, he painted his own, even to his double-forked beard. Did he feel compelled to depict himself, no less than St. Paul, as a soul once wavering in faith and now stunned in the presence of God?

"No one understood him," said Romain Rolland, "yet all imitated him. . . . Nothing like Michelangelo had ever appeared before."

Michelangelo's Conversion of St. Paul *graces the Pauline Chapel in the Vatican.*

David

PAINTER IN PRISON

In 1794, JACQUES LOUIS DAVID (Dah-*veed*), the most illustrious artist in France, was condemned to death. A revolutionary Jacobin, David had served as court painter to King Louis XVI. Elected a deputy to the National Convention, David voted to put the King to death. When the Revolution turned on its own, as revolutions have a habit of doing, the great Robespierre and his followers were arrested — David among them. They were jailed in the Hôtel des Fermes.

David's ex-wife, an ardent Royalist who had divorced him after his vote for the King's death, came to visit him. Born Charlotte Pecoul, this beautiful patrician had married David when he was 34 and she only 17. She belonged to a fine and wealthy family; now, with her husband in the shadow of the guillotine, she went from door to door, her children beside her, using her name and influence to plead for David's life.

The painter was both moved and inspired. To him, Charlotte's intercession was more than connubial; she was a patriot, rising above her own convictions, trying to reconcile the embittered factions of France. He conceived of a heroic canvas about the Sabine women who had thrown themselves between warring men to end bloodshed.

It was not unusual for an artist of the eighteenth century to seek a moral in antiquity. The excavations at Pompeii and Herculaneum had excited the intellectuals of Europe, who were infatuated with what Edgar Allan Poe later called "the

glory that was Greece and the grandeur that was Rome." Poetry, sculpture, architecture, oratory— even dress—paid homage to the rediscovered past. And revolutionists, aflame with the ideas of liberty and justice, modeled themselves on Greek heroes and fancied themselves Romans reborn.

But what made David think of the Sabine women? The old legend, embroidered through the centuries, maintained that the followers of Romulus, short of women, raided the Sabine hills northeast of Rome and carried off enough females to insure the populating of their newborn city. Three years later, the Sabine men descended on Rome to rescue their womenfolk from what later generations called "a fate worse than death." But the Sabine women, who had by now borne many children, flung themselves between their Roman husbands and their Sabine ex-husbands, lovers, brothers, fathers, kin.

This was the symbolic tale David decided to paint. He would reach the heart of France through an allegory about women and war, political conflict and national unity. He asked friends to bring books from the *Bibliothèque Nationale* to him, in jail, so that he could study the costumes and weapons of the ancients. He set to work.

Charlotte's eloquence won David a reprieve from death and release from prison. He moved to an atelier in the Louvre. Famed society women, hearing of David's painting-in-progress, offered themselves as models for the Sabine heroines.

They were so proud of the honor that they appeared at the Opera and public halls wearing their hair in the style of David's painting, and in gowns copied from his costumes.

David finished *The War Between the Romans and Sabines* in 1799. Parisians paid more than 65,000 francs, in admissions, to view it. Neither art nor politics alone accounted for such success: the painting titillated public curiosity because some of the heroines were undraped, and the lovely females—well, everyone knew that David's models had been ladies of high station.

A new political crisis threw David into prison again, and again his Charlotte won his freedom. When Napoleon became emperor, he made David "Our First Painter." Came Waterloo. David was exiled. At 68, he left France for Belgium—where he was honored, acclaimed and sought after by legions of French, Dutch and German pupils. No French painter exercised so great an influence on the art of Europe.

David drew beautifully; he painted with distinction; he organized complicated canvases with masterly control. But he could not escape that air of pretentiousness which invests art when the aesthetic is harnessed to the political.

For all its power, rhythm and brilliance, the gigantic painting that began in prison pays the price which allegory exacts from any creator—it is already one step removed from emotions, personally felt and directly communicated.

Jacques Louis David worked on this immense canvas—
12½ x 17 feet!—for five years. After David was
exiled from France, Louis XVIII bought
The War Between the Romans and Sabines *for a then princely*
50,000 francs. It now hangs in the Louvre.

Matisse

MAGICIAN IN COLOR

ONE HOUR BEFORE this startling picture was painted, the three children of Henri Matisse were playing on the wharf at Collioure, a small Mediterranean resort. Pierre, aged 4, who had filled his pinafore with sand, was gravely pouring it into the sea, when Jean, a year older, impatiently pushed him. Pierre fell off the pier and began to drown. Their older sister, Marguerite, cried for help, and a fisherman yanked Pierre out. Marguerite carried the terrified boy home.

Madame Matisse comforted the children, gave Pierre a warm bath and some sweets—and cautioned them to breathe not a word to their father. For nothing, not even a near-drowning, must disrupt her husband's work or the even, orderly life he demanded. She was the most devoted of wives—Matisse's first and favorite model, the lady whose later portrait in a hat of strident colors ("The hat was black, of course," Matisse mischievously revealed) was to create a furor.

Madame Matisse lay down on the couch; Marguerite went out to the balcony. Matisse came into the room. It was a scene of languor and repose. Matisse set up an easel, selected a canvas from the many he always kept stretched and ready, took his paints and precisely arranged rectangular palette (they were always perfectly neat and ready, too) and happily painted this picture. It made history. For it was this painting that marked the birth of Fauvism in the 1905 show, when Matisse, Rouault, Vlaminck and Dufy stunned the critics with the riotous colors, the disregard of form, the flat-tened space which "these Fauves" ("wild beasts") had the "gall" to exhibit as art.

Matisse always remained the staid father of a bourgeois family. In 1891, he had promised his father (a grain merchant who wanted Henri to be a lawyer) that though he wanted to be an artist, he would never, never become a Bohemian. Years later, when his fame was international, Matisse begged a reporter: "Do tell the Americans that I am a normal man, a devoted husband and father with three fine children. . . ."

There was another side to the story. This methodical, robust, witty little man who looked like a shopkeeper and adored practical jokes was wracked by anxiety throughout his life. He had a horror of wasting time and a premonition that some mysterious force had given him his talent—and might take it away. "There was always a feeling of deadlines about him," his son Pierre says.

When Matisse was 20, recovering from an appendectomy that interrupted his law studies, his mother gave him some paints. He copied a lithograph. "I felt transported into a paradise in which I felt gloriously free." He was so frightened by the thought that it was too late for him to become an artist that he plunged into painting "head down."

He first studied under Bouguereau, painting conventional pictures he loathed. "Exactitude is not truth," he said. When he saw Goya's brilliant, slashing work, he exclaimed, "I can paint that way!" One day, he noticed how much light a friend got into pictures by juxtaposing Impressionist colors. He saw how Cézanne simulated perspective with color alone. He saw how Gauguin and Van Gogh expressed emotion through violent hues and distorted drawing.

Matisse abandoned shadows, discarded perspective, rejected the old masters' gradations of dark and light—and bent color itself into the service of contour. He wanted his pictures to be gay and sensuous, but he planned them like an engineer. He drew so that no line was superfluous, and painted so that no brush stroke was fortuitous.

He went to Morocco, fell under the spell of Oriental motifs and reveled in bizarre patterns and exotic colors. He went on to sculpture, lithography, stained glass, tapestries, ballet sets. And when he was too old and ill to work at an easel, this man who always used spectacles (and imagination) to surmount his nearsightedness, lay in bed, took scissors and glue and colored paper, and turned out brilliant *papiers collés*—pasted-up cutouts of colored paper.

What happened to the others in our story? Pierre Matisse, who almost drowned, is a leading art dealer in New York. Jean, who pushed him in, has become a noted sculptor. The girl on the balcony married a distinguished scholar. Matisse died in 1954, aged 85. His wife died four years later, at 83. *Interior at Collioure* marked his first step toward "what I dreamed of . . . an art of balance, of purity and serenity, devoid of depressing subject matter . . . art that is an appeasing influence, like a good armchair in which to rest. . . ."

Interior at Collioure *(23½″ x 28⅝″) was painted in 1905 and created
a furor when exhibited. It marked the birth of the
controversial "Fauvist" school. Here, Matisse used color to smash
through the bonds of form and perspective. This free, fresh, lyrical
painting is in a private collection in Ascona, Switzerland.*

Botticelli

A STRANGE AND SPECIAL BEAUTY

HE FOUNDED NO SCHOOL, led no movement, attracted few imitators. In an era bursting with drama and brilliance, his life was devoid of both. He lived in the Renaissance, yet remained Gothic in spirit—a marginal man who saturated his paintings with an odd, dreamy grace and his own sweet-sad melancholy.

Sandro Botticelli's patrons, the Medici of Florence, must have regarded his talent as essentially decorative, for they commissioned him to paint many "fancy pictures for bed fronts and chests." The Pope called him to Rome, where, with a battery of artists, he worked on the Sistine Chapel; but his frescoes created no great stir. He was entirely overshadowed by his contemporaries—Leonardo da Vinci, Michelangelo, Raphael, Titian.

Botticelli was born in Florence in 1444 or '45. It was a city unmatched for the brilliance of its culture, the splendor of its life, the juiciness of its pleasures. The Florentines loved pageants and panoply. One of the most spectacular *divertissements* occurred in 1475, when Giuliano de'Medici, the younger brother of Lorenzo the Magnificent, sponsored a great tournament in the Piazza Santa Croce. The coveted crown of "Queen of Beauty" was bestowed on Simonetta Cattaneo, the young wife of Marco Vespucci, but known to all Florence as Giuliano's beloved.

Giuliano was murdered in the cathedral of Florence by political rivals, and the bereaved Lorenzo asked Botticelli to immortalize Giuliano—and the girl he loved, who had died soon after Giuliano's tournament. Tradition has long had it that

Simonetta's features appear in Botticelli's marvelous *Birth of Venus*, in *Mars and Venus* and in the Uffizi Gallery's great 6'8" x 10'4" *Primavera* (of which the right-hand third is reproduced on the opposite page).

Some historians believe Simonetta was the model for the goddess of love; some believe her immortalized in the figure of Flora shown here, a pensive, dolorous maiden, a wreath in her hair, a garland around her neck, strewing roses from the folds of that superbly adorned gown. Was this really Simonetta—this delicate, haunting girl who appears again and again in Botticelli's work?

Not that he was in love with her; his name was never linked in romance to any woman's. Indeed, when his cousin once urged him to marry, Botticelli replied: "One night I dreamed that I was married, and the bare idea made me feel so miserable that for fear I should fall asleep and dream the same dream, I got up and rushed about the streets of Florence like a madman."

Simonetta died before Botticelli painted the *Primavera* (around 1478). Whether she was Botticelli's model or not, we may never know; nor does it matter. *Some* face so bewitched Botticelli that he idealized it into an image of such fresh and unique beauty that it stands out as utterly his own invention. Few faces so aptly illustrate the line of Francis Bacon: "There is no excellent beauty that hath not some strangeness in the proportion."

Botticelli practically stopped painting after 1500. A man neurotic by any standard, he was caught up in the fantastic drama of the monk

Savonarola, whose apocalyptic sermons against luxury and licentiousness threw Florence into such agonies of guilt that huge bonfires were lighted in the public squares and the lords and ladies threw the objects of their vanity—jewels, ornaments, costumes—into the flames. Botticelli is reported to have tossed some of his own "secular" paintings into the fires. His house became a meeting place for Savonarola's followers.

So little dent did Botticelli make on his time that his death, in 1510, went unnoticed, and his name was misspelled in the official register. And when, almost 90 years later, the Grand Duke Ferdinand published a list of masters whose paintings he forbade Florentine citizens to remove from their homes or churches, Botticelli's name was not included.

Until the late 19th century, Botticelli was forgotten. Today, his paintings are among the most popular of any 15th-century artist's. For he had the rarest of gifts—the capacity to lure us into the realm of his own strange and special beauty. His flowing lines, his stylized postures and intertwined forms, his subordination of color to pattern transform his paintings into a kind of archaic tapestry. He remains forever remote from us, a self-absorbed figure, not reaching out to the viewer, but spinning his own private and ambiguous harmonies. Perhaps that is why "we feel a pleasure in Botticelli that few if any other artists can give us," says art critic Bernard Berenson. "He was the greatest artist of linear design Europe has ever had. . . . He got music out of design."

Sandro Botticelli's great allegory of spring,
the Primavera, over 10 feet long and almost
7 feet high, remains one of the most beloved
paintings in the world. For almost 400 years,
Botticelli's name was hardly noticed, his
paintings unacclaimed. Few artists invested
their work with such singularity of style and
such altogether unique "atmosphere." The
grace, melancholy, and sheer singing loveliness
of the Primavera make it one of the crowning
masterpieces in the Uffizi Gallery, Florence.

Holbein

EYES FOR A KING

THE KING: Henry VIII. The lady in the portrait: Anne of Cleves. The painter: Hans Holbein.

Few artists ever had a more peculiar assignment; few paintings ever played so curious and historic a role.

In 1539, Henry VIII—massive, gluttonous, majestic—was looking for wife number 4. He had divorced Catherine of Aragon, beheaded Anne Boleyn and seen Jane Seymour die after childbirth. He now sent a mission to Cleves, near Cologne, to look over 23-year-old Lady Anne.

Politics, not love, dictated the move: Henry wanted Anne's father, the Duke of Cleves, as an ally against the Catholic powers of the Continent. And Henry sent Hans Holbein along with the mission to paint the girl, saying, "I put more trust in your brush than in all the reports of my courtiers."

But Sir Thomas Cromwell, one of the King's advisers, told Holbein, "You will, I am sure, bring back a most *beautiful* portrait of the Lady Anne." Cromwell wanted to ensure a Protestant alliance.

Holbein met the Lady Anne in her castle, near Cologne, on a hot August afternoon. She was no vision of loveliness. She was, in fact, large-boned, bovine, vapid—and pock-marked. She knew no language but German—fortunately, Holbein's native tongue—and she bombarded the painter with questions. Would it be hard to learn English? Did King Henry like singing or the lute or cards? She neither sang nor played the lute nor knew card games—which, in Lutheran Cleves, were most

grievous sins. She *was* good-natured, patient, honest. She was also dull.

Holbein faced a perplexing dilemma. If he prettified Anne, he would please Cromwell, but risk the wrath of the King. If he painted her as plain, he would offend not only Cromwell, but the girl who might become Queen.

She sat for him in elegant court clothes, perspiring from the heat, and babbled along in German all the while. The left-handed Holbein worked rapidly and with phenomenal precision, using red chalk to mark the reference points: the eyes, the chin, the sweep of the sleeves. Then he began to paint over the sketch and—with irony? in self-protection?—enveloped this uninspiring girl in an aura of magnificence, bold color and flawless texture, powerful composition and exquisite detail. The insipid features were framed in sumptuous velvet, glowing jewels and incandescent brocade.

Holbein finished the painting in less than a week; he knew it was a masterpiece. He returned to England, where Henry VIII took one look at the portrait and signed the marriage contracts. Arrangements were made for royal nuptials that would dazzle Europe.

Anne crossed the Channel and arrived at Rochester the day before New Year's Eve. Henry awaited her at Greenwich, where a glittering pageant was planned. Suddenly, the King ordered eight friends to accompany him—all dressed in gray—and rode to Rochester impulsively. He

wanted to see Anne before the public celebrations. A courtier rode ahead to announce him.

The King burst in on Anne, who knelt before him—ungainly and bony and pock-marked. "So marvelously abashed and stunned was he," it is recorded, that he forgot to give the girl the furs and jewels he had brought along as presents. He returned to Greenwich in a rage. To Cromwell, he stormed: "Were it not for fear of driving her father into the hands of the Emperor Charles, I would never marry her. Is there no remedy?"

There was no remedy. They were married on January 6, 1540. The next morning, Henry exclaimed, "She's no better than a Flanders mare!"

On July 9, Henry had the marriage declared null and void. He gave Anne two royal residences, 3,000 pounds a year and the unusual title of "Adopted Sister."

The girl from Cleves became "more joyous than ever and was wearing a new dress every day."

Sir Thomas Cromwell was arrested for "treason" and executed in the Tower of London.

Holbein, surprisingly, remained court painter to the end of his days.

And the King? Henry chose his next two wives only after personal inspection. Only one of them had to be beheaded.

Hans Holbein painted this magnificent tempera and oil of Anne of Cleves (25⅝" x 18⅞") in 1539. Millions have admired it; but few knew its story, as arresting as the picture itself. The painting now hangs in the Louvre, Paris.

Della Francesca

A GENTLE GRANDEUR

FEW TOURISTS BOTHER TO VISIT the provincial town of Arezzo, 38 miles from Florence. Yet Arezzo contains the Church of San Francesco, on whose 60-foot-high walls, over 500 years ago, Piero della Francesca painted *The Story of the True Cross*, a series of frescoes so beautiful—in color and design and in what can only be called a gentle grandeur—that they rank among the crowning achievements of the Renaissance.

We know little about the life of Piero della Francesca. He won little renown in his own time; for 400 years, his reputation was overshadowed by contemporaries whose brilliance history never surpassed—Leonardo, Fra Angelico, Michelangelo, Botticelli, Giovanni Bellini, Mantegna, Fra Filippo Lippi. Today, Piero ranks among the immortals.

Piero was born in the Umbrian town of Borgo San Sepolcro around 1415. He studied mathematics as a boy, was apprenticed to the Florentine studio of Domenico Veneziano, and was deeply influenced by Uccello. He spent most of his life around Borgo, where he adorned chapels, painted altarpieces and executed portraits. His famous profiles of the Duke and Duchess of Urbino still stand among the most memorable and appealing portraits in the history of art.

He was an extremely slow painter. One contract granted him eight years to complete an altarpiece—and he took no less than 15. Much of his work has disappeared; his frescoes in Rome, to which he was once summoned by the Pope, were blithely removed from the walls of the Vatican so that Raphael might use the surfaces.

In a day when art and science moved hand in hand, Piero sought to enlist geometry in the service of painting. He mastered his Euclid, became an intimate of Luca Pacioli, a celebrated mathematician, and wrote a learned treatise on perspective and rectilinear bodies.

Piero contributed as much as any painter of his time to the solution of technical problems of distance, depth and space. He was among the first to use light itself as an ingredient of perspective, as a bridge between figures and background. He often made little figures out of clay, draped them with fabrics and used them as models. His painted forms all look solid, beautifully rounded, anchored in space, deftly related to what lies before and beyond them—a triumph of painting skill in the mid-15th century.

He loved color and costume, rich brocades and exotic headdresses, of which he must have seen aplenty in the pageants and parades of Renaissance Italy. He was also among the first to use color to convey feeling. Unlike the Gothic artists, who worked with a restricted palette, Piero moved across the spectrum with delight, inventing delicate harmonies—pinks, soft grays and browns, mellow rusts, pale yellows and shadings of blue such as no other Italian had attempted.

But none of this explains the distinctive and enduring beauty of Piero's work. "He neither loves nor hates," wrote Lionello Venturi, "nor even smiles or weeps. . . . His art is a monument of contemplative beauty. In it, life goes imperturbably on, as if time had never been. . . ."

The marvelous angelic minstrels on the opposite page, singing the first Christmas carols in this beguiling *Nativity*, are caught in a moment of action that is rare with Piero; yet even their joy is imbedded in the curious and fascinating repose that is his hallmark. His Virgin is a pretty, statuesque young woman—not the pallid Madonna of so many artists before him. He linked the rhythms of the distant landscape to the odd carpet of herbage and into the folds of the gown on the kneeling Virgin and back into the draped tunics of the angels, who have the strength of sculpture.

His clarity, his assurance, his supreme composure are all to be seen in *The Nativity*, of which the English critic R. N. D. Wilson wrote: "He evokes a feeling of suspended action, a pause in the drama, infinitely solemn, in which the participants become mysterious spectators of the scene they are enacting." His world is always cool, composed, lucid; he is never agitated or sentimental; he never overstates; he is never flamboyant. He achieves nobility without pretentiousness.

The Nativity has been damaged in cleanings and restoration, but we still see in it what the late Bernard Berenson meant when he said that the miracle of Piero's charm is that he can hold us spellbound by his very impersonality.

The Nativity (49¾″ x 48½″) was the center part of a triptych whose
side wings are today in the cathedral in Borgo San Sepolcro.
Painted around 1470, the picture was badly damaged in various
cleanings before it came to London's great National Gallery
(here reproduced by courtesy of The Trustees); there were once
strings on the instruments, and some inept restorer failed to
replace the pupils in the eyes of the shepherd standing at right.

Rousseau

THE COUCH IN THE JUNGLE

OF COURSE YOU ASK, "What is a naked lady on a sofa doing in the middle of a jungle?" The question was often asked of Henri Rousseau in 1910, when he finished this strange, moon-swept landscape. To one critic, Rousseau—a benevolent, sentimental, incurably romantic, hopelessly naïve man—replied, "This woman asleep on the couch dreams that she has been transported into the forest, listening to the sounds from the instrument of the enchanter. This is the reason for the couch in the jungle." But to another, the painter merrily confided, "The sofa is there only because of its glowing red color." (The "glowing red" has turned to dark maroon, alas, over the years.)

Attached to the back of the painting was a verse Rousseau had written; it begins, in Bertha Ten Eyck James's translation:

> Yadwigha in a lovely dream,
> Having most sweetly gone to sleep,
> Heard the snake-charmer blow his flute,
> Breathing his meditation deep.
> While on the streams and verdant trees
> Gleam the reflections of the moon,
> And savage serpents lend their ears
> To the gay measures of the tune.

Who was "Yadwigha"? She was a Polish maiden whom the quixotic Rousseau met — or claimed to have met — in Paris, and over whom he fondly sighed years later. After he was smitten with her charms, the fair Yadwigha either returned to Poland or disappeared or died. No one knows.

Some even consider Yadwigha's attractions more the product of fantasy than truth. With the fey Rousseau, indeed, it was hard to tell where reality ended and imagination began.

He was a small, gentle, mustached Frenchman who loved to play the violin for his friends, but would get so carried away, while playing, that he would hop from one foot to the other. He served in the French Army—by playing the flute in the 52nd Infantry Band. At 40, he decided to devote himself solely to painting.

He seems to have been bewitched by one Yadwigha after another. He had seven children by his first wife, to whom he was blissfully married for 20 years, and when she died, he pined and yearned —and launched upon ardent love affairs, none of which, with surpassing innocence, he made the slightest attempt to conceal.

He loved to spin romantic tales about the French invasion of Mexico in the 1860's, attributing his virgin forests and primeval jungles to impressions he gained as a musician in the army of Maximilian. No evidence was ever found to support these stories. His exotic plants and flowers, his quaint birds and beasts were more likely the result of the hours he spent poring over botanical handbooks and catalogues or, with childlike concentration and delight, at the Botanical Gardens. His imagination was so powerful that, while painting a jungle scene or some fantastic beast, his heart would pound with terror. He would have to

stop work and rush to the window and gasp for air.

His naïveté passeth understanding. Two of his paintings had to be removed from the 1907 Salon des Indépendants—and it is not hard to see why: One showed the Kaiser parading through the streets, stark-naked; the other depicted the Czar and the Mikado wrestling, stark-naked too.

The papers called him a half-wit; critics derided the lyrical scenes he painted with such tenderness. But Gauguin, Redon, the young Picasso saw that a bright and original talent had broken through the preoccupations of the Impressionists (disregarding form and design) with the unconcerned certainty of his innocence.

His life was a confluence of art and *amour*. After his second wife died, he felt the grand passion once more—for an unresponsive widow who was, literally, the death of him: At 66, the lovesick Rousseau went serenading the lady under her window during a Parisian downpour, sacrificing sense to infatuation, got soaked to the skin, came down with pneumonia and died.

He called this last great painting (in which one artist counted 50 shades of green alone) *The Dream*. But all his work derived from the dreams he cherished. His apparently artless "primitivism" created an inimitable atmosphere of enchantment. The simple-hearted man who did not hesitate to put the nude Yadwigha on a couch in a jungle possessed what every artist seeks and only the rarest few attain: a truly fresh vision.

Henri Rousseau's last great painting, The Dream (oil, 80″ x 118½″), is in the Museum of Modern Art, New York, a gift of Nelson A. Rockefeller.

Hals

"HE FORCED IMMORTALITY UPON THEM...."

HE WAS 84 YEARS OLD when he painted the chilling masterpieces you gaze upon now. He was destitute, living on an allowance from the Paupers' Fund of Haarlem, Holland. He had been a noted painter, never wealthy, some of whose best pictures sold at auction for a few shillings.

One day, the regents of the Haarlem poorhouse voted to sit for two group portraits—one, of the trustees of the men's almshouse; the other, of the women's trustees. It may have been out of pity that they asked the aged Frans Hals to paint both. Or perhaps, being old themselves, they hoped for a flattering portrayal from a grateful pauper.

They did not know their man. Age had not dimmed the penetrating power of Frans Hals's eye, or the pitiless candor of his brush. He had never painted anything but portraits. He had never sought the commissions so popular with wealthy Dutch burghers—sparkling interiors, meticulous still lifes, pretty landscapes, charming domestic scenes. Hals had spent a long and raucous lifetime painting "vulgar" people—laughing soldiers, brawling fishwives, lusty wenches, boozy barflies, grinning harpies. He had never pandered to the *nouveau riche*. His pictures were revelations of character, not celebrations of social station.

Now, in the year 1664, this 84-year-old "hasbeen" acquired two huge canvases, each over eight feet long, and set to work. In the group portrait of the male regents, he painted one who was

bulbous-nosed and tipsy, his hat askew; he showed another so insipid that the portrayal might have been a caricature. As for the women, he arranged the five old matriarchs in a peerless composition, under a stark nocturnal light, accenting—in black and gray—the desiccation of these worthy, withered biddies, highlighting the gnarled fingers and wrinkled skins, seeing, behind faces ennobled by age, the inflexibility of Puritans. It was "superb—but terrifying," a masterpiece in a mood that can only be called mortuary. Intentionally or not, he "avenged himself upon the complacent nonentities," says André Malraux; he also "forced immortality" upon them.

The two group portraits won Hals no praises. They were quietly put away in the Old People's Home, where they remained, practically unknown, for 250 years—until 1913, to be exact, when the remains of the poorhouse became the core of a special museum to memorialize Frans Hals's art. The regents hang there today, staring at each other across a room.

Their almost frightening impact was described by Paul Claudel: "Are these the living or the dead? [These] five fearsome old ladies seem to be sitting in judgment on us. . . . Neither in Goya nor in El Greco is there anything so convincing nor so appalling. . . . All the accounts have been squared; no money is left on the table—only that book whose pallid cover gleams like dry bone

and whose fore edge has the glow of burning coal."

Long before 1913, painters had recognized Hals's mastery of portraiture. Manet and Van Gogh marveled at Hals's capacity to "state the subject instantly, at one stroke." The Impressionists hailed him and Velázquez (who was painting in Spain during the same years) as forerunners of the modern, original minds who boldly fragmented their pigment, seized upon swift impressions, broke up color for the eye of the beholder to reassemble.

Hals's life was as boisterous as his art. A happy carouser, he was often drunk, broke and in debt. His first wife, by whom he had two children, died after a beating he gave her. His second bore him ten children. He trained seven of his sons to be painters.

He never put a lifeless stroke on canvas. He specialized in spontaneity. He did not gloss over his brushwork, as painters before him had done. He thrust the decisive components of character—a wicked grin, a nervous hand, a flabby mouth, a foolish nose—right toward the viewer, with a kind of mocking force. Many of his pictures look unfinished, and this, too, was part of the deft simplicity with which he achieved such directness.

Frans Hals's people seem to move out of their frame. They are as alive or—as in the unforgettable five women staring at you—as unyielding as the day he painted them.

For 250 years, these powerful group portraits remained virtually unseen. In 1913, they became the central exhibits in the Frans Hals Museum in Haarlem, the Netherlands. The Male Regents of the Haarlem Almshouse, *above*, is 67½" x 101¼". The Female Regents, *to the right*, were immortalized on a canvas almost as large: 66¾" x 98".

Caravaggio

WHO WAS THIS MADONNA?

In 1605, the fathers of the church of Santa Maria della Scala in Rome commissioned a brilliant, violent artist named Michelangelo Amerighi da Caravaggio to paint the death of the Virgin.

This Caravaggio was a most "ugly runt" of 32 with a temper of fire—a short, powerful, intractable brawler with a thick mustache, a black goatee and eyes that blazed like coals. He had fled from Milan to Venice after a street fight, and from Venice to Rome after another.

Caravaggio approached *The Death of the Virgin* with utter self-confidence. He made no preliminary sketches or drawings or designs. He simply took an immense canvas, 12 feet tall and 8 feet wide—and set to work. The measure of his assurance was matched by the magnitude of his skill.

A year later, the painting was completed. The pious fathers of Santa Maria della Scala took one horrified look at the picture and refused to accept it. This painting was sacrilegious: this Madonna was no ethereal Virgin, conscious of immortality, breathing intimations of beatitude. This was a plain, ordinary woman, poorly clothed, barefooted, who looked like—why, like a woman of the streets. Here were none of the familiar contrivances of humility—no signs of exaltation, no ascension to glory in the heavens amid a covey of angels. This Mary was a lifeless body on whose face lay only the reluctant serenity of death.

And the saints around the Madonna—these were not majestic figures, men of noble birth, patrons of the arts. These men looked like beggars, unshod creatures from the alleys of the Eternal City—poor men mourning a woman who *looked* dead. Rumors even raced through Rome that Caravaggio, that wild man, had used the body of a woman, drowned in the Tiber, as a model for the Madonna. The fathers of Santa Maria della Scala would have none of this appalling vulgarization of holiness. They would not even allow the Painters' Guild to see what Caravaggio had done.

But the great Flemish master Peter Paul Rubens, working in Rome, saw *The Death of the Virgin* and persuaded his patron, the Duke of Mantua, to buy it. The picture was exhibited in Rome for one week. Thousands—lured by rumors about the notorious painter—flocked to see it.

What they saw was staggering—the reduction of the supernatural to the recognizable, a drama of emotion, deeply felt and nobly transmitted. This was a painting born in the amplitude of a vision that broke through the conventional posturings and mannerisms which were stifling religious painting. The heroic scale, the commanding arrangement of the figures, the daring lighting (which influenced Rembrandt), the power of the conception—these registered an impact on the viewer that could not be forgotten. Here was a work which exemplified Caravaggio's creed: Art must be related to life, to the living. "The greatest art," his motto went, "is to owe nothing to art."

The year he finished *The Death of the Virgin*, Caravaggio killed Ranuccio Tomassoni in a quarrel—about a point in tennis—and fled to the Sabine Hills. From there, he stole to Naples, then Malta, where he lived under the protection of the Duke of Malta. He was even knighted. But the violence of his temper undid him once more. He assaulted a cavalier, was imprisoned, scaled the walls and escaped—to Syracuse, then Messina, then Palermo. Some knights of Malta caught up with him in Naples and beat him up so badly that he was reported dead. Caravaggio set sail for Port Ercole—and was hauled off the boat, in a case of mistaken identity, and imprisoned again. Released, he spent a night wandering on the seashore, cursing and raging. He died a few days later in the throes of malaria at the age of 36.

The Death of the Virgin was purchased by King Charles I of England for £600, and was later sold to Louis XIV. Today, it hangs—honored, admired, much beloved—in the Louvre.

And who was the Madonna in the painting? She was a woman who had flung herself into the Tiber in despair. Caravaggio—moved by the legacy of suffering on the face—had taken the body to his studio and used it as his model.

Michelangelo Amerighi da Caravaggio (1573-1610) painted The Death of the Virgin *in 1606. It hangs in the Louvre, Paris.*

Redon

THE MAGIC CASEMENTS

"I HAVE LIVED WITH a Redon 'bouquet' for 35 years," says Claude Roger-Marx, French collector and critic, "and its charm never fades. Forty anemones (they seem like a thousand) in shades of purple, violet, mauve, blue, lemon yellow, pink-veined white . . . they seem just brought in from a garden. Yet what is it that sets them apart from all other painted flowers? Why do they seem not wholly of this earth?"

They seem not wholly of this earth because Odilon Redon—lonely, shy, withdrawn—painted "double impressions," by which he meant an inspired fusion of "reality seen" with the lovely, lyrical images released within himself by "reality *felt*." Redon insisted that even his most enchanted visions (and there is no better word than "enchanted" to describe them) were true—that is, depicted a world that actually exists. His particular genius contained the power to cast a spell upon us which makes that inner world—radiant and mysterious—exist for us.

For 30 years, while Degas, Monet, Renoir, Matisse revolutionized painting, liberating color, endowing it with unprecedented range and freedom, Redon explored his own fantasies and showed little interest in Impressionism. He worked entirely in black (as did Seurat, for many years). "One must respect black," he wrote. "It awakens no sensuality. It is the agent of the mind. It provides no scope for mere pleasantries."

He undertook no "big" subjects, no majestic cathedrals or commanding landscapes, no dramatic portraits or shimmering meadows. He painted flowers—mystical, luminous flowers—and faces seen in dreams (as in the haunting *Ophelia* on the opposite page). He endowed his flowers with a kind of exaltation. He said he sought "the magic casements" through which we can enter "the unseen world."

Redon was born in Bordeaux in 1840. A sickly, delicate child, he was raised in the country, not by his parents, but by an uncle. He felt condemned by illness to "a tragic and fatal isolation." Once he wrote: "As a child I sought out shadows, hiding behind the big curtains in the dark corners of the house . . . living inside myself."

He got little love from his mother, a Creole from Louisiana, and he felt little love for her. It was his French father "who taught me to see apparitions, strange beings, chimerical and wonderful, in the shifting clouds and sky."

From the time he began to draw, Redon observed nature with care; he learned that it was only after he had copied a petal, a stone, a blade of grass with scrupulous fidelity that he felt "fired with the urge to create something imaginary." Reality was his touchstone to imagination, his gate to the strange harmonies he discovered within and beyond the seen.

For three decades, Redon limned his brooding, secretive fancies—but only in the quiet chords of black and white. He was 40 years old before he married—a Creole, like his mother, one Camille Falte, who had come to Paris from an island in the Indian Ocean. She made him a home in which, for the first time, he discovered that happiness was possible. An exotic woman who loved color, Mme. Redon filled their apartment with flowers of every shape and hue, placing fresh bouquets they could scarcely afford in her husband's workroom. "I have found in my wife," he said, "the lodestar of my life." Slowly, color entered his work.

Redon was 55 when a friend brought him a gift—a box of pastels. The man who had been an artist all his life was as captivated by the crayons as if he were a child seeing them for the first time. Encouraged by Gauguin, he began to use color more freely. "Black exhausts me. Pastels and red chalk—these soft materials bring me joy."

They brought him more than joy. They opened new heavens to his fantasies. He began to paint flowers—but what flowers! They seem to breathe, to glow and tremble before the eye. He painted blossoms, buds, leaves as if they had moods. And he did this through chromatic contrasts and complementary tones so fresh, so poetic that his flowers became nothing less than odes to beauty.

The power to bewitch the beholder, to reveal divinity in the commonplace, is the subtlest talent an artist can possess. Redon described it in these words: "My originality consists in placing the logic of the possible at the service of the invisible."

Odilon Redon's matchless capacity to capture
the spiritual essences of flowers is nowhere better
seen than in this glowing Ophelia (pastel, 25″ x 36″),
which is in the collection of Mrs. Albert D. Lasker,
in New York. Redon executed many Ophelias, in
his incomparable pastels and in oil. His romantic,
inward "double impressions" often led him to
place the pensive profile of a maiden among the
flowers he endowed with such enchantment.

Rubens

"SHE WOULD NOT BLUSH..."

IN 1630, the illustrious Peter Paul Rubens, a widower, wrote a friend: "I have taken a young wife of honest but middle-class family. Everyone tried to persuade me to make a Court marriage, but I feared Pride, that inherent vice of the nobility. I chose one who would not blush to see me take my brushes in hand...."

Rubens was 53. His bride, Helena Fourment, was only 16. She was the niece of the wife with whom he had spent 17 blissful years. Helena's beauty was so renowned that she was called "Helen of Flanders." She was the very incarnation of those plump, billowy charms the prosperous Flemish admired. And Rubens had been painting her, in a way, long before he ever saw her, for she bore an astonishing resemblance to that ideal of beauty he had already immortalized on canvas.

The girl "who would not blush" inspired Rubens to new creative heights. He painted her again and again—as the Virgin, as Mary Magdalene, as the nude Susanna in the bath, as a nymph with golden tresses and pink-and-pearl complexion. He caught her loveliness in enchanting portraits—alone or with their children (she gave him four). She was only 24 when he draped her in fur to create what is acclaimed one of the enduring masterpieces of art (opposite page).

The painter's most difficult technical problem, says Sir Kenneth Clark, the British critic, is to catch with his "sticky pigments and smearing brush . . . that strange substance (flesh) . . . neither white nor pink, of a texture smooth yet variable, absorbing the light yet reflecting it, delicate yet resilient, flashing and fading.... Perhaps only three men, Titian, Rubens and Renoir, were sure how it should be done."

But where Titian was classical, and Renoir (300 years later) romantic, Rubens rendered the female form with exuberant and unprecedented candor. He painted his ripe, full-blown beauties without a trace of the salacious. In private life, he was more than moral; he was, in fact, prudish. What fascinated him was the technical problem of rendering with paint the depth and roundness of sculpture. The Greeks had accented the sensuousness of flesh with gossamer veils which clung to the body. Rubens used the dimples and wrinkles of skin itself as modeling to catch light and convey the sense of movement and living tissue.

Rubens was no Bohemian, no tortured soul, no mystic seeking exaltation in art. He brought to painting immense vitality, a love of life, passion for drawing and "the ease of genius." He spoke six languages, was a student of science, consorted with noblemen and scholars. He often had Plutarch or Cicero or Virgil read aloud to him while he worked at his easel. Handsome, cultivated, brilliant, he served as a diplomat on special missions to Spain and England, where Charles I knighted him.

He and his beloved Helena, 37 years his junior, owned a castle, the Château de Steen near Brussels, and a palatial house in Antwerp with vast gardens and lawns on which peacocks roamed.

He owned his own gallery of masterpieces, collected in Italy and later sold to the Duke of Buckingham. Platoons of pupils and assistants, among them Anthony Van Dyck, worked in his studio factory. Yet for all his wealth and fame, Rubens arose every morning at four, heard Mass, then painted as long as the daylight held.

"No undertaking," he once wrote, "however vast in size and diversified in subject, ever daunted my courage." He created complex canvases of gigantic scale and splendor (some 14′ x 10′) in which the figures are interlaced in magnificent rhythms—bursting with life, swirling with sheer kinetic excitement.

He produced some of the noblest religious pictures in art, a score of stupendous paintings on the life of Marie de'Medici, the great Constantine tapestries for Louis XIII, the monumental paintings of Henry IV, a magnificent ceiling in London's Whitehall Palace and some of the loveliest portraits and landscapes we know.

Rubens's prodigious talent "outlined the direction of painting for two centuries," said a curator of the Louvre. English artists used his portraits as models of perfection; his landscapes inspired Constable and Corot; his magnificent coloring—as in the radiant Helena in the fur coat—broke the trail for Watteau, Delacroix and Renoir.

Above all, this many-sided genius realized the almost limitless aesthetic range of the female form. In Clark's words: "Rubens did for the female nude what Michelangelo had done for the male."

Rubens's portrait of his young second wife, Helena Fourment, *one of the most celebrated works of art, was painted around 1638. Virtually life-size (69″ x 33″), it hangs in Vienna's great* Kunsthistorisches Museum.

Braque

"THE QUIET MASTER"

"A PAINTER DOES NOT try to tell a story," Georges Braque once said. "He tries to paint a pictorial fact." *Atelier VIII* (opposite page) is the eighth version Braque has painted of the "pictorial facts" which surround him in his own studio. Experts consider it the finest painting Braque has created since the war; and in it, the Frenchman who is called "the quiet master" of modern art has tried to sum up many of his original contributions to the rendition of form, plane, depth and texture.

"All my *Ateliers* are souvenirs of my studio," Braque once said. "A bottle, a glass, apples, my palette—these form the 'climate' of my work. . . . What you see on the canvas is the fruit of imagination. . . . 'Why?' But why must you ask an artist for a *reason?* Why approach a painting with logic? . . . I painted what I felt; I cannot explain how and why. Inspiration is like love. It is what you feel, without reasons and logic."

Years ago, Braque—an inveterate keeper of notebooks—crystallized this thought in an aphorism: "One should be content to discover, without explaining." He has made some of the most exhilarating discoveries since the Impressionists.

Pablo Picasso and Braque were inseparable friends and collaborators from 1907 to 1914; together, they dropped a bombshell in the salons of Paris with paintings which an acidulous critic said looked as if they were made up of nothing but "little cubes." The name "Cubism" stuck to one of the newest and freshest departures in painting.

What Braque and Picasso tried to do in their pictures was to take objects apart, break them into basic structural components, and rearrange them on canvas—as geometric forms which would show, in Braque's memorable phrase, "not what you see, but *what you know is there.*" Their styles were so similar that Picasso once lost a bet by mistaking one of Braque's pictures for his own.

Braque painted a jug, a pitcher, a guitar, not from the conventional single point of observation, but as a composite of images—presenting the object as if it were being simultaneously observed from the sides, the top, the bottom, even the inside. He placed his abstracted shapes against a cascade of "little cubes," interweaving them, letting the planes overlap, achieving that striking dynamic effect which Janet Flanner called "immediate distance . . . the surprise of space." And this was done at a time when, as he said, "Matisse, Picasso and I had a terrible struggle to find ourselves—after a genius like Cézanne."

Braque wanted a picture to stand like a piece of architecture; he wanted to paint things so that they looked more solid, more permanent than in reality itself.

"One should not imitate what one wants to create," he once explained. "I do not wish to copy nature—I am more concerned with the possibility of being on an equal level with her."

While the rambunctious *Fauves* were drenching their canvases with slashing reds and blues and oranges, Braque began to use colors which painters had always scorned as dull—dead blacks and browns, flat grays, lusterless greens. But he combined them in new and muted harmonies that assumed an austere loveliness. He became the greatest painter of still life in our time.

Braque at 80 was still a tall, graceful, well-built man with a magnificent head, flowing white hair and luminous eyes. He used to love to box, and was an excellent cyclist. (The wheel in the lower left of *Atelier VIII* still forms part of the "climate" of his work.) He has great personal dignity and an aristocrat's manner. A man of the utmost probity and discipline, he has been happily married for over half a century. In his art, as in his many writings, he combines a powerful intellect with strict discipline and impeccable taste. One of his most famous sayings is: "I love the rule that corrects emotion."

His father was a house-painting contractor.

and decorator, and as his apprentice, the young Braque developed phenomenal skill in reproducing materials with brush and color: He painted the most lifelike parquetry floors and rosewood panels, oak frames and marble pillars.

Braque still grinds and mixes his own colors, and whether he is at his Paris studio or in his farmhouse in Normandy, he works from eight o'clock in the morning to about one in the afternoon. "Morning light is best," he says.

He manipulates brown-paper louvers that hang above his easels to control the light as he works. Space and light have always intrigued him; on the walls of his house, he hangs platters, spoons, forks, wrought iron—observing with unsated fascination how light glints off surfaces. He makes hundreds of sketches, notes and comments in notebooks which rest on a lecternlike stand next to his

easels. "I draw on paper a great deal," he explains. "But when I work on canvas, I improvise. I do not reason. I follow my instinct."

He sometimes cuts a form out of paper to reduce a contour to its ultimate simplicity—as he did for the massive white bird above, in which he tried to distill the sensation of flight. He first applies his pigment in layers so thick that the groundwork on one picture alone took 32 *pounds* of paint. He wants to make a picture "touchable."

Someone once said, "Picasso thunders; Braque creates silence." This singular quiet, this cool mood of balance and repose, this characteristic mixture of lucidity and elegance, radiates off a Braque canvas. It is a tribute to both his craftsmanship and his taste that the complex and crowded *Atelier VIII* becomes more serenely exciting the longer our eyes explore it.

Braque calls this painting Atelier VIII. *It is considered the finest of the many "souvenirs of my studio" which the great artist has done since World War II. In it are the things with which he surrounds himself in his studio. This huge painting (4′ 11″ x 7′ 4″) is in a private collection in France and has rarely been reproduced.*

Delacroix

"A HURRICANE IN HIS HEART..."

THE SWIRLING SKETCH above was drawn in a matter of moments, in North Africa, in 1832; the marvelously flamboyant *Arab Rider Attacked by a Lion* (opposite) was carefully painted in Paris over 17 years later. The difference in dates and places is at the heart of the story of Delacroix.

He was born an aristocrat, the son of an ambassador, but the rumors never died that he was really the illegitimate offspring of Talleyrand, to whom, in fact, he bore a startling resemblance. Handsome, graceful, brilliant, Eugène Delacroix was welcome in the poshest salons of Paris. He was a connoisseur of literature and the theater, a friend of Dumas, Chopin, Balzac, Stendhal.

He began to draw when quite young, then fell desperately in love with that most absorbing and perverse mistress: painting. There is no better way to describe his passion for art. Once, after seeing a picture by Géricault, he ran through the streets, "delirious with enthusiasm." While painting, he often refused to eat, fearful of interrupting the flow of creativity. He never married: "Art," he said, "is a celestial compensation for my isolated life." (His life was not *that* "isolated"; he scored many a success with the ladies, and his diaries speak of his pretty housekeeper, who "gives me her heart unreservedly.")

He envied writers and musicians: Painting, he lamented, is "the mute art." So for forty years, from the time he was 24, he poured into his journals ideas, observations, commentary on the nature of art and the perplexities of an artist. He

rebelled against the classical style, with its stiff glorification of repose, that was then in fashion. He extolled romanticism.

"A painting," he declared, "should be a feast for the eye." He publicly attacked Ingres, the traditionalists' idol. He even dared acclaim Rembrandt, who was then disparaged, a far greater painter than Raphael, who was revered. "Exactitude is not art," Delacroix insisted. "Most painters [apply] perfection to the art of boring."

The first painting he exhibited was *The Massacre of Chios*, a tumultuous picture full of violent movement and supercharged emotion, which an enraged critic called "A Massacre of Painting"; another sneered that it was painted "with a drunken broom." Delacroix dismissed the slurs: "I became the abomination of painting, but I was enchanted with myself."

In 1832, he joined a mission of the French Government to the Sultan of Morocco. The trip lasted only six months, but it forever changed his life and work. Delacroix was enthralled by the savage splendor of North Africa; he filled innumerable sketchbooks with excited drawings such as the one above. For the next 32 years, in his studio in Paris, he painted his memories of exotic costumes and Bedouin tribesmen, gleaming minarets and harems and Moorish gardens, Negro slaves and musicians on horseback.

The further time carried him from Morocco, the better his work became. To heighten psychological impact, he began to experiment with color,

putting shadowy greens into red, setting vivid blues against orange, making violet complement yellow—defying that fidelity-to-life that had reigned over painting for 400 years. Fifty years later, when Van Gogh and Seurat devoured his journals, the Post-Impressionists acclaimed him a trailblazer.

A stunning draughtsman, Delacroix wondered why a painting always loses some of the vitality of a sketch, and concluded that a spectator reads into a sketch possibilities that no artist can entirely realize.

Six times in a row, the French Academy denied him membership; when he was finally elected, in 1857, it was too late to mean much to him. His romanticism had fallen out of favor. At the end, he refused to exhibit his work at all.

He died in 1863. He had created 850 large paintings, thousands of drawings, huge wall paintings in the Chamber of Deputies—and his incomparable journals. No less than a fifth of his pictures celebrate his fascination with Arab horsemen. "For forty years," wrote critic Theophile Silvestre, "he sounded the whole scale of human passion—grandiose, terrible, calm—his brush going from saints to warriors, from warriors to lovers, from lovers to tigers, from tigers to flowers. . . . He had a sun in his brain and a hurricane in his heart."

Arab Rider Attacked by a Lion, *oil on canvas. (18" x 14¾"), is in the Potter Palmer Collection, the Art Institute of Chicago. The drawing (above) is from the Meta and Paul J. Sachs Collection, the Fogg Museum, Harvard University.*

Titian

THE GRAND AND THE OPULENT

IN 1518, Alfonso d'Este, Duke of Ferrara, husband of Lucrezia Borgia (and therefore son-in-law of Pope Alexander VI), commissioned the Venetian master Tiziano Vecelli to paint him a bacchanal. Alfonso grew displeased because Titian took so long and delayed so often. For Titian liked to work on many pictures simultaneously, turning from one to another when the spirit moved him, returning to his canvases with a fierce expression "as though they were mortal enemies."

When the *Bacchanale* was at last completed, Titian was acclaimed for his genius once again. Of particular interest was the figure of the lovely bacchante reproduced here, of whom the historian Ridolfi wrote many years later: "The painter drew a woman loved by him named Violante, alluding to her name with a violet that he drew in her bosom, and in small letters wrote 'Tiziano'." Titian also placed the number 101 in his charming *billet doux*. No one is sure what this number means. Was it intended only to identify the work? Was it, perhaps, his 101st message of love?

Violante was said to be the daughter of Palma Vecchio, who often painted her, and with whom Titian had once studied. But Palma Vecchio never married and is not known to have had any children, legitimate or otherwise. In a time and land where love and license interplayed, the parentage of the fair Violante is of small consequence. Titian seems to have been in love with her from 1515 on, and we recognize her in several of his most famed

paintings, including the *Sacred and Profane Love*.

Titian was a man of his time. Around 1520, he brought a girl named Cecelia from his home town, Cadore, to Venice, where she and Titian lived together quite happily. She presented him with two sons. When Cecelia came down with an illness that appeared fatal. Titian called in a priest —to legitimize both his union and his offspring. The good father pronounced the necessary words over the dying Cecelia, who then recovered, blossomed and bore Titian two more children, including the golden-haired Lavinia, the glorious "Titian beauty" he immortalized in many paintings.

Titian loved the wealth and luxury of Venice, a city that dazzled the eye and gratified the senses. The citizens of the great city on the Adriatic vied with each other in the magnificence of their *palazzi*, the elegance of their dress, the sophistication of their lives. Titian lived like a prince, traveling far and wide to execute his commissions, accompanied by retinues of servants, admirers and students. He owned a fine house near Venice to which kings and dukes and noblemen from all over Europe beat a path. After sitting for Titian, Charles V would permit no other artist to paint his portrait. After Titian had finished the third portrait, the Emperor exclaimed: "This is the third time I have triumphed over death!"

Titian was as productive as he was successful. He poured his talent out in luminous portraits, great altarpieces, religious paintings of grandeur,

glowing Saviours and Madonnas and Magdalenes, paintings on mythological themes that popularized allegory, fabulous battle scenes (he worked for 20 years on those in the Palace of the Doges).

His name became the hallmark for splendor of style and richness of color. He created magical, shimmering effects, piling on layers of gleaming pigment, using a heavy groundwork when he wanted light to be absorbed into rich, glowing shadows, using thick surface layers over transparent colors when he wanted the light to be reflected back into the eye of the beholder. He loved the sensual and captured the essences of the voluptuous. His gleaming flesh tones, the sheen of his textures, the iridescence of his light influenced El Greco (who studied under him), Rembrandt, Rubens and, much later, Renoir.

He gave landscape artists models for depth and distance, and himself painted the first Italian picture specifically designated as a "landscape". He was careless and impatient with drawing: Michelangelo stood before the wonderful *Danae and the Shower of Gold* and remarked: "It is a pity that men in Venice did not learn to draw well from the beginning. If this man had been assisted by design as he is by nature, no one would do better work, for he has a fine spirit and beautiful manner."

Titian's boundless productivity stretched into his middle nineties. This handsome, superb figure of a man, who always painted with opulence, died at 99, not of old age, but of the plague.

...acchanale by Titian (circa 1518, oil, 69"
...76"). This opulent masterpiece hangs in the
...rado Museum, Madrid. The artist chose
... sign his work with a card, bearing his "Tiziano"
...d the number 101, tucked into the bodice of
...s mistress, Violante (detail, right).

Miró

WORLD BEYOND REASON

In 1925, a young Spanish painter named Joan Miró startled the salons of Paris with a picture, *Carnival of Harlequin,* which he described (see opposite page) in a vivid and unpunctuated burst of words. *Carnival of Harlequin* was among the very first paintings to be called Surrealist. It carried art into the realm of pure fantasy—unfettered by reason or realism or convention. Miró and his defiant fellow countryman Salvador Dali had signed a manifesto with other artists who described their creed as Surrealism. The name could hardly have been more precise: "beyond realism."

Now it was not unusual for artists to paint the products of their imaginings: Leonardo, Bosch, Blake, Goya—each drew weird figures and macabre figments. But even their most fantastic creations were anchored in the recognizable. What Miró did was plunge art into the chasms below consciousness, into that jumbled wilderness of dreams and memory where time is obliterated, where "sense" and proportion do not exist, where only symbols live—and take meaning from the special vocabulary of fantasy.

Miró's whimsical style and strange forms were not tricks to gain attention. In all his 65 years, he has never made the slightest attempt to be popular, or to accommodate his work to public favor. Miró always felt more at home with reverie than with reality. When he was a student in Catalonia, a perspicacious teacher made him draw objects by feeling them without looking at them. Nothing could have served Miró better: He was bewitched not by the world around, but by the world within.

To free his imagination, Miró, like a medieval religious mystic, deliberately induced hallucinations in himself—by starvation. When he came to Paris in 1919, the son of moderately well-off parents, he forced himself to live on one meal a week, chewing gum to deaden his appetite and munching dried figs for energy.

"Instead of setting out to paint *something,*" he declared, "I began painting—and as I paint, a picture begins to assert itself under my brush. A form suggests itself, a sign—for a faun or a bird. Even a casual wiping of my brush may suggest the beginning of a picture. The first stage is free and unconscious; but the second is carefully calculated, controlled through that desire to discipline myself which I have felt from the beginning."

In the droll, nursery-rhyme domain of Joan Miró, mischievous stars float around crescent moons, ladders forever reach into the sky, bizarre amoebae and grotesque nuclei burst out of the canvas in brilliant clots of color.

His world is entirely subjective. He paints objects as if they were metaphors, independent of each other in size or scale, floating in vagrant patterns through a flattened space he invented. He regards painting as a form of poetry, and early in his career seized that freedom from the literal we call "poetic license." He paints his free associations, in an atmosphere somewhere between delight and delirium.

Miró is an absent-minded, modest little man who looks more like a businessman than a painter. He lives on the island of Majorca, off the coast of Spain, and likes to paint in a room so tiny he can scarcely move around in it. He has never lost the omnivorous curiosity of a child. His house is full of toys, which he collects with endless fervor and studies with endless absorption. He is especially fascinated by jack-in-the-boxes, which he has bought by the hundreds; they appear in his paintings again and again.

He is a friend of Pablo Picasso's, who bought one of Miró's first pictures and whom he greatly admires. Whenever he visits his fellow Spaniard and fellow rebel, they never talk about painting—but hasten, instead, to the nearest movie. Both are passionate *aficionados* of the cinema.

Ernest Hemingway bought one of the earliest of Miró's paintings and, to show his friendship for the then little-known artist, offered to teach him how to box. Hemingway said that behind the gentle exterior of the unobtrusive Miró lurked a force that might someday want to beat someone up.

Miró paints with a beguiling combination of gravity and humor, as if painting were a game, all freedom and fancy, in which the goals are revealed in delicious surprises as the game unfolds. His art, one writer remarked, seems to get younger as other artists get older.

A hostile critic said of *Carnival of Harlequin,* "Miró paints for children." He is wrong: Miró paints for the child in all of us.

Carnival of Harlequin One of the first Surrealist paintings, this picture (26″ by 36½″, oil on canvas) hangs in the Albright-Knox Art Gallery, Buffalo. Miró described it once in a burst of Surrealist prose. If we separate the images, and remove certain indelicacies, here is what he said: "The ball of yarn unraveled by the cats dressed as Harlequins of smoke ... twisting about my entrails, stabbing them during the period of famine which gave birth to the hallucinations registered in this picture ... beautiful flowering of fish in a poppy field noted on the snow of paper ... throbbing like the throat of a bird at the contact of a woman ... in the form of a spider with aluminum legs ... returning in the evening to my home at 45 rue Blomet, a figure which has nothing to do with 13 which has always exerted enormous influence on my life ... by the light of an oil lamp, fine haunches of a woman ... with a flame which throws new images on the whitewashed wall ... at this period I plucked a knob from a safety passage which I put in my eye like a monocle ... gentlemen whose foodless ears are fascinated by the flutter of butterflies ... musical rainbow ... eyes falling like a rain of lyres ... ladder to escape the disgust of life ... ball thumping against a board ... loathsome drama of reality ... falling stars crossing the blue space to pin themselves on the body of my mist which dives into the phosphorescent Ocean after describing a luminous circle."

Vermeer

THE SPHINX OF DELFT

IN 1842, a young French journalist named Etienne Thoré happened to see a small painting by an obscure Dutchman who had died in 1675. Thoré was so carried away by the beauty of the picture that he began to ask questions about the painter, one Jan Vermeer, and discovered to his astonishment that even museum experts could tell him little. Vermeer, a contraction of van der Meer, is a common name in Holland, and this Vermeer, who had lived and worked in Delft, was often confused with a painter named Vermeer from Utrecht, or with yet another from Haarlem. For more than 150 years, art dealers had deliberately attributed the few Vermeer canvases that came their way to more famous painters whose names fetched higher prices—Metsu, de Hooch, even Rembrandt.

Thoré conducted a one-man quest for facts about Vermeer—in the Netherlands, Germany, Belgium, England—for 24 years. He was frustrated at every turn: Most histories of Dutch painting did not mention Vermeer's name, and one encyclopedic work in nine fat volumes contained only one mystified reference: "It is quite inexplicable how he attained the excellence many of [his pictures] exhibit."

In 1866, Thoré published three articles, under a pseudonym, on the unknown master he dubbed "The Sphinx of Delft." They created a sensation in art circles and launched an excited movement of rediscovery for a painter who had died almost two hundred years earlier. The search has never ended. Yet even today, all we know about Jan (Johannes) Vermeer can be summarized on a page.

He was born in Delft in 1632, spent his life in that pleasant and prosperous town, was admitted to the artists' guild at 21, married Catharina Bolenes, sired 11 children and died in 1675, leaving many debts and a pathetic estate: a few paintings, a suit of armor, two easels, three paintbrushes, 10 pieces of canvas, "three bundles with all sorts of colors," and a stick with an ivory handle. His widow gave the baker two paintings, to repay a debt of 617 florins, and gave her mother the picture which is reproduced on the opposite page.

How strange a fate befell this painting! It was probably sold at an Amsterdam auction in 1696, passed into the collection of Gottfried van Swietin, was purchased from a saddler in 1813 for 50 florins by the Austrian Count Czernin, who thought he was buying a Pieter de Hooch, and, over a century later, found its way to a German mountaintop called Berchtesgaden, in the home of Adolf Hitler, who paid 1,650,000 reichsmarks, or about $660,000, of other people's money for it. (It was a bargain: The American industrialist Andrew Mellon reportedly offered $2,000,000 for it.) In May, 1945, a unit of Gen. George Patton's Third Army found the picture hidden, in an immense cache of Nazi loot, in a salt mine near Salzburg. U.S. Army authorities returned the Vermeer to the Austrians, and it now has an honored place in the Kunsthistorisches Museum of Vienna.

Vermeer painted less than 40 pictures—virtually all in the same room, the room we here behold, with its black-and-white floor, its old map of the Netherlands on the wall, its bourgeois furniture, its brocaded curtain and that window at the left through which streamed the clear, pure, incredible light that has been the marvel and the despair of artists ever since.

The radiant work on the opposite page, sometimes called "the finest technical achievement in art," displays Vermeer's absolute mastery as an artist, the miraculous luster of his ivory-and-enamel finish, his alluring control of space to lead the eye into magical perspectives, his surrounding of figures with air and light, a light so incandescent that one viewer stepped in back of a Vermeer to see if it was illuminated from behind.

The modest, unknown man whom some call "the perfect painter" died before he was 43 years old. He left no romantic legends, no glamorous infidelities, no trace of the Bohemian or the flamboyant. He simply painted—with patience and devotion, transforming the genre form from mere humorous illustration, creating his own harmonies of the precise and the poetic, striving for a purity of mood and a perfection of technique that went to "the *rightness* of things," capturing for eternity the hushed, lovely moods of simple people in tender moments. He was so absorbed in his work, and so unaware of its immortality, that he did not leave a single self-portrait, or a single letter of self-revelation. Probably the only time he painted himself was in this picture—and then it was with his back to the viewer, and to history.

This 47″ x 39″ oil, variously called The Artist in His Studio,
Fame and the Artist *and* The Allegory of Painting,
is the pride of Vienna's Kunsthistorisches Museum.

Boccioni

"MADNESS IS WHAT WE NEED...."

In 1909, an Italian poet named Marinetti wrote a now-celebrated *Manifesto of Futurism* in the French journal *Figaro*. "We want to exalt aggressive movement, feverish insomnia, the quick step, the somersault, the slap in the face, the punch. . . ." Five brash young Italian painters carried Marinetti's torch from literature to painting. They attacked tradition, extolled violence, exalted the machine, glorified war and even cried, "We demand a total suppression of the nude in painting for 10 years!"

Umberto Boccioni—handsome, gifted, neurotic—was the most articulate of these *enfants terribles*. He poured scorn on the masters—past and contemporary, calling Raphael "disgusting" and Michelangelo "disgraceful," attacking Picasso and Braque for "freezing" art into static images, denouncing Cézanne and the Cubists for reducing beauty to dry, geometric forms. The artist, Boccioni proclaimed, should "glorify the life of today, incessantly and tumultuously transformed by the victories of science. . . ."

Each time the Futurists read a manifesto at a public meeting, a riot broke out. "We no longer consider man the center of universal life," Boccioni flatly asserted. "The suffering of a man holds the same interest to us as the suffering of an electric lamp, which, with spasmodic starts, shrieks out the most heartrending expressions of color."

Boccioni was driven by passionate and uncontrollable longings. "I feel a savage cry," he wrote, "an irresistible urge . . . a maddening rage. I want to overthrow, to smash, to attack, to wound myself, to cut, to bleed! Madness is what we need—

delirious madness, screams, tears!"

Behind all their rambunctious defiance, the Futurists did have an interesting conception: The Impressionists had seen that light transformed objects, and subordinated form to light; the Futurists asserted that forms themself interact ("When our bodies sink into a sofa, the sofa also penetrates us") and wanted to subordinate both form and light to movement—the movement of many images synthesized in a moment of "simultaneity."

In 1910, Boccioni became fascinated by vast construction works on the outskirts of Milan. He spent days there sketching—the steel frames rising, the pouring of cement, the tremendous exertions of men and horses. He was wild about horses, though he had never ridden one.

Boccioni completed *The City Rises* (opposite page) in six months. He used slanting shafts of light to dramatize the tension, and bold ribbons of color—hot blue, white, orange—to accentuate the swirling rhythms. It had "a flowing radiance," says James Thrall Soby, "as if painted with an electric brush."

Paradoxically, the man who glorified the machine found his cardinal symbol of power in the plunging, surging horses of *The City Rises*. He gave them flickering wings of color, and moved his splendid central figure to a tiny culvert across which a train steams. . . . It was to have a meaning no one could have foreseen.

When the World War I broke out, Boccioni and the Futurists staged antineutralist demonstrations in Italy. He went to jail for five days. In 1915, he and Marinetti joined a bicycle battalion

and fought against the Austrians in a mountain campaign. Later, Boccioni was assigned to an artillery regiment stationed near Verona, where, at the home of a distinguished Italian lady, he met a beautiful girl of noble birth. She was wild about horses, too, and invited him to come to Rome, where they could pursue romance via fox hunting.

Boccioni prepared for his visit like a mad man. The 34-year-old painter took the fieriest horses he could find in the regiment; he spent every free moment riding, hour after hour, so long and so violently that the skin on his thighs was rubbed raw and it was agony for him to sit in the saddle. But he was determined not to "disgrace" himself when he met his sweetheart in Rome.

One day, he rode a horse into a culvert that resembled the one he had painted five years earlier. A train roared overhead. The horse panicked and bolted. Boccioni—sore and chafed from riding—could not control it. He was thrown and fractured his skull. He never regained consciousness.

The City Rises, *painted in 1910-11 by Umberto Boccioni, is among the best—and best-known—works of the Italian Futurists, one of the many schools that sprang up after the Impressionist revolution in art. This painting (6' 6½" x 9' 10½") is in the Museum of Modern Art in New York, Mrs. Simon Guggenheim Fund. Charred in the fire of April 15, 1958, it has since been restored. The crayon and chalk study for the painting, probably made at the construction site, is in the same collection.*

Velázquez

"THEY *SEEM TO BE LOOKING AT* US."

ON NOVEMBER 25, 1648, Diego Rodríguez de Silva y Velázquez, court painter to Philip IV of Spain, left Madrid by carriage for Italy, to purchase paintings for the King's gallery. With Velázquez was his servant, Juan de Pareja, a Moor, himself a competent painter, taught by his master.

Though Velázquez was handsomely received by Pope Innocent X and the nobility of Rome, he was offended, for the Italians had seen little or none of his work and paid him homage, not as an artist, but as Philip's emissary. When the Pope asked Velázquez to paint his portrait, the proud Spaniard resorted to an extraordinary bit of bravado: He first painted the Moor (opposite page), then instructed him to take the portrait around to Rome's leading artists and noblemen — so they could compare the picture with the model and judge Velázquez's genius for themselves.

The portrait of the Moor made so powerful an impression that it was promptly placed on exhibition in the Pantheon, and Velázquez was elected to the august Academy of St. Luke. When he painted Innocent X, the Pope was so pleased (the portrait is still called the finest in Rome) that he offered Velázquez a handsome fee. But the Spaniard reminded His Holiness that a man of noble blood could never accept money, save in the service of his sovereign: Innocent gave Velázquez a medal instead.

This magnificent painter came from Seville, the son of Juan Rodríguez de Silva; in accordance with Spanish custom, he used his mother's patronym—Velázquez. He was a born painter, ironically trapped by his status: An aristocrat, he could not earn his living as an artist; he could only hope for a post in the court.

He came to Madrid with a letter to one of Philip IV's courtiers, and soon painted the King's portrait. From that day on, Philip let no one else paint him. He brought Velázquez and his family into the palace. For 37 years, Velázquez lived and worked in the royal household, painting the infantas and the little princes, the noblemen, buffoons and dwarfs. He completed no less than 34 portraits of the King (possibly, no painter ever painted a monarch so often) and was ultimately appointed palace marshal. A passage led from Philip's apartments to Velázquez's studio, and the King often dropped in to talk to his court artist, or watch him work, or dabble in painting himself.

Philip offered Velázquez a knighthood; the painter chose the illustrious Order of Santiago. A year of investigation followed, to prove Velázquez free of any taint of heresy, trade, or Moslem or Jewish forebears. Two knights traveled to Portugal to inquire into his father's family origins; two rode to Seville; witnesses in Madrid testified that Velázquez had never accepted money for his work. Still, the panel of four judges found Velázquez not noble enough. Only after the King petitioned the Pope himself for a dispensation was Velázquez invested with the honors of Santiago.

Yet it was neither his lineage nor his knighthood that brought Velázquez immortality; it was his painting. For he transmitted to canvas a miraculous "living" quality, in peerless revelations of character. He worked directly in oil, indifferent to drawing, making few preliminary sketches, correcting as he went along, searching for the decisive, if transient, expression. He saw that light and shadow change with the recession of distance, and manipulated them with masterful assurance to create both modeling and the illusion of perspective. He was the absolute master of his materials and his purpose, and excluded the expected detail—which only distracts. (Note the deliberate ambiguity of the Moor's lace collar, the bold mass of black to represent hair.)

The astonishing directness that is Velázquez's hallmark, as in the challenging stare of this Moor, is what struck Ortega y Gasset when he wrote of his countryman's portraits:

"We cannot communicate with them; we are alone with beings who often irritate us . . . because *they* seem to be looking at *us*."

This remarkable portrait of Juan de Pareja (30" x 25¾6") is in the Earl of Radnor's collection at Longford Castle in Salisbury, England.

Raphael

THE NAME ON THE BRACELET

FROM MANY LANDS, painters came to Rome to study with young Raphael Sanzio. At 30, the boy wonder from Urbino was fit to stand beside Leonardo and Michelangelo in as astonishing a triumvirate as ever lived at the same time in the same land. Painter, sculptor, architect, Raphael was the most beloved artist in Rome. There seemed no end to his blessings. He was handsome, charming, cultivated and so generous that, even among the bickering artists of the Vatican, his goodness was legendary. He lived like a prince, and when he set forth from his palace in the Borgo Nuovo, as many as 50 artists would accompany him in an entourage of homage.

Raphael brought to painting a golden grace and self-assurance. He learned from everyone—Perugino, Leonardo, Michelangelo—enriching his range and perfecting his style with a virtuosity that seemed boundless. He loved the classics and imposed classic restraint on the rich, sensuous material of the high Renaissance. He placed his figures in space with a freedom that opened new horizons in composition. His Madonnas, so human yet so ethereal, managed to wrest the intimate from the sublime, and so won the public heart that to this day they remain our ideal image of the Virgin.

Raphael was not as complex as Leonardo, nor as tormented as Michelangelo. He was "a very amorous person," wrote Vasari, first biographer of painters, "delighting much in women and ever ready to serve them." And therein lies our tale. For Raphael often complained that he could not find maidens beautiful enough to paint.

One day, a group of his students, looking over the wall of a baker's garden, saw a girl so beautiful that they hurried back to their master to rave about her comeliness. Raphael was first amused, then intrigued, and secretly went to the garden to see for himself. When he looked over the wall, he beheld the baker's daughter bathing her feet—in the Tiber, say some, in a fountain, say others. For days, Raphael could not get her out of his mind. He returned to the garden and courted her, and she became his beloved.

Her name was Margherita Luti, but Raphael called her "La Fornarina." It means "the baker's daughter." She went to live with him, in his house, and all Rome talked of their infatuation. Raphael painted her many times, and the gossip ran that he could not work unless she was at his side.

Now Raphael's patron, Cardinal Bibbiena, had long urged him to marry Maria Bibbiena, the Cardinal's niece. Raphael finally agreed, but asked that the betrothal be delayed. He delayed for four years. Why? Because of his passion for the baker's daughter? Because he did not want to marry at all? Or because he did not want to spoil his chances of becoming a Cardinal? This was no idle dream: Pope Leo X owed Raphael considerable money, showered him with commissions, made him chief architect of St. Peter's, and hinted that he would bestow the red hat on "the divine painter." Raphael's conflict was resolved when the Cardinal's niece, who was as mad about Raphael as he was about La Fornarina, died—the day before their official betrothal.

In the spring of 1520, Raphael fell ill of a violent fever. The doctors bled him. His friends told him it was a passing ailment, but Raphael knew he was dying. Dismay raced through all strata of the Holy City. "Thereupon he made his will," wrote Vasari, "and like a good Christian sent his lover from the house . . . Then [he] confessed, and in much contrition completed the course of his life, on the day whereon it had commenced, Good Friday." He was only 37.

He was buried in the Pantheon. A plaque of Maria Bibbiena was placed next to his tomb, as he had (out of duty?) requested. There is no plaque of La Fornarina. But it is her face that is enshrined in the *Sistine Madonna*, probably the most popular picture ever painted, and in the unforgettable portrait on the opposite page, with "Raphael Urbinas" on the bracelet which encircles her arm. Some experts think the hands and bust were painted by Raphael's favorite student, Giulio Romano; but that wonderful, direct, knowing expression could have come only from Raphael's brush. Over 400 years after her lover's death, the radiant portrait, *La Fornarina*, now in Rome's Galleria Nazionale, tells us what Vasari meant when he wrote: "Other masters paint pictures, but Raphael paints life itself. His figures all but breathe."

La Fornarina (23⅗" x 31½") hangs in the Galleria Nazionale in Rome

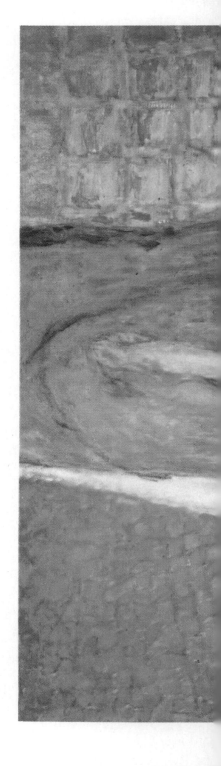

Bonnard

"THE SAVOR OF THINGS..."

HE WAS ALMOST 70—and he gazed fondly at his wife, old and worn and ill, as she lay in the tub of the sun-splashed bathroom of their villa, atop a hill overlooking the Mediterranean. He remembered her as she was years ago—young, lovely, pensive —and that was the way he finally painted her, with surpassing affection, in the radiance of remembrance. He painted the same scene in five different pictures, for she had an absolute mania about cleanliness and would spend innumerable hours in the bathtub.

They had lived in blissful domesticity for perhaps thirty years before they were married. Only then did he learn that her name was not Marthe de Melliny, which she had deliberately used to conceal her humble origins, but Maria Boursin. She was pathologically shy, "quasi-invisible," said a friend, with a susceptibility to tuberculosis and a morbid temperament. But she lived like a queen in Pierre Bonnard's adoration.

He avoided posing his subjects; he liked to watch his models as they dressed or rested or washed up; and he caught their spontaneous movements in sketches that were undecipherable to any eye but his. Then, when he painted, he let his imagination play freely around what he remembered and had recorded. He was indifferent to theories; he was in love with painting itself.

He was up at five each morning, mixing his colors on an old dinner plate. "He understands and loves everything," wrote Paul Signac, "the pie for dessert, the eye of his dog, a ray of sunshine

coming through his window blind, the sponge in his bathtub." He liked to walk or bicycle or drive through the countryside at the slowest possible pace, drinking in the smallest details. He said he painted only what "attracted" him, but he was attracted to the most ordinary things: a striped tablecloth, a face seen in passing, the heavy furniture in a crowded parlor. "His observation was so penetrating," said a friend, "that for him *one* vista was worth thousands."

He was a tall, thin, reticent man who wore glasses to correct a nearsightedness which may have enhanced his singular way of blending form and color so that the one seems to flow into the other in unexpected harmonies. "Bonnard," said Edgar Degas, "loves the accidental." He more than loved it; he invested ordinary moments with a sense of surprise. His pictures often look "as if people had wandered into them." He made the commonplace poetic. He was incapable of boredom.

He painted—anywhere and everywhere. He would nail a large piece of canvas to a wall and work on four or five pictures at once; later, he cut up the canvas and took the separate subjects to be framed. He often tacked canvas on the wall of a hotel room and cheerfully plunged into work— a momentous feat of concentration, if one considers the ghastly colors and shrieking patterns of French hotel wallpaper.

Bonnard was born in a pretty Paris suburb in 1867. Even as a child, he had the sunniest of dispositions. He was raised in country comforts

and spent his summers on the family estate at the foot of the Alps. To please his father, he studied law—but enrolled in an art school. He resisted instruction, out of some simple, stubborn refusal to be influenced by others. He failed his law exams, quite happily, and rented a studio on the Rue Pigalle. Quiet, modest, likable, he attracted many young artists and poets, who crowded his studio. They called themselves "The Nabis"—from the Hebrew word *nabi*, meaning "prophet." Bonnard's special friend was Edouard Vuillard, with whom he tramped through the galleries; together, they discovered Japanese art, with its superb drawing and economy, its unconventional perspective and deliberate asymmetry in composition.

He painted. He painted stage sets, panels, screens for private homes; he illustrated sheet music and books of poetry; he turned out countless black-and-white lithographs for the *Revue Blanche*. The first thing he sold was a poster (for

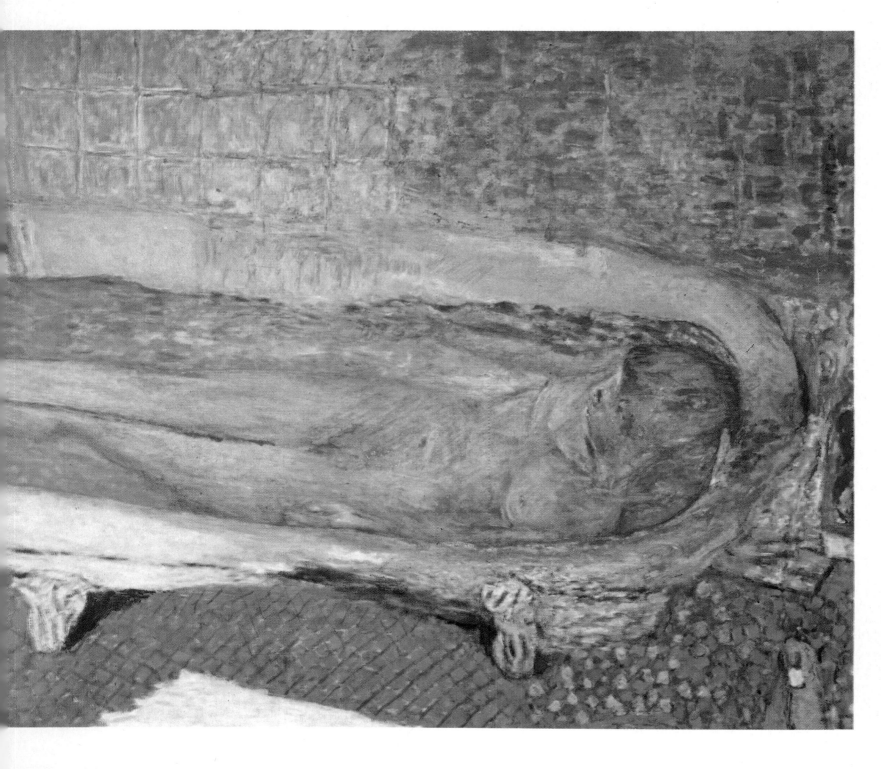

a champagne company), a poster which so excited a deformed dwarf named Toulouse-Lautrec (who had not yet himself produced one) that he tried to interest buyers in Bonnard's pictures. He was not successful. Neither was Bonnard. His first one-man show was a fiasco. Even Camille Pissarro sneered at his work. He was neither dismayed nor deterred. He was not driven by vanity.

It was the heyday of the Symbolists, the Fauvists, the Cubists, but Bonnard could join no school or movement. "I only try to do something personal," he said. He had such a horror about hampering originality, his own or anyone else's, that even when he was world-renowned, he would not teach. "Paint what *you* want, as you want it," he told an aspiring pupil. "Treasure your freshness."

He has been called "the last of the Impressionists," and critics say he recaptured form. But what he did most was retain an entirely personal perception that found mystery in ordinary scenes and moments. "It is summer, it is almost always summer in Bonnard's scenes," said one critic. "The melody of happy times blazes in his style."

He was never entirely satisfied with his work. Even after the great museums bought his paintings, he would visit them with a concealed paint box and, while a friend diverted the guards, would change a spot of color, add a daub here, correct a line there.

He painted—always with joy and dedication. As he aged, his glowing canvases became more abstract, concerned with mood, small miracles of atmosphere—warm, radiant, vibrant.

"Savor!" he once exclaimed. "I seek to paint the savor of things." What better description is there of the tender *Nude in the Bathtub*, with its flowing pattern, its luminous tiles and mosaic floor, that astounding straight line of the leg and that tranquil, bemused figure of his beloved— caught in a shimmer of quiet?

This version of Nude in the Bathtub *(37" x 58") was completed around 1937. It hangs in the* Musée du Petit Palais *in Paris.*

Van Eyck

WEDDING CERTIFICATE

THEY ARE TAKING the marriage oath, these two, in 1434, and few pictures capture the customs of their time with such fidelity and charm. Despite the bride's abdominal amplitude, she is not (as legend has it) pregnant; it's just that the capacious velvet gowns of those days were so heavy that maidens had to hold up the folds in the manner here depicted by the Flemish master Jan van Eyck.

This is a wedding—though no priest is present. Catholic dogma permitted a bride and groom to bestow the sacrament of marriage upon themselves, in private if they chose, until 1563, when the Council of Trent, realizing it was too easy for mortals to renege on connubial vows, decreed that a priest and two others had to act as witnesses.

This serene, beautifully organized painting was a marriage certificate. Above the mirror, van Eyck carefully lettered, in legal script, *Johannes de Eyck fuit hic* ("Jan van Eyck was here") to attest that he witnessed the wedding. On the curved mirror, in remarkable and much admired perspective, van Eyck painted himself with a second witness.

The marriage is being performed under canon law. The groom raises his hand in solemn oath and joins hands with his bride. One candle burns in the chandelier, though it is broad daylight, because a candle was required at oaths and because the "marriage candle" either preceded a bridal procession to the church or, as here, was lighted in the newlyweds' home.

Each detail had special meaning for the devout. The fruit on the window signifies the inno-cence of man before his fall in Eden. The dog is a symbol of marital faith (loyal little dogs are found on the tombs of many medieval ladies). The spot-less mirror and crystal beads stand for Marian purity. Atop the chair is a tiny statue of St. Marga-ret, patron saint of childbirth. Around the mirror frame, van Eyck drew ten scenes in exquisite mini-ature from the Passion. The discarded shoes of the groom and the discarded red slippers of the bride remind us of God's words to Moses from the flam-ing bush on Mount Sinai: ". . . put off your shoes from your feet, for the place on which you are standing is holy ground" (*Exodus*, 3:3).

Jan van Eyck, who handled light and space with new authority, is generally considered the father of painting as we know it today. He was born between 1385 and 1390 in the Flemish town of Maeseyck. His older brother Hubert was a dis-tinguished painter in the court of Philip of Charo-lais. Jan lived as a gentleman of the court and sired ten children in a calm and fecund lifetime. He "took delight in alchemy," says Vasari, great gossip-historian of painting, meaning that van Eyck experimented with varnishes to protect the tempera (a mixture of powdered color and bind-ing) which had been used as a painting medium since the Egyptians and Greeks.

Vasari, who is sometimes reliable, tells this titillating story: One day, van Eyck took a panel he had painted and put it out in the sun to dry. Either the heat was too great or the wood badly joined; the painting was ruined. Searching for a varnish that would dry in the shade, van Eyck found that linseed oil and the oil of nuts, boiled together with other mixtures, produced a hard, lustrous varnish. Then, van Eyck had the inspira-tion of mixing the oils right into his colors. A new world opened up for painting. Oils made it pos-sible to work over, correct and develop a picture by building it up, adding paint upon paint, with pigments of unheard-of brilliance and depth.

When artists saw the opulent glow and sheen of van Eyck's work, Vasari chortles, they were astounded. Van Eyck refused to reveal his secret. One of his paintings was exhibited in Naples, and among those who thronged to see it was the Sici-lian painter Antonello da Messina, who went to see van Eyck, showered him with presents and praise, and got the aging artist at last to take him into his confidence. Messina returned "to communicate to all Italy," says Vasari, " a secret so useful, beautiful and advantageous."

But who were the bride and groom? Her name was Jeanne Cenami; his, Giovanni Arnol-fini. They were sedate and prosperous folk, of no great fame or station, but they won an unexpected place in history through the man they hired to paint this immortal record of their marriage.

This double portrait, The Marriage of Giovanni Arnolfini and His Wife *(panel, 33″ x 22½″), is one of the treasures in the National Gallery, London. Reproduced by courtesy of the Trustees.*

Chagall

THE BLUE AIR OF LOVE

"THIS PICTURE WAS PAINTED in Russia in 1914 upon my return from Paris," Marc Chagall writes from Vence, France. "At that time, I was much concerned by the question of marriage. Excuse me for talking about such sentimental things after so many years. . . .

"I wanted the coloring to be restrained, that is why it is in gray. The red angel is not only the herald of dramas about love, but is also a premonition of events which later came about—the Revolution in Russia, my marriage to Bella. . . . The child which is seen on the cheek of the fiancée can surely be interpreted as a presentiment of the birth of my daughter Ida.

"I do not mean that I thought of all these details consciously. There are problems below consciousness which are the base of every art. It is by the unconscious that a work of art more fully communicates itself."

The story of Chagall and the girl in this painting is as touching a romance as can be found in fiction. He fell in love with her before he ever laid eyes on her. He was courting a girl in the village of Vitebsk, Russia, when a friend of hers came to the door. Chagall heard a voice "that warbled like a bird, like a voice from another world." The girl left before he could see her, but Chagall could not get her out of his mind. When he beheld her for the first time, he wrote, "I knew that this is she, my wife. Her silence is mine. Her eyes are mine. When she looks at me, it seems that she has known my childhood, my present life, my future too. She never saw me before, but it is as if she had always been watching over me."

Her name was Bella and he married her shortly after painting *The Wedded With an Angel.* For 29 years, Chagall's work was a running hymn to their love. Bella figures in his paintings again and again. "I had only to open my window and the blue air, love and the fragrance of flowers entered with her. . . . She hovers over my canvases, and directs my art. I never complete a canvas before asking her yes or no." She died in 1944.

The Wedded With an Angel is but one glimpse into the beguiling world that Chagall has amplified and enriched for more than 40 years. He creates an intensely personal atmosphere, a childlike purity in which the real, the improbable, the dreamed and the imagined are intertwined.

Chagall was born in Vitebsk in 1889, the eldest of eight children. His childhood was dominated by poverty, hunger and religious devotion. His parents belonged to a small Jewish sect known as Hasidim, who hold to a mystical belief in the omnipresence of God and believe that communion with Him is found not in abnegation, but in an ecstasy achieved through joyous dancing and singing in praise of the Lord. Memories of Chagall's childhood—his father, his mother (he called her eyes "a city of tears"), his uncle who played the fiddle (badly, but happily), his grandfather, who often sat on the roof of the house to catch the eve-ning breeze—all these run through his work in sweet-sad sentiment. They appear with a thousand other fragments of his life and feelings in a tender world where fiddlers sit in trees (see opposite page) or flowers glow with incandescence against ink-black skies.

Chagall has always searched for what he calls "an innocent, newborn language." He dislikes words like "fantasy" and "symbolism" applied to his work. But what better words can describe the fancies which flow from his brush? His lovers literally walk on air, or soar, enraptured, into the heavens. He puts wings on clocks (for does not time fly?) and sends blue cows over ghostly moons. His lampposts walk, his fish swim in space, his winged sleighs and goats float over housetops. He puts the head of a hen on the body of a woman and merrily colors faces blue or green (are no emotions as visual as embarrassment's red?).

"There are no stories in my pictures," Chagall insists. "No fairy tales, no popular legends. . . . To call anything that appears illogical a fantasy or a fairy tale is to admit that one does not understand nature. Our whole inner world is reality—perhaps more real than the apparent world."

The mischievous, endearing, topsy-turvy world of this naïve and original artist may startle our eyes at first, but only the hopelessly literal can fail to sense the familiar in Chagall's lines and patterns: for each of us has encountered all this before—in the whimsical world of dreams.

This is the first time that Marc Chagall's The Wedded With an Angel *has been reproduced. Chagall himself describes (see text) the special meaning to him of the red angel, the lovers and the child on the cheek of the bride. Rarely seen, this striking picture (4′ x 4′8″) is in the Hermitage collection, Leningrad, U.S.S.R.*

Goya

THE PAINTER AND THE DUCHESS

THE RING on her middle finger reads "Alba"; the ring on her index finger says "Goya"—and points to the name of the artist inscribed in the sand at her feet in an imperious gesture that emphasizes her certainty of his love. And he was at her feet, wildly in love with the Duchess of Alba, this remarkable, willful, passionate and spoiled noblewoman, one of the wealthiest in Spain and easily the most notorious.

Goya was 51; she was 34. He was married and had sired no less than 20 children, only one of whom, Xavier, survived. He was snub-nosed, ugly and deaf—not unlike Beethoven in both his appearance and his affliction. She had 30 names to her full title, 31 separate palaces, mansions, homes and estates, insulted her Queen regularly and had a succession of love affairs that made her name the scandal of all Europe.

This bold and luminous portrait was painted in 1797, in Sanlúcar in the province of Andalucía. The Queen had just banished the Duchess from Madrid for two years. Goya, the official court painter, defied the wishes of his sovereigns by fleeing into exile with his *enamorada*. It was characteristic of his insight, and her sense of irony, that for this portrait, he clothed her not in the costume of the court but in that of a *maja*, a common woman, dressed up for a holiday.

The Duchess was in exile because of an astounding act. She had announced a great ball in honor of Queen María Luisa, an ugly and stupid woman, bitterly jealous of the Alba fortune and beauty. The Duchess sent spies to Paris to find out the exact details of the gown the Queen had ordered for the occasion. And when the Queen swept into the Alba palace, there to greet her was a corps of servant girls each dressed in the identical gown the Queen was wearing.

Goya and the Duchess of Alba were madly in love—but not for long. He was replaced in her affections by others. Goya raged and fumed and revenged himself by sketching her as a two-headed deceiver, accepting the kisses of one man while dispatching a message to another.

The hatred between the Queen and the Duchess of Alba did not subside after the Duchess returned to Madrid. The Queen learned that the Duchess was building a lavish new wing to her great house, San Cristóbal, and hired incendiaries to burn it down. They failed twice. The Duchess, singularly gifted in malice, now invited the entire court to a grand fête at San Cristóbal. And for the benefit of the royal company, a spectacular array of fireworks was provided. The display was marvelous to behold, and reached a fantastic climax:

The letter "C" (for King Charles IV) burst into the night sky—and all applauded; then the letter "L" (for Queen Luisa) exploded in the darkness—and all responded; and then the letter "M" appeared—to the horror of the assemblage. For all knew that "M" stood for Manuel de Godoy, the Queen's lover! And before the full impact of even this unprecedented act of insolence had worn off, the palace itself broke into flames in a dozen places, as servants, under the orders of the Duchess, set fire to the entire edifice, while she calmly announced, "I wanted to arrange it myself so my friends would not have to trouble themselves."

The arrogant, splendid, tempestuous Duchess of Alba fell ill soon after (half of Madrid believed the Queen had poisoned her) and died. Her will, when opened, was the crowning affront to her world: She left her entire fortune—all her palaces, her parks, her jewels, her land—to her servants. She had always maintained that servants were fools to let the nobility treat them as slaves.

The Queen and her prime minister, none other than Manuel de Godoy, promptly declared the dead duchess insane, and her will the gesture of a revolutionary. Her lands were confiscated, and in time the Queen was seen wearing the Alba jewels.

And Goya? What of this moody, marvelous painter, who always worked at white heat, contemptuous of patience and processes, using whatever odd objects came to hand—a piece of cork or crayon, charcoal or pen, dipping his brush into ink mixed with tobacco, applying his colors with sponges, a broom, rags, spoons, delighting in the uses of the accidental, the blots or splotches or speckles? What happened to Goya? He painted with merciless candor and a hatred for the corruption of the monarchy, the clergy, the Inquisition. He painted masterful observations of the horrors of war and the cruelties of men.

Before Goya died, he turned over all his belongings to his son. He had kept only two paintings out of the hundreds he had painted in his lifetime —and one was this one, of the sensuous, insatiable Duchess who had been his tormentor and his love.

The Duchess of Alba,
*by Francisco José de
Goya y Lucientes
(79⅛″ x 58¼″), hangs
in the Hispanic Society of
America, in New York.
After this photograph was
taken, a cleaning of the
picture revealed
another word at the
Duchess's feet:* solo *(only).*

Bihzad

MASTER OF THE MINIATURE

THIS GEM, by the Persian master Bihzad, portrays the curious final measures which the great King Timur (a descendant of Genghis Khan and known to us as Tamerlane) took against the Kipchaks who invaded Persia in the year 1395. Tamerlane is on horseback atop the cliff, under the umbrella held over his royal head by an attendant, sending his bowmen down in large baskets to hunt out the last soldiers of the enemy army, hiding in a cave in the face of the precipice.

Bihzad painted this fascinating episode some 100 years later, for a *Book of Victory* about Tamerlane. The scene takes on special interest because Bihzad himself once was hidden in a cave—during a battle between Shah Ismail I and another band of invaders. In those days, conquerors regarded artists as loot, spoils of conquest. Before Shah Ismail went into battle, he hid Bihzad in a cave along with Mahmud an Nishapuri, a great calligrapher. After his victory, Ismail gave thanks to God for sparing the lives of his precious artists.

We knew very little about the artists of old Persia, but enough to recognize Kamal ud-Din Bihzad as one of the masters. He was born in about 1450 and was for a time in the service of Mir Ali Shir, a famed writer and friend of the Sultan. Then Bihzad won the patronage of the distinguished Sultan, Husayn Mirza, and became the head of the Academy of Artists at Herat, the center of Timurid civilization. Around 1507, Shah Ismail, founder

of the Safavid dynasty, brought Bihzad to the flourishing city of Tabriz, then appointed him director of the Royal Academy, with authority over "all the copyists, painters, gilders, margin-drawers, gold-mixers, gold-beaters and washers of lapis lazuli." Bihzad's talent was so great, his style so beautiful and appealing, that his influence spread through all of Persia and India and Turkistan.

In those days, calligraphy was the dominant art form of the East; all art revolved around intricate and exquisite handwriting. A painter was a draftsman of script, a letterer, concerned with design and pattern alone, placing tiny leaves, flowers, flecks of color, birds and beasts and gorgeous peacocks in the margins around a text to enhance the decorative effect. Mohammedan conquerors superimposed the restrictions of their faith, which forbade the realistic representation of humans, on Persian art. The Mongol invasions led to a special Perso-Mongol style, blending calligraphy with the charming landscapes and stylized portraiture of the Orient.

Persian painting was limited mainly to miniatures—illustrations for tiny books, or drawings intended to be mounted in albums. Artists illustrated manuscripts about national legends, ancient stories of love and war and glory, fables from the East and Araby, the *Shah-Namah (Book of Kings)* and the poetry of Firdusi and Nizami. Painters ignored the third dimension; they used color with-

out gradations of tone; they knew little of perspective; they included whatever details suited them, without regard to what was actually visible from a single point of observation.

Bihzad's influence was so great that he modified the rigidities which calligraphy enforced on Persian art. He was a gifted observer of nature. He manipulated figures with new freedom and shaded his painting of flesh and dress with a subtlety not seen before. He made landscapes intimate and inviting. He used a richer palette than any artist before him—pinks and vermilion, maroons and brick reds, wonderful hues of yellow and green and blue.

He was one of the rare painters in Persia to achieve recognition in his lifetime. The historian Khwandamir wrote: "His fingers, endowed with miraculous qualities, have wiped out the pictures of all the artists among the sons of Adam. A hair of his brush has given life to the lifeless form. . . . This marvel of the age . . . is encompassed with the boundless consideration of the Rulers of Islam."

So Tamerlane's stratagem against the Kipchaks who hid in a cave, not unlike the one in which Bihzad himself was hidden, has come down to us in this fairyland vignette, with its clean vertical planes and its beguiling colors. In an area of only 40 square inches, Bihzad of Herat created a jewel whose grace abides through history and whose charm has conquered time.

*Destruction of the Remnants
of the Kipchak Army (here
enlarged from its actual size, only
8" x 5") was painted by Kamal
ud-Din Bihzad 450 years ago for
the Zafar-Namah, a book that
recounts the glories of Tamerlane.
Courtesy of the
John Work Garrett
Library, Johns Hopkins
University, Baltimore.*

Van Gogh

GENIUS AND CHAOS

DID HE KNOW it was the last self-portrait he would ever paint? For it, he donned the very clothes he would wear in a few days, when they released him from the asylum at St.-Rémy. He would go to Auvers, outside Paris, where Dr. Gachet could perhaps cure him.

Vincent Van Gogh knew he was insane—ravaged by terrible depressions, violent hallucinations, maniacal seizures. In one fit, he had shouted so long that his throat remained swollen for days. In another, he tried to commit suicide by swallowing all his paints. Once, he attempted to kill his friend Gauguin—then cut off his own ear and sent it to a brothel girl.

His life was a battleground for such suffering as few men have endured. He could not hold a job —in Holland or London; he quarreled with his employers, insulted customers. He devoured the Bible, drank heavily and poured out his misery in a flood of heartbreaking letters to his younger brother, Theo, who supported him for years.

Each time Van Gogh sought love, he met disaster. He proposed to his landlord's daughter, who rejected him brutally. He had one unhappy affair with a spinster cousin, another with a wretched creature who tried to kill herself, and befriended a drunken prostitute with whom he lived, for a time, in a ghastly parody of domesticity.

He often wore strange clothes (homemade trousers, a fantastic soldier's tunic) and was heartsick that people thought him a crackpot. To Theo, he protested, "There is in me harmony, calm, music." He haunted London's slums, preaching that suffering is greater than happiness, sorrow nobler than joy. Yearning to be a man of God (his father was a Calvinist pastor), he returned to Holland. He failed the seminary entrance exams and became a lay preacher instead, in the worst mining villages in Belgium, where he nursed the sick, slept on hovel floors, gave away his own pathetic possessions, preached such wild, rambling sermons as to be dismissed for "religious mania."

But he loved art. He had explored museums wherever he was. Now, he tramped the roads of the lowlands, sketching landscapes, peasants, fishermen. Not knowing where to live or how to earn a living, he came to Theo in Paris. He had begun to paint with such passion, with such hot colors, that Toulouse-Lautrec suggested he move to the south of France. In Arles, he began to paint sun-drenched fields and flowers in astounding bursts of energy. Fascinated by stars and night, he would set up an easel outdoors and work by the light of a circle of candles placed around the brim of his hat.

His madness became so unmanageable that he was hospitalized. And when he left, after a few weeks, children hooted at him and neighbors demanded that he be taken to an asylum by force. He committed himself to St.-Rémy.

Painting was his one lifeline to sanity now. He tried to fix his disordered mind on "the reassuring, familiar look of things"—on a chair, his shoes, a pipe, his room—and he rendered these ordinary objects with electrifying freshness of color and intensity of vision. He clung to the *tangibility* of what he saw, as if to strengthen the edge that divides the real from the insane, strongly outlining a head, a petal, a lapel. Yet his internal chaos broke through in tormented, swirling lines and the agitated aureoles of his backgrounds.

He used color as a language for feeling itself, speaking of "green saddened by gray," or yellows that represent "pure love." He saw red and green as "those terrible things—man's passions." He painted with such force and originality that he brought unheard-of expressiveness to portraiture. And in his last self-portrait (opposite), he caught his own terrible, set, psychopathic glare with shattering impact. The portrait had special meaning to him, for, although he sent all his other paintings on to Theo, he kept the self-portrait and himself brought it to Dr. Gachet . . .

On July 27, 1890, Van Gogh took a revolver, went into the fields and shot himself through the heart. Even his aim mocked him: He had only wounded himself. So he dragged himself back to his room and lay there, smoking a pipe, waiting for death. Theo hurried from Paris and pleaded with him to try to live. His last words were: "There will never be an end to human misery." He was 37 years old.

He had sold only one picture during his lifetime. Today, the millions who adorn their walls with his joyous sunflowers and irises, his moving portraits and singing landscapes, have made him as beloved as any painter who ever lived.

This startling Self-Portrait (25½" x 21¼"), painted shortly before Van Gogh's suicide, is now in the Musée du Jeu de Paume, Louvre.

The churning, bursting, imaginative universe of
Vincent Van Gogh reached astounding expressiveness
in the paintings of his last years. Starry Night
(29″ x 36¼″) is one of the most dramatic pictures
in the Museum of Modern Art, New York (acquired
through the Lillie P. Bliss bequest). This
powerful, profoundly original picture was
painted in 1889, shortly after Van Gogh entered the
sanitarium at St.-Rémy. Van Gogh's obsession
with religion often manifested itself in paintings
that illuminate for us his own intensely mystical
visions of the sun, the moon, the heavens themselves.

Klee

THE LAND OF DEEPER INSIGHT

HE WAS A SMALL, PALE, gentle man who worked on half a dozen pictures at a time, sitting before the easels for hours, smoking his pipe, lost in "inner watching," trying to weave intelligence and reverie into fresh harmonies. To Paul Klee, painting was "a trip into the land of deeper insight."

He was born in Switzerland, the son of a music teacher, and became so good a violinist that he could not decide whether to devote his life to music or painting. He once said that his work owed more to Bach and Mozart than to any of the masters of art. He had a unique intensity of vision. When he saw a child asleep, he saw "the circulation of his blood, the regular breathing of his lungs . . . and in his head a world of dreams in contact with the powers of fate." When he saw a man strolling down the deck of a ship, he saw the man's movement, the motion of the ship, the rotation of the earth, the orbit of all the stars wheeling in the heavens—until his mind encompassed a vast system of "movements within the cosmos, centered on the man on the steamer."

In 1902, Klee visited Italy, like many another student; and in the aquarium in Naples, he was suddenly bewitched by the dreamlike universe under water, in which fish and flora moved like phantoms through lyrical light. Here was a world "where things fall upward," where a flower looked like a fish, a turtle like a rock. Again and again, his paintings echoed the enchantment he felt in that aquarium, as in the haunting *Fish Magic* (opposite page).

He went through life fascinated by the whole world of wonder around him. In Tunis, he fell under the spell of Bedouins in a desert dotted with Moslem minarets. "I am possessed by color," Klee wrote. "I do not need to pursue it. This is the great moment: I and color are one. I am a painter." He drew strange and exquisite dream cities, for which he invented names: Beride, City of Water, Prhun, Uol, Air-Tsu-Dni.

"Art does not render what is visible," he said. "Art *makes* visible."

He wanted art to "sound like a fairy tale, a holiday, a change of atmosphere and view, a transfer to another world. . . ." And in his search for that other world, he began to paint not only what the unimaginative could not see, and not simply those new impressions with which the French had liberated art: Klee wanted to paint ideas, meditations, feelings, fantasies. He said that he tried "to push myself away from the earth."

His pictures are all quite small, and he used every conceivable material—paper, canvas, silk, glass, linen, burlap, tin. Intrigued by shapes and textures, he studied mosaics, shells, masks, stained glass, coral, moss, butterfly wings, Chinese poetry, Coptic embroideries, Eskimo drawings, the pictographs by bushmen and American Indians.

His work, at first sight so naïve, rested on immense discipline, masterful drawing, acute and original perceptions. He taught himself to paint with both hands, and once told his students in the famed *Bauhaus* in Weimar: "My hand is merely a tool, guided by something higher, more distant, somewhere."

He created 8,926 pictures and drawings—no one of which does justice to his range and inventiveness. He was, in turn, charming, satirical, mischievous, morbid. He produced scenes of absolutely new strangeness, in which specters and symbols—some lovely, some weird, some delicious, some frightening—seem to drift toward us, in instants of incandescence, from a haunted labyrinth. And sometimes his intensely personal images, which float between memory and inspiration, reveal startling flashes of that dread which is in the faces of those "consecrated to suffering." It was in the nature of Klee's inimitable talent that he saw in the moon "a dream of the sun."

"No other painter of the last half-century," says the *Dictionary of Modern Painting*, "has exercised such a widespread influence. Even more than the variations of Picasso, whose genius recapitulates the history of form, Klee's art opens on the future. . . ."

He died in 1940, and on his tombstone is carved: "I cannot be understood in purely earthly terms. For I can live as happily with the dead as with the unborn. . . ."

Klee painted Fish Magic *(30½″ x 38½″) in 1925. It is in the Arensberg Collection of the Philadelphia Museum of Art.*

THE ARTIST

Biographical information and bibliographies

BIHZAD: Portrait. Library, Istanbul Univ. Miniature.

BIHZAD

Kamal ud-Din Bihzad or Behzad
c.1440/1450-1527/1535
Persian Miniaturist and Teacher

(Only three manuscripts illustrated by Bihzad are positively identified by experts. He was so widely admired that other artists would imitate his miniatures, to honor him—and Bihzad, to return the compliment, or put the seal of his approval on their work, would sign them.)

1440 or 1450	Born in Persia. In the service of Mir Ali Shir, writer and minister of the Sultan.
c.1467	Wins patronage of Sultan Husayn Mirza (also Husayn Bayqara). Illustrates the *History of Timur*. Becomes head of the Academy of Artists at Herat, center of Timurid civilization.
1467	Illustrates the *Zafar Namah*, miniature manuscript (see text).
1478	Illustrates the *Khamsa* of Nizami.
1485	Illustrates the *Khamsa* of Amir Khusrau.
1487	Illustrates the *Bustan* of Sa'di (or the *Bostan* of Saadi, now in the Royal Library, Cairo).
1493	Illustrates the *Nizami* manuscripts (now in the British Museum).
1496	Illustrates the *Amir Khusrau* manuscript.
1506	Paints portrait of Sultan Husein Mirza.
c.1507	Shah Ismail, founder of the Safavid dynasty, brings him to Tabriz and appoints him director of the Royal Academy.

1514   Shah Ismail hides Bihzad and a calligrapher, Shah Mahmud an Nishapuri, in a cave on the eve of battle against the Turks. After the battle, the Shah thanks God that Bihzad and the calligrapher have not been captured.
1527/1535 Dies.
Suggested reading:
Bihzad and His Paintings, by T. W. Arnold (Oxford).
Persian Painting of the Fifteenth Century, by Ralph Pinder-Wilson (Faber & Faber).
Persian Miniatures, by M. S. Dimand (Metropolitan Museum of Art).
See also Oriental Art in general reading list (page 163).

BOCCIONI

Umberto Boccioni 1882-1916
Italian Futurist

1882	Born on October 19 in Reggio Calabria, of parents who come from Romagna.
1897	Follows his father, a police employee, to Catania. Completes his studies (begun at Padua) at the Technical Institute. Obtains diploma in drawing, with rather poor marks.
1898	Quarrels with his father, who objects to his literary and artistic bent, and moves to Rome. Studies painting, literature, journalism. Publishes stories and articles. Studies under Balla. Attends course in drawing from the nude, at the Academy of Fine Arts.
1902	Wins a prize in a painting competition and goes to Paris, to study Impressionism.
1904	Spends seven months in Russia, in St. Petersburg and Tzaritzin, as guest of Russian family.

BOCCIONI: Self-portrait, 1910. Collection of Mr. and Mrs. Harry L. Winston, Birmingham, Mich. Wash and pen.

1905-1907	Returns to Italy. Works in Padua and Venice, exhibits in Florence and Rome.
1906-1908	Keeps a diary, in which he records the "Futurist" direction of his thoughts. Settles in Milan with his mother and sister. In economic difficulties; does sketches for magazines and advertising.
1909	Shows work at the Exhibition of Lombard Painters.

1910	Writes the *Manifesto of Futurist Painters* and reads it in the Chiarelli Theatre, Turin. The evening ends in a riot. Exhibits pastels and drawings in Milan. Brings out the *Technical Manifesto of Futurist Sculpture*. Exhibits 42 works (paintings, drawings, etchings) in Venice.
1911	Finishes *The City Rises* (see text).
1912	Exhibits with Futurists at the Bernheim-Jeune Gallery in Paris. Shows several sculptures at the Salon d'Automne.
1913	Exhibits Futurist paintings with Soffici, Carra, Severini and others in Rome. Speaks in foyer before very large crowd. Shows entire plastic production in Paris. Futurists stage violent evenings in Italy. Opening in Rome of the *Galleria Futurista permanente* of the "first Italian exhibition of Futurist sculpture."
1914	Exhibits 10 sculptures and 46 drawings in Florence. As First World War begins, joins Marinetti, Russolo and Carra in staging demonstrations against Italy's neutrality; spends five days in jail.
1915	Enrolls as volunteer in a bicycle battalion, together with Marinetti and Russolo. Fights in the mountains. When his battalion is disbanded, returns to Milan. Writes a column, *Arti Plastichi* for a weekly.
1916	Is conscripted and assigned to an artillery regiment in Verona. Writes friends that he is riding particularly fiery horses and gaining his sergeant's praise. Seriously hurt in fall from horse. Dies the next day, August 16, without regaining consciousness.

Suggested reading:
Futurism, by Joshua C. Taylor (Museum of Modern Art, New York).
Twentieth Century Italian Art, by James T. Soby and Alfred H. Barr, Jr. (Museum of Modern Art, N. Y.).
See also Modern Painting in general reading list (page 163).

BONNARD

Pierre Bonnard 1867-1947
French Post-Impressionist

1867	Is born at Fontenaye-aux-Roses, suburb of Paris, on October 13. Receives private school education.
c.1885	At his father's bidding, studies law. Also enrolls at the Académie Jullian to study art, later at the École des Beaux-Arts.
1888	Meets Vuillard, Sérusier and Maurice Denis, fellow painters, who gather regularly and call themselves "The Nabis." Because of his interest in Japanese prints, Bonnard is named "the very Japanese Nabi."
1889	Fails law exams and gets father's permission to become a painter after a first poster sale to the France-Champagne Co. Is deeply influenced by Gauguin's work.
1890	Completes military service, takes a studio with Vuillard and Denis. His work is admired by Lautrec.
1891	Shows five canvases and four decorative panels at the Salon des Indépendants. Also exhibits with Vuillard, Roussel and Denis at Le Barc de Boutteville.

1893	Contributes lithographs to the *Revue Blanche*; again shows at the Indépendants.
1895	Vollard publishes an album of his lithographs, *Some Aspects of Parisian Life*; he designs a stained-glass window for Tiffany.
1896	Has first one-man show, at Durand-Ruel Gallery in Paris.
1899	Participates in last Nabis group show; enters into agreement with Bernheim-Jeune to handle the bulk of his work.
c.1900	Meets Marthe de Melliny (real name, Maria Boursin), the model for most of his women. They live together for about 30 years as man and wife before finally marrying.
1903	His colors begin to brighten as he spends more and more time in the country.
1905	Five of his works at the Salon d'Automne greatly impress André Gide.
1907	Makes short trips to Belgium and Holland for study.
1910	Visits Italy to study and paint.
1912	Buys a small house at Vernonnet in the Seine Valley. A critical study of his work is published; he declines the Legion of Honor.
1915	Becomes dissatisfied with his work; writes, "I have sent myself back to school. I want to forget all I know."
1922	Is shown at the Venice Biennale.
1923	Wins third prize at the Carnegie International exhibition in Pittsburgh.
1926	Visits U.S. as member of Carnegie International jury. Has one-man show of 20 recent

BONNARD: Self-portrait, 1938. Collection Georges Wildenstein, N. Y. Oil.

works at Bernheim-Jeune's. Buys a small villa at Le Cannet, in the south of France.

1929	Spends more and more time in the south, very little in Paris.
1936	Wins second prize at Carnegie International.
c.1937	Completes one of several versions, done over the years, of *Nude in the Bathtub* (see text). Large group of works shown at Paris World's Fair.
1940	His wife Maria dies, as does his oldest painter-friend, Vuillard.
1946	Is given major retrospective at Bernheim-Jeune's. Agrees to second large retrospective at the Museum of Modern Art, New York, to celebrate his eightieth birthday.
1947	Dies on January 23 at Le Cannet.

Suggested reading:
Bonnard, by John Rewald (Museum of Modern Art, New York).
Pierre Bonnard, by Claude Roger-Marx (Fernand Hazan). In French.
Bonnard, by Charles Terrasse (Floury). In French.
See also Post-Impressionism in general reading list (page 163).

BOSCH: Self-portrait, detail, Carrying of the Cross. Kunsthistorisches Museum, Vienna. Oil.

BOSCH

Hieronymus Bosch van Aeken c.1450-1516
Flemish Fantasist, Mystic

c.1450	Born in 's Hertogenbosch (or Bois-le-Duc, as the Dutch called it) in the province of Brabant, "12 leagues distant from Antwerp." His father, grandfather and at least two uncles are also painters. The family is well-to-do.
c.1470	Perhaps serves as apprentice to a master painter in Delft or Haarlem.
c.1478	Marries Aleid van de Meervenne (also known as Aleido van Merberme), of a wealthy local family.
1480	Paints two wings of an altarpiece for the Confraternity (Brotherhood) of Our Lady, a work left undone by his father at his death.
1486	Is admitted to membership in the lay Brotherhood of Our Lady, as "Hieronymus, son of Anthony of Aachen." Acts in religious plays, sings in the choir, works as painter and designer for the group.
1488	Is sworn in as "a notable" of the Brotherhood. Occupies a half-timbered house, in the center of town, which also contains his studio.
1493	Supplies the master glassworkers with designs for several stained-glass windows in the chapel of the Brotherhood in the Cathedral of St. John. (These windows were later destroyed by iconoclasts.)
c.1494	Is commissioned to supervise the polychroming of an altarpiece for the Brotherhood.
c.1504	Paints a *Last Judgment* for Philip the Fair.
1516	Dies in 's Hertogenbosch; receives a regal funeral as master painter of the Brotherhood.

Suggested reading:
Bosch, by Robert L. Delevoy (Skira).
Hieronymus Bosch, by Howard Daniel (Hyperion Press and Duell, Sloan and Pearce).
The Millennium of Hieronymus Bosch, by Wilhelm Fränger (Faber & Faber).
See also Flemish and Dutch Painting in general reading list (page 163).

BOTTICELLI

Alessandro (Sandro) di Mariano Filipepi 1444?-1510
Florentine Early Renaissance Master

1444-1458	Born in Florence, the son of Mariano di Vanno Filipepi, a tanner. Acquires the nickname Botticello, or "little barrel." A 16th-century writer reports that he was "always unquiet, never satisfied with schoolwork . . . so that his father, annoyed by so extravagant a brain, as a last resort apprenticed him to a goldsmith."
1458-1467	Apprenticed to Fra Filippo Lippi, whose style dominates Botticelli's early works.
1470	Opens his own workshop and is commissioned to paint *Fortitude*, one of the seven virtues, as decoration for the Florentine Guild of Merchants.
1472-	Is admitted to painters' Guild of St. Luke.
1474	Hires Filippino Lippi as apprentice. Completes *St. Sebastian* for a Florentine church.
1475-1478	Paints a tournament banner for Giuliano de' Medici. Wins the patronage of the Medici. For Pierfrancesco, cousin of Lorenzo the Magnificent, decorates villa at Castello by painting *Primavera* (*Spring*, see text). Paints *The Adoration of the Magi*, including in it portraits of the Medici and a self-portrait.
1481	Is summoned by Pope Sixtus IV to Rome, to help decorate the Sistine Chapel with a series of frescoes. Illustrates first Florentine edition of Dante's *Divine Comedy*.
1482-1487	Returns to Florence. Decorates the Palazzo Vecchio (town hall). Paints altarpiece, *The Madonna With Six Saints*, also *The Madonna of the Magnificat*, *Birth of Venus* (his second work for Pierfrancesco's villa at Castello), *Mars and Venus*, *Virgin With Pomegranate*.
1488	Paints two great altarpieces, *The Coronation of the Virgin* and *The Annunciation*. Paints *Pallas and the Centaur*, probably for Lorenzo the Magnificent.
1493-1498	A brother, Simone di Mariano, returns from Naples to live with Botticelli. Simone be-

BOTTICELLI: Self-portrait, 1478, detail from The Adoration of the Magi. Uffizi, Florence. Oil.

comes a follower of the Dominican monk Savonarola. Botticelli, though profoundly influenced by Savonarola's austere philosophy, manages to retain Medici patronage. Savonarola is executed in 1498; Simone is banished from Florence. Botticelli is allowed to remain. His creativity declines. Completes drawings for illustrations of Dante's writings. Paints *Calumny of Apelles*.

| 1500-1509 | Virtually stops painting. Serves on a commission to select site for Michaelangelo's *David*. |
| 1510 | Dies. Is buried in the Church of Ognissanti. |

Suggested reading:
Botticelli, by André Chastel (N. Y. Graphic Society).
Botticelli, by Giulio Carlo Argan (Skira).
Life of Sandro Botticelli, by Herbert P. Horne (Bell & Sons).
Botticelli, by Lionello Venturi (Phaidon).
See also The Renaissance in general reading list (page 163).

BRAQUE: Portrait by Picasso, 1909. Collection, Edward A. Bragaline, N. Y. Oil.

BRAQUE

Georges Braque 1882-
Modern French Master

1882 Born on May 13 at Argenteuil-sur-Seine, near Paris. His father is a decorator, house painter and amateur artist.

1890 The family moves to Le Havre.

1893 While still in school, attends evening classes at École des Beaux-Arts.

1899 Is apprenticed to his father; learns technique of painting simulated wood and marble for interiors.

1900 Goes to Paris. Settles in Montmartre. To qualify as an artist-craftsman (and thus reduce his period of military service), apprentices himself to a painter-decorator.

1901 Is stationed near Le Havre during military service.

1902 In Paris, studies at École des Beaux-Arts for two months, under Bonnat, and at the Académie Humbert.

1904 Takes first studio; gives up academic studies.

1906 Exhibits six paintings at the Salon des Indépendants. Spends the fall at L'Estaque, becoming part of the *Fauve* movement, which is under the influence of Van Gogh and Gauguin.

1907 Shows with *Fauves* at the Salon des Indépendants—sells all his paintings. Meets Kahnweiler, the art dealer, who contracts for all of his works. Meets Picasso. Completes oil painting, *Large Nude*, his first step toward Cubism.

1908 Spends the spring and summer at L'Estaque. Is influenced by Cézanne. Exhibits at Kahnweiler's. Paints *Guitar and Compote Dish.*

1909 Exhibits at the Salon des Indépendants. His work is described as "jumbles of cubes"— origin of the term "Cubism."

1910 Begins using oval canvases. Enters, with Picasso, period of Analytical Cubism. Paints *Woman With a Mandolin.*

1911 Incorporates letters into paintings. Spends the summer with Picasso at Céret. Does *Man With a Guitar.*

1912 Spends summer with Picasso at Sorgues. Develops Synthetic Cubism. Does first *papiers collés.*

1913 Paints *Still Life on Table.*

1915 Is wounded in action in World War I. Undergoes head surgery. Receives two citations, including the *Croix de Guerre.*

1917 Spends summer at Sorgues. Begins to use large, bold color areas.

1919 Exhibits in Paris and is established as a leader of modern painting.

1922 Shows at the Salon d'Automne. Is in his Neoclassical period.

1923 Designs sets for a Diaghilev ballet.

1925 Marries Marcelle Lapre. Does illustrations for *Le Piège de Méduse.*

1930 Builds a cottage at Varengeville, near Dieppe. Embarks on "thin period."

1932 The Boston Museum includes his Cubist pictures among the first modern works it buys.

1933 Ends his "thin period."

1937 Takes first prize at the Carnegie International exhibition for *The Yellow Tablecloth*, painted in 1935.

1939 Begins to experiment with sculpture, in chalkstone, metals, plaster.

1940 Flees to the Pyrenees to escape German invasion, but then returns to Paris. Refuses to show his work in Germany; declines to design emblem for the Vichy government.

1943 Exhibits sculpture and paintings at the Salon d'Automne.

1945 Is awarded the Legion of Honor.

1946 Exhibits with Rouault in London.

1948 Wins First Prize at the Venice Biennale with *The Billiard Table.* Elected to Academy of Fine Arts, Argentina.

1949 Exhibits 114 paintings, drawings, prints, illustrations, sculptures at the Museum of Modern Art in New York.

1949 Publishes *Cahier de Georges Braque*—his ideas and pen-and-ink drawings from 1917 to 1947.

1953 Decorates a ceiling for the Louvre. His studio, "the climate of my work," is the subject of several works (see text).

1958 Is awarded $30,000 prize by the Rome Academy of Fine Arts.

1961 Exhibits at the Louvre—its first exhibition of a living artist—where his studio on the Rue du Douanier is reconstructed.

Suggested reading:
Braque, by Douglas Cooper (Drummond).
Georges Braque, by Henry Hope (Museum of Modern Art, Cleveland Museum of Art).
G. Braque, by John Richardson (N. Y. Graphic Society).
G. Braque, by John Russell (Phaidon).
Men and Monuments, by Janet Flanner (Harper).
See also Cubism and Modern Painting in general reading list (page 163).

BRUEGEL

Pieter Bruegel or Brueghel c. 1525/1530-1569
also known as The Peasant Bruegel, Pieter the Droll, Bruegel the Elder.
Flemish Landscape and Genre Painter

BRUEGEL: Self-portrait, detail. Albertina, Vienna.

c.1525- Born in the village of Brueghel, near the
1530 Dutch-Belgian border, from which the family name may come. During his youth, the family moves to Antwerp.

c.1545- Is apprenticed to Pieter Coecke van Aelst,
1550 whose woodcuts stimulate Bruegel's interest in landscapes. Studies also under Hieronymus Cock, a successful engraver.

1551 Becomes a member of the Guild of St. Luke, the painters' guild in Antwerp.

1552- Travels to Italy via France and returns to Ant-
1553 werp via Switzerland, with sketchbooks full of landscapes, but no strong or visible Italian influence on his technique.

c.1554 "He lived with a housekeeper-concubine, whom he promised to marry when she stopped lying; he recorded her lies with notches cut into a stick; and having no stick for his own sins, he renounced her when the notches overflowed."—Will Durant, *The Reformation,* page 832.

1554 Goes to work for Hieronymus Cock. For many years, draws pictorializations of proverbs, genre scenes and representations of hell's horrors for Cock's engravings.

1557 First dated painting: *River Landscape With the Peasant Sowing.*

1559- Paints *The Battle Between Carnival and
1563 Lent, Children's Games, The Triumph of Death, The Fall of Rebel Angels, "Dulle Griet" (Mad Meg).* Marries Marie Coecke (age 17), daughter of his teacher, Pieter Coecke van Aelst. Bruegel had carried her in his arms when she was a child.

c.1563 Settles in Brussels.

1563- Paints *The Tower of Babel, Christ Bearing
1564 the Cross, The Death of the Virgin.*

1564 His son Pieter Bruegel the Younger is born. (He will be called "Hellfire" Bruegel because of the scenes of hell and conflagration he paints. *He* has a son, Pieter III, 1589-1638/39, who is a mediocre artist.)

1565- Paints *The Harvesters, Hunters in the Snow,
1567 The Wedding Dance, The Land of Cockayne, The Blind Leading the Blind.*

1568 His son Jan Bruegel is born. (He is later called "Velvet" Bruegel—because of the smooth finish of his small pictures of animals and plants. *He* has two sons, eight grandsons and four great-grandsons—all of whom become painters.)

1568 Paints *Birds' Nests, Peasant Dance, Peasant Wedding, Tempest at Sea, The Beggars* (see text).

1569 The Brussels City Council recognizes Bruegel's standing by exempting him from housing Spanish soldiers; gives him an advance on a commissioned painting. Dies in Brussels on September 5.

Suggested reading:
Pieter Brueghel The Elder, by Virgil Barker (Arts Publishing Corporation).
The Fantasy of Pieter Brueghel, by Adriaan Barnouw (Lear).
Peter Brueghel The Elder, by Gustav Glück (Braziller).
Brueghel, the Paintings, by Fritz Grossmann (Phaidon).
See also Flemish and Dutch Painting in general reading list (page 163).

CARAVAGGIO

Michelangelo Amerighi da Caravaggio 1573-1610
Italian Baroque Master

1573 Born in Caravaggio, Lombardy, on September 28.

1584 Under guardianship of his brother Battista,

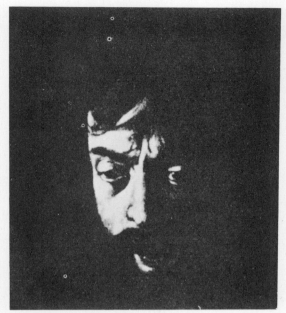

CARAVAGGIO: *Self-portrait, detail, head of Goliath. Borghese Gallery, Rome. Oil.*

goes to Milan to study art, for four years, under Simone Peterzano.

1589- Leaves Milan for Rome, via Venice. Very ill,
1590 enters a pauper's hospital in Rome.

1591- Wins patronage of the Cardinal del Monte,
1592 marking the end of his poverty. Does a first *St. Matthew Writing the Gospel*—which is rejected as "too low-class" a characterization of the saint.

1592- Paints *Love as Conqueror* and *The Lute*
1595 *Player.*

1593 Is admitted to the painters' Guild of Saint Luke.

1596 Paints a still life, *Fruit Basket.*

1598- Completes *Calling of St. Matthew* and second
1599 *St. Matthew Writing the Gospel.*

1600- Paints *Crucifixion of St. Peter.*
1601

c.1605 Works on *The Virgin of the Serpent.*

1605 Paints *St. Jerome Writing.* Flees Rome for a month after having attacked a lawyer. Begins *The Death of the Virgin* (see text).

1606 Kills Ranuccio Tomassoni in a quarrel over a tennis match. Flees to the Sabine Hills, then to Naples.

1607 Paints *The Seven Works of Mercy.*

c.1607 Goes to Malta.

1608 Is knighted, but, after assaulting a cavalier, is thrown into prison. Escapes and flees first to Syracuse, then to Messina and Palermo.

1609 In Naples, is beaten so badly by some Knights of Malta that he is reported dead.

1610 Sets sail for Port Ercole. Hauled off the boat in a case of mistaken identity. Imprisoned. Released. Spends a night wandering on the seashore. Contracts malaria. Dies on July 18.

Suggested reading:
Caravaggio, His Incongruity and His Fame, by Bernard Berenson (Chapman and Hall).
Caravaggio Studies, by Walter Friedlaender (Princeton University).
Caravaggio: His Life, Legend and Works, by Roger Hinks (Faber & Faber).
See also The Great Centuries of Painting in general reading list (page 163).

CÉZANNE

Paul Cézanne 1839-1906
French Post-Impressionist

1839 Born on January 19 at Aix-en-Provence. His

father, a hat maker, later turns banker.

1844- Receives a classical education. At school, be-
1856 comes a good friend of Émile Zola, a classmate. Attends the School of Drawing in Aix. Also studies music.

1858 Wins second prize at the School of Drawing.

1861 His father, having urged him to study law, finally allows him to go to Paris and study art. Attends the Académie Suisse (is rejected by the École des Beaux-Arts). Disgusted with Paris, returns to Aix and works in his father's bank.

1862 Returns to Paris; becomes friendly with Renoir, Monet, Sisley.

1864- Divides his time between Aix and Paris. Sends
1870 paintings to the Salon every year and is rejected every year.

1870 Stays at L'Estaque, near Marseilles, during the Franco-Prussian War. Lives with a model he met in Paris, Hortense Fiquet (later Mme. Cézanne).

1871 Returns to Paris.

1872 Son, Paul, is born. Visits Pissarro at Pontoise and is greatly influenced by him.

1874 Exhibits in the First Impressionist Exhibition: *The Hanged Man's House, A Modern Olympia, Landscape at Auvers.* He is the most laughed-at artist, by both critics and public.

1876 Spends the summer at L'Estaque. Refuses to join the Second Impressionist Exhibition.

1877 Exhibits 17 paintings at the Third Impressionist Exhibition.

1878 Returns to L'Estaque. Stays with his mother, who is very ill. Zola lends him some money. Breaks with Impressionism.

CÉZANNE: *Self-portrait, 1879-82. Berner Kunstmuseum, Berne. Oil.*

1880 Returns to Paris. Spends summer with Zola.

1881 Goes to Pontoise with Pissarro, then to Aix-en-Provence.

1882 Accepted at the Salon. Renoir visits him at L'Estaque.

1883- Paints *The Blue Vase, The Bather, Village of*
1888 *Gardanne.*

1886 Marries Hortense Fiquet. Zola, in his novel *L'Oeuvre,* bases the character of an unsuccessful painter on Cézanne, who breaks with Zola. Father dies, leaving Cézanne well off.

1887 Exhibits at Brussels with the "XX" Group.

1889 Exhibits at the Paris World's Fair.

1890-1900 Paints *Still Life With Apples* (see text).

1890- Paints five versions of *The Card Players,*
1895 *Baigneuses* series, *Still Life With Basket of Apples, The Boy in a Red Vest,* etc.

1891 Trip to Switzerland; has first diabetic attack.

1894 Spends the fall at Monet's. Meets Rodin and Clemenceau.

1895- Exhibits (at Ambroise Vollard's) *The Boy in*
1900 *a Red Vest* and portraits of *Gustave Geffroy.* Paints *Pines and Rocks, Still Life With Onions and Bottle.*

1898 His mother dies.

1898- Paints *Women Bathers*—his largest painting,
1906 on which he works for at least eight years.

1899 Settles in Aix. Exhibits three paintings at the Salon des Indépendants.

1900 Shows at the Centennial Exhibition. The Berlin Nationalgalerie buys a painting.

1901 Exhibits at the Salon des Indépendants and in Brussels.

1902 Émile Zola dies. It affects Cézanne deeply, despite their break.

1904- Exhibits 33 paintings at the Salon d'Automne
1905 and at the Salon des Indépendants.

1906 Caught in a rainstorm, he collapses, is picked up by a laundry cart and taken home. Dies on October 22, at Aix-en-Provence.

Suggested reading:
Cézanne, by Roger Fry (Hogarth Press).
Paul Cézanne, by Gerstle Mack (Knopf).
Paul Cézanne, by John Rewald (Simon & Schuster).
Paul Cézanne, His Life and Art, by Ambroise Vollard (Crown).
See also Post-Impressionism in general reading list (page 163).

CHAGALL

Marc Chagall 1889-
French Fantasist and Expressionist

1889- Born on July 7 to Zakhar and Ida Chagall at
1906 Vitebsk, Russia. Has eight sisters and one brother. Parents belong to a Jewish sect of religious mystics called *Hasidim.* Chagall takes lessons from a cantor and sings in the temple. Is briefly apprenticed to a photographer, but persuades father to provide tuition for a school of painting and design.

1908- Is urged by a friend to study in St. Petersburg,
1909 where Jews are allowed to live only by special permission. Fails entrance examinations for a school of arts and crafts. Enrolls in another, wins a contest and obtains a grant of 10 rubles per month for a year. His time in St. Petersburg is marked by abject poverty. Serves a short term in prison for not having correct residence papers. Vinaver, a lawyer, buys two of his paintings and promises to support Chagall in Paris by providing a monthly income.

1910- Journeys to Paris. Lives near slaughterhouse.
1913 Meets many artists and poets, including La Fresnaye, Delaunay, Modigliani, Apollinaire. Extremely productive; produces hundreds of paintings.

1914 First one-man show in Berlin, for which he provides 200 paintings. Charles Malpel, an art dealer, contracts to buy seven paintings each month for 250 francs. Paints *The Green Rabbi* and *The Wedded With an Angel* (see text).

1915- Returns to Vitebsk. Marries his childhood
1917 sweetheart, Bella Rosenfeld. World War I breaks out. Bolshevik government appoints him Minister of Arts for the province of Vitebsk. Founds an art school. Later resigns. Paints *Birthday* and *Self-Portrait With a Wineglass.*

1919- Commissioned to paint murals for the Jewish

CHAGALL: Self-portrait, 1959. Galerie Maeght, Paris. Gouache.

1921	State Theatre in Moscow. Designs sets and costumes for three plays by the great Jewish humorist Sholom Aleichem.
1922-1923	Returns to Paris after futile attempt to retrieve the paintings he had sent to the Berlin exhibition in 1914. Does engravings for *Mein Leben*, German edition of his autobiography. Ambroise Vollard, art dealer, commissions him to illustrate Gogol's *Dead Souls*.
1924	First retrospective exhibition, in Paris. Paints *Jew With Torah*.
1926	First one-man show in the United States, in New York.
1927-1930	Vollard commissions him to illustrate the *Fables* of La Fontaine—100 plates.
1931	Visits Palestine, Egypt, Syria prior to illustrating the Bible.
1933	Studies El Greco in Spain. Travels in Italy, England, the Netherlands.
1935	Visits Vilna, Poland, to refresh memories of old-fashioned Jewish life.
1936-1938	Paints *Time Is a River Without Banks*, showing concern over totalitarianism and persecution of the Jews.
1939	Receives the Carnegie International's third prize for painting.
1941	The Museum of Modern Art invites him to the United States, to escape from Vichy France. Arrives on June 23.
1942-1943	In Mexico, creates sets and costumes for a Tschaikovsky ballet.
1944	Bella Chagall dies of virus infection. Deeply grieved, he ceases working.
1945	Designs costumes and sets for Stravinsky's ballet *The Firebird*.
1946-1947	Retrospective exhibition at the Art Institute of Chicago and the Museum of Modern Art in New York. Returns to Paris. Further showings in Paris, Amsterdam, London.
1948	Receives the International Prize for Engraving at the 24th Biennale in Venice. Paints *The Blue Horse*.
1949-1951	Buys villa at Vence, near Cannes, on French Riviera. Travels to Israel for exhibition. Begins working in pottery. Executes murals for the Watergate Theatre in London.
1952-1955	Marries Valentine Brodsky. Two trips to Greece.
1957	Exhibition of his paintings, prints and watercolors, sponsored by the Museum of Modern Art, New York, to celebrate his 70th birthday.
1959	Is commissioned to create 12 large windows

for the synagogue of Hadassah Medical Center in Jerusalem. The windows represent the twelve tribes of Israel.

1961	Windows for the Hadassah synagogue are exhibited in the Louvre and the Museum of Modern Art, New York.
1962	Travels to Israel for dedication of the synagogue windows.

Suggested reading:
Chagall, by Michael Ayrton (Faber & Faber).
Marc Chagall, by Walter Erben (Praeger).
Marc Chagall, by James Johnson Sweeney (Museum of Modern Art, New York).
Chagall, by Lionello Venturi (Skira).
See also Modern Painting in general reading list (page 163).

CLOUET

François Clouet c.1510-1572
French Renaissance Court Painter

Note: Though many paintings are attributed to Clouet, by long and unbroken tradition, there are no contemporary and original attestations of his work—hence, there is no certainty about many of the accepted attributions.

c.1510	Born at Tours, France, son of Jean Clouet, official Court Painter to François I of France.
1541	Earliest reference to François Clouet.
1545	Jean Clouet dies. François inherits the titles *valet de chambre* and *peintre du Roi*. Is allowed to inherit the property and possessions of his father, though not a "subject of the King."
1547	François I dies. Clouet is commissioned to

CLOUET:
Self-portrait.
Courtesy Burlington Magazine, London.

make an effigy of the King, which includes taking a death mask of face and hands and dressing him in his mourning clothes. Executes paintings to be used in church decorations and banners for the funeral.

1547	Henry II ascends the throne, and Clouet enters his service at the same wages he had received under François I—240 livres a year.
1550	Paints *Diane de Poitiers* (see text).
1554	Decorates the King's carriage, which is hailed a masterpiece.
1559	Becomes inspector of the mint—supervising the minting and creating the designs of most coins. Makes a last will and testament, dividing his wealth between his two daughters (born out of wedlock, Clouet never married) and his sister. Both daughters become nuns.
1568	Accepts patronage of Claude Gauffier de Boisez, Seigneur d'Oiron, and his wife.
1571	Prepares death mask of Henry II and paintings for church ceremonies.
1572	Dies on December 22, shortly after the Massacre of St. Bartholomew.

Suggested reading:
Stories of the French Artists from Clouet to Delacroix, by P. M. Turner & C. H. C. Baker (Chatto & Windus).
Les Clouet, peintres officiels des rois de France, by

Étienne Moreau Nelaton (Levy). In French.
See also The Renaissance and National Surveys of Painting *(French Painting)* in general reading list (page 163).

CRANACH

Lucas Cranach, the Elder 1472-1553
Real name, Lucas Muller
German (Saxon) Court Painter

1472	Born in Kronach in Bavaria. Father, a painter, probably his first teacher. Marries Barbara Brengbier, daughter of a burgher of Gotha. (Has three sons by her; all become painters: John, Hans, Lucas Cranach "the Younger").
c.1503	Moves to Vienna, where landscape painting is much in vogue.
1504	Paints *Rest of the Virgin During the Flight Into Egypt.*
1505	Does first woodcut, representing the Virgin and three saints in prayer before a crucifix. Is appointed court painter to Frederick the Wise of Wittenberg, Prince Elector of Saxony.
1508	The Elector gives Cranach the symbol of a winged snake as a coat of arms.
1509	Goes to the Netherlands on a diplomatic mission and paints the Emperor Maximilian and the boy who afterwards becomes Charles V. Paints a life-sized nude. Frederick the Wise does not approve. Cranach does not paint a nude again until he is 60.
1513	Is influenced by Dürer engravings that arrive in Saxony.
1519	Is elected a town counselor of Wittenberg.

CRANACH: Self-portrait, 1550. Uffizi, Florence. Oil.

1520	Paints Luther as an Augustinian friar.
1525	Is present at the betrothal festival of Luther and Catherine Bora.
1529	Paints *Portrait of Martin Luther.*
c.1529	Paints *Stag Hunt.*
1530	Paints *Earthly Paradise.*
1533	Receives payment for "sixty pairs of portraits of the elector and his brother."
1537	Is elected Burgomaster of Wittenberg. Heartbroken by the death of his son Hans, he turns the wings of the serpent downward on his coat of arms.
c.1537	Paints *The Nymph of the Spring* (see text).
1540	Is reelected Burgomaster of Wittenberg.
1541	Elector Jean Frederick I embraces Lutheran-

141

ism and enters the religious wars. Cranach follows his patron in the campaign against the Duke of Brunswick. The Elector is wounded, imprisoned and condemned to death. Charles V, on his way to Wittenberg, finds himself face to face with Cranach and, in remembrance of the portrait Cranach had painted of him when he was eight, forgives both Cranach and Jean Frederick I.

1552 Moves to Weimar.
1553 Dies at Weimar, October 16.

Suggested reading:

Cranach L'Ancien, by Gabriel Rouches (Braun). In French.
Lucas Cranach, by Christian Zervos (Cahier d'Art). In French.
See also National Surveys of Painting (*German Masters of Art*) in general reading list (page 163).

DAVID: *Self-portrait. Grand Palais, Paris. Oil.*

DAVID

Jacques-Louis David 1748-1825
French Neo-Classicist

1748 Born on August 31, in Paris, the only child of a prosperous ironmonger and Marguerite Buron, from a prominent French family.
1757 Father is killed in a duel, in an *affaire gallante.* An uncle, François Buron, guides his education. On the advice of his first cousin, François Boucher, the famous painter, he is sent to a school specializing in rhetoric.
1766 After he fails to be "practical" about a career in architecture, medicine or law, his family allows him to study art. His first teacher, J. M. Vien, professor of the Royal Academy, encourages him to develop a classical style.
1774 Wins the *Prix de Rome* with his painting *Loves of Antiochus and Stratonice.*
1775 Goes to Rome. Begins to choose subjects from classical tragedies. Greatly admires Raphael.
1781 Returns to France.
1782 Marries Charlotte Pecoul, 17, member of a wealthy family. Relieved of economic problems, he devotes himself entirely to painting.
1783 Is admitted to the Royal Academy.
1784 Paints *The Oath of the Horatii.*
1788 Paints *Death of Socrates.*
1789 Paints *Brutus.* His works become propaganda symbols for the Jacobins. Supports the Revo-

lution and joins with younger artists to abolish the Academy, incurring enmity of established painters.

1790 Paints *The Oath in the Tennis Court,* his first important painting of the revolutionary period; in it, he includes portraits of Mirabeau, Bailly, Robespierre. The National Academy accepts the picture. Joins a Jacobin Club.
1791 Wife leaves him after he votes for King's death, takes custody of their two daughters; he has custody of two sons.
1792 Is elected a Deputy to the National Convention. Becomes a member of the Committee of Public Industries and member of the Committee on Arts.
1794 Robespierre is condemned to death (July 27). David, politically associated with him, is arrested and sentenced to death (July 30). His estranged wife intercedes, going from door to door, pleading for his life, her children beside her. In prison, he begins *The War Between the Romans and Sabines,* inspired by his wife (see text).
1794 Freed, imprisoned again; once more his wife
1795 wins his release. Is named one of 48 members of the National Institute of Arts and Science.
1799 Finishes *The War Between the Romans and Sabines.* Charges admission fee for viewing and earns some 65,000 livres.
1800 Napoleon names him Government Painter. Leery of politics, he declines.
1803 Is made a Chevalier of the Legion of Honor.
1804 Is given title "Our First Painter" by Napoleon. Begins *The Coronation,* on which he spends four years, and *Distribution of the Eagles.*
1814 Napoleon is defeated. David is displaced from throne of art.
1815 Signs petition welcoming Napoleon back.
1816 After Waterloo, is exiled. Leaves France for Brussels.
1825 Dies on December 29, at Brussels.

Suggested reading:

David, Ingres, Gros, Géricault, by Pierre Courthion (Skira).
Pageant-Master of the Republic, by David Lloyd Dowd (University of Nebraska).
The Painter Jacques-Louis David, by Helen Rosenau (Nicholson & Watson).
Jacques-Louis David and the French Revolution, by William R. Valentiner (Sherman).
See also Nineteenth Century in general reading list (page 163).

DEGAS

Edgar Hilaire Germain Degas 1834-1917
French Impressionist

1834 Born in Paris on July 19. His father, Auguste De Gas, is a banker; his mother, a Creole from New Orleans.
1845- Studies at the Lycée Louis-le-Grand, passes
1853 his baccalaureate. His mother dies in 1847.
1853- Studies law, but is allowed to study art as
1854 well. First visits his grandfather's home in Naples.
1855 Enters the École des Beaux-Arts in Paris.
1856- Visits Rome, Naples and Florence.
1857
1858 Revisits Rome and Florence; begins studies for painting of his uncle Bellelli's family.
1860- Concentrates on legendary and mythological
1862 subjects.
1861 Paints *Semiramis Founding a City, Spartan Girls Wrestling.*
1862 Meets and becomes friends with Manet. Begins series of pictures on jockeys and horse racing.

DEGAS: *Self-portrait. Calouste Gulbenkian Foundation, Lisbon, Portugal. Oil.*

1865 Exhibits a pastel, *War in the Middle Ages,* at the Salon.
1866- Paints *Steeplechase, Family Portraits, Por-*
1868 *trait of a Young Woman, The Orchestra at the Paris Opera.*
1869- Paints *Degas' Father Listening to Pagans, At*
1872 *the Race Course.*
1870 During the Franco-Prussian War, serves in the artillery near Paris.
1871 Paints *Count Napoléon Lepic With His Children.*
1872 Begins to watch opera dancers rehearse. Becomes friendly with Renoir, Monet, Pissarro, Bazille. Sails for New Orleans to visit his brothers. Paints *The Cotton Office, Woman With a Vase of Flowers.*
1873 Returns to Paris.
1874 Is active in organizing the First Impressionist Exhibition. Shows ten of his works.
1875- Does gouache-and-pastel *Café Concert: The*
1877 *Song of the Dog.* Paints *Absinthe*—perhaps his most famous café scene.
1878 The Pau Museum in southern France buys *The Cotton Market,* his first work to hang in a museum.
1880 Visits Spain. Paints *Portraits of Criminals, The Dancing Class.*
1881 Exhibits his first sculpture at the Sixth Impressionist Exhibition.
1882 Paints series of milliners and laundresses.
1883 Paints *Before the "Takeoff."* Does many studies and finishes paintings of women bathing, a subject he returns to again and again.
1885 Vacations in Normandy. Begins worrying about losing his sight.
1886 Visits Spain. Exhibits at the Eighth (and last) Impressionist Exhibition. Does *The Tub* (see text).
1889 Trip to Spain and Morocco.
1893 His eyesight worsens. Works with great difficulty.
1898 Begins to live as a recluse, seeing only a few old friends: Henri Rouart, Daniel Halévy, Bartholomé.
1914 The large Isaac de Camondo collection of Degas enters the Louvre.
1917 Dies in Paris, blind, on September 27.

Suggested reading:

Letters of Edgar Degas, Edited by Marcel Guérin (Studio Publications).

The Life and Work of Edgar Degas, by J. B. Manson (The Studio, Ltd.).
Degas, by Daniel Catton Rich (Abrams).
See also Impressionism in general reading list (page 163).

DELACROIX

Ferdinand Victor Eugène Delacroix 1798-1863
French Romanticist

1798　Born on April 26 at Charenton-St. Maurice, near Paris. His father holds high offices under the First Empire, both as a Minister and Ambassador. His mother is of German stock.

c.1815　Enters the studio of Guerin, "a hopeless academician," meets Géricault, whose vigor, talent and romanticism impress him.

1822　Begins his journal, which he keeps, with certain gaps, until his death at 65. Paints *Dante and Virgil*, his first important picture.

1824　Exhibits his first large Romantic canvas, *The Massacre of Chios*, at the Salon.

1825　Takes three-month trip to England to study Bonington's and Constable's use of color.

1831　Exhibits painting, *Liberty Leading the People*, at the Salon.

1832　Takes six-month trip to Morocco, as part of a special French mission. The exoticism of North Africa provides a lifetime of subject matter.

1835　Jenny le Guillon becomes his loyal housekeeper and friend, until his death.

1837　Meets Chopin; becomes a close friend of his and George Sand.

1841　Paints *The Jewish Wedding*, a subject from his North African tour.

1849　Paints *Arab Rider Attacked by a Lion* (see text).

1857　After being refused election to the Academy six times because of the influence of Ingres's devotees, he is elected.

1859　Eight of his works are badly received at the Salon, and he refuses to exhibit again.

1860　Paints *Horses Coming out of the Sea*.

1863　Paints *Collecting the Arab Tax*, his last important picture, a few months prior to his death. Dies on August 13, at Champrosay.

Suggested reading:
The Journal of Delacroix, edited by Walter Pach (Crown).
Eugène Delacroix: His Life and Work, by Charles P. Baudelaire (Lear).
Eugène Delacroix, by Dorothy Bussy (Duckworth).
Delacroix, by Paul G. Konody (Stokes).
See also Nineteenth Century in general reading list (page 163).

DELACROIX: Self-portrait. Uffizi, Florence. Oil.

DELLA FRANCESCA

Piero della Francesca c.1415-1492
Florentine Early Renaissance Master

c.1415　Born in Borgo San Sepolcro, Umbrian town. His father, Benedetto de' Franceschi, died before his birth—hence his name follows the feminine form of his widowed mother's.

c.1429　Considers becoming a mathematician, but decides in favor of a painting career.

1439　Apprenticeship in Florence, in studio of Domenico Veneziano. Is attracted to Uccello's mathematical studies of perspective.

1442　Returns to Borgo San Sepolcro, is elected Town Counselor.

1445　Begins work on commission of a polyptych, the *Madonna della Misericordia* (not finished until 1461).

c.1449　Probably makes first visit to Ferrara on invitation of the court and meets Rogier van der Weyden.

1451　Completes a fresco in Rimini for Sigismondo Malatesta.

1452　Embarks on a cycle of frescoes, *The Story of the True Cross*, for the Church of San Francesco at Arezzo. (Work not completed until 1466.)

1454　Receives commission from the friars of Santo Agostino at Borgo for an altarpiece. Known to be a slow worker, he is given eight years

DELLA FRANCESCA: Believed to be a self-portrait, detail, The Resurrection. *Palazzo Communale, Borgo San Sepolcro, Italy. Fresco.*

to complete the work (not finished until 1469, almost 16 years later).

1459　Works in Rome—for first and last time; receives payment for his part in "the painting of several pictures in the Chamber of His Holiness, the Pope." (None remain today.)

c.1462　Paints celebrated profile portraits of Duke of Urbino and his wife.

1469　Is called to Ferrara by Duke Borso to execute some palace frescoes, none of which remain today.

c.1470　Completes *The Nativity* (see text), the central panel of a triptych for the cathedral in Borgo.

1471　Is cited for failure to pay taxes in Borgo.

c.1472　Works more formally under the patronage of the Duke of Urbino, as a kind of "master of the works." Probably shared in the designing of the sculptured cornices, entablatures and capitals of the Ducal Palace at Urbino.

c.1478　Stops accepting new commissions. Devotes himself to writing.

1482　Rents a house in Rimini in order to complete an old commission.

c.1485　Dedicates two treatises (on rectilinear bodies and perspective) to the new Duke of Urbino, citing that he had given his best works to his father.

1487　Makes a will at Borgo, written in his own hand.

1492　Reputed, by Vasari, to be blind in his last years. Dies a man of considerable property. Is buried in the Badia at Borgo San Sepolcro.

Suggested reading:
Piero della Francesca, Kenneth Clark (Phaidon).
Piero della Francesca, Roberto Longhi (Boston Book & Art Shop, Inc.).
Piero della Francesca, or The Ineloquent in Art, by Bernard Berenson (Macmillan).
Piero della Francesca, by Lionello Venturi (Skira).
See also The Renaissance in general reading list (page 163).

DÜRER

Albrecht Dürer 1471-1528
German Renaissance Master

1471　Born at Nürnberg, the third of 18 children. His father, Albrecht Dürer the Elder, a goldsmith, teaches him the craft of goldsmiths.

1486　Is apprenticed to Michael Wolgemut for three years.

DÜRER: Self-portrait, 1498. Prado, Madrid. Oil-tempera.

1490　Travels for four years, visiting Colmar, Basel and Strasbourg. Paints portrait of his father (see text).

1494　Returns briefly to Nürnberg. Marries Agnes Frey, who is chosen for him in his absence. (They will have no children.) Visits Venice, studies Mantegna, mathematics, reads Poligiano's Latin poetry.

1495　Back in Nürnberg for ten years, produces great quantity of paintings as well as wood and copper engravings.

1502　His father dies.

1504　Paints *The Adoration of the Magi*. His mother comes to live with him.

1505　Obtains a loan of 100 florins and goes again to Italy, there receiving great respect and adulation. In Venice, is influenced by work of Giovanni Bellini.

1511-　Paints *The Adoration of the Trinity* and does
1514　engravings: *Knight, Death and Devil, St.*

Jerome in his Study, Melancholia I.

1515 The Emperor Maximilian gives him a modest pension of 100 florins a year.

1520 Travels in the Netherlands, where the artists of Antwerp honor him with a banquet. From Antwerp, he writes Erasmus to come to the aid of Luther.

1522 Paints *Man of Sorrows,* his final self-portrait.

1525 Publishes *Instruction in Measurement.*

1526 Completes *The Four Apostles* and presents the panels to the city of Nürnberg. Executes a portrait-engraving of Erasmus.

1528 Dies on April 6, after periodic attacks of malarial fever.

Suggested reading:
The Life and Art of Albrecht Dürer, by Erwin Panofsky (Princeton).
Albrecht Dürer, by Lionel Cust (Seeley).
Life of Albrecht Dürer, by Mrs. Charles Heaton (Macmillan).
Albert Dürer, His Life & Works, by W. B. Scott (Longmans, Green).
See also The Renaissance and National Surveys of Painting *(German Masters of Art)* in general reading list (page 163).

EL GRECO: Self-portrait, detail, 1586, The Burial of Count Orgaz. Church of Santo Tomé, Toledo. Oil.

EL GRECO

Domenikos Theotokopoulos 1541-1614
Spanish Mannerist and Religious Expressionist

1541 Born at Candia, Crete, which at this time is governed by Venice.

c.1560 Comes to Venice. Works in the studios of Titian and, probably, of Jacopo Bassano and Tintoretto.

1567 Titian, now in his eighties, writes to Philip II, King of Spain, regarding a commission given him for the Escorial palace: a *Martyrdom of St. Lawrence.* He tells Philip he is being helped by "a certain young disciple of great merit." (Authorities feel certain he refers to El Greco.)

c.1570 Arrives in Rome, is commended to Cardinal Farnese as "a young Candian, a pupil of Titian . . . exceptionally gifted in painting." On way to Rome, stops at Reggio, where he is deeply moved by works of Correggio.

c.1575 Leaves Rome for Madrid, possibly attracted by rumors of the possibility of major commissions from Philip II at the Escorial.

c.1577 Paints an altarpiece, which Philip rejects; moves to Toledo. Is commissioned to paint a *Holy Trinity,* for the Church of Santo Domingo el Antiguo, and the *Espolio,* for the Cathedral.

1578 A son, Jorge Manuel, is born to El Greco and Doña Jerónima de las Cuevas, who remains El Greco's lifelong companion.

1580 Is commissioned to paint *The Martyrdom of St. Maurice* for the Escorial. Philip II orders the prior of the local convent to supply him with fine-ground colors.

1584 Is paid 800 ducats for *The Martyrdom of St. Maurice,* but Philip refuses to hang it.

1585 Rents 24 rooms in the palace of the Marquis of Villena.

1586 Completes one of the major works of his career, *The Burial of Count Orgaz,* for the Church of Santo Tomé, Toledo (see text).

1588 Sues parish of Santo Tomé for payment of *The Burial;* wins suit.

1596 Council of Castile orders an altarpiece for the College of Doña María de Aragón in Madrid.

1597 Contacts dealers at Seville and Genoa for the export of his pictures.

1600 Completes the altarpiece for the College of Doña María de Aragón in Madrid.

1603 Signs contract for several works for the Hospice of the Caridad at Illescas, between Madrid and Toledo.

1605 Begins two-year lawsuit over payment of Illescas's commission.

1607-1611 Completes several commissions for the municipality of Toledo.

1614 Dies in poverty and semiobscurity, on April 7. Is buried in Santo Domingo el Antiguo, Toledo.

Suggested reading:
El Greco, by Ludwig Goldscheider (Phaidon).
El Greco, by Elizabeth du Gué Trapier (Hispanic Society of America).
El Greco, by Paul Guinard (Skira).
See also The Great Centuries of Painting and National Surveys of Painting *(Spanish Painting)* in general reading list (page 163).

FRA ANGELICO

Guido di Pietro da Mugello, Fra Giovanni da Fiesole
1387-1455
Florentine Early Renaissance Master

1387 Born Guido, son of Peter of Mugello, a moderately well-off farmer, in Vicchio, Tuscany.

1407 Joins the Holy Order of the Dominicans at Fiesole, outside Florence, with a younger brother.

1408 Takes his vows and the name Fra Giovanni.

1409 Flees with other brothers of the order to Foligno, during the Great Schism.

1414 Survives the plague and enters a monastery at Cortona, where he stays till 1418. Here, it is believed, he studies painting, in the workshop of a miniaturist.

1418 Returns to Fiesole and a belated apprenticeship in painting, perhaps with Masolino.

1428 Completes an altarpiece for his monastery, San Domenico, at Fiesole.

1431 Paints the masterly *The Annunciation,* at Cortona.

1433 Is commissioned by the Guild of Flaxworkers at Fiesole to paint a triptych "inside and out with gold, blue and silver of the best and the finest that can be found."

1436 Cosimo de' Medici presents the convent of San Marco, in Florence, to the Dominicans of Fiesole. Fra Giovanni is commissioned to

do his major lifework in the cloister, chapter house, corridors and the cells of individual monks.

1438 Begins frescoes of *The Crucifixion,* to move through 44 cells.

1440 Paints *Madonna and Saints* for the high altar of San Marco.

1443 Pope Eugenius IV sees Angelico's work, at the consecration of San Marco. Invites him to paint a chapel in the Vatican.

1446 Arrives in Rome. Pope Eugenius dies. Angelico decorates the Chapel of Pope Nicholas V with rich frescoes.

1447 Spends summer at Orvieto, painting the vault

FRA ANGELICO: Believed to be a self-portrait, detail, St. Dominic, 1437-1445. The Mocking of Christ. San Marco, Florence. Fresco.

of a chapel in the cathedral. Never completes this work.

1448 Leaves Rome.

1449 Becomes Prior of San Domenico, Fiesole. Perhaps is dubbed "Angelico" from a Latin poem by a Dominican of his time, calling him "Angelicus Pictor" ("painter of angels").

c.1450 Undertakes a new commission from Cosimo de' Medici—for the Chapel of the Annunziata, 36 scenes from the life of Christ (see text).

1452 Returns to Rome.

1455 Dies in Rome on March 18. Is buried in the Dominican Monastery of Santa Maria Sopra Minerva.

Suggested reading:
Fra Angelico, by Giulio Carlo Argan (Skira).
Fra Angelico, by John Pope-Hennessy (Phaidon).
Fra Angelico, by Jean Dominique Rey (Scribner).
Fra Angelico, by Wilhelm Hausenstein (Methuen).
See also National Surveys of Painting *(Gothic Painting)* and The Renaissance in general reading list (page 163).

FRA FILIPPO LIPPI

Fra Filippo Lippi (also called Lippo Lippi)
c.1406-1469
Florentine Early Renaissance Master

c.1406 Born in Florence, the son of a butcher.

c.1408 Orphaned, is raised by an aunt who does not welcome the responsibility.

1414 His aunt enters him in the Carmelite Order.

1421 Takes his vows in the order.

1425	Becomes acquainted with Masaccio, who has strong humanizing and secular influence on Lippi's art.
1430	Is listed as a painter by his order.
1437	Paints a *Madonna*, his earliest dated work.
1439	Describes himself as "the poorest friar in Florence." Lives with, and supports, six nieces.
1442	Is made a rector by Pope Eugenius IV.
c.1454	Cosimo de' Medici secures a position for him as Perpetual Abbot of a church near Florence.
1455	Is accused of forging a receipt for wages paid to an apprentice. Put to the rack, he "confesses," loses his perpetual abbotship and is pronounced "guilty of many and great wickednesses." Leaves Florence for Prato, nearby.
1456	Is commissioned to paint frescoes illustrating the lives of St. John the Baptist and St. Stephen for the Cathedral of Prato. Also becomes Chaplain to the Convent of Santa Margherita in Prato, whose Abbess commissions him to paint the *Madonna of the Girdle*. Asks Abbess to permit Lucrezia Buti—about 16—to put off her habit and pose in worldly

FRA FILIPPO LIPPI: Self-portrait, detail, c.1447, The Coronation of the Virgin. *Uffizi, Florence. Oil.*

clothes, as the Madonna (see text).
c.1457	Lippi's and Lucrezia's son, Filippino, is born. He will become an artist.
1458	Lucrezia returns to the convent and renews her vows.
1461	Lucrezia leaves the convent and returns to Lippi. Cosimo de' Medici persuades Pius II to release Lippi and Lucrezia from their monastic vows and allow them to marry. They have another child, Alessandra, the goddaughter of Alessandro Botticelli, Lippi's apprentice. (She is the model for Botticelli's *Venus—The Goddess of Love*.)
1464	Finishes the frescoes of *St. John the Baptist* and *St. Stephen*.
1468	Works on frescoes representing the Coronation of the Virgin and other scenes from her life and the life of Christ, in the Cathedral of Spoleto.
1469	Dies on October 9, in Spoleto and is buried there at the request of local authorities.

Suggested reading:
The Joyous Friar, by A. J. Anderson (Stokes).
Filippo Lippi, by Paul G. Konody (Jack).

Fra Filippo Lippi, by Edward C. Strutt (Bell & Sons).
Fra Lippo Lippi, by Margaret Livingston (Putnam).
See also The Renaissance in general reading list (page 163).

GAUGUIN

Paul Gauguin 1848-1903
French Post-Impressionist

1848	Born in Paris on June 7. His father is a liberal journalist. His mother, Aline Chazel, is of Peruvian ancestry.
1851	Family goes to Peru. Father dies at sea.
1855	Returns to Orléans from Lima, Peru.
1865	Enters the French merchant marine as a cadet, after unhappy time in a Jesuit seminary. Sails often to Brazil.
1871	His mother dies. Enters stock-brokerage business in Paris.
1873	Marries Mette-Sophie Gad, a middle-class Danish girl. Begins painting as a hobby. Collects Impressionist paintings.
1876	His painting, *Viroflay Landscape*, is accepted by the Salon. Meets Pissarro.
1880	Exhibits seven paintings and one bust at the Fifth Impressionist Exhibition.
1881	Exhibits at the Sixth Impressionist Exhibition.
1882	Exhibits at the Seventh Impressionist Exhibition.
1883	Leaves the stock-brokerage business and moves wife and five children to Rouen, where he and Pissarro paint.
1884	Goes to Denmark with family. Tries to get financial aid from his wife's family, but fails. His exhibit in Denmark is closed by order of the Academy.
1885	Leaves his wife and children. Returns to Paris with son Clovis. Extremely poor, works as a bill sticker in Paris railroad stations. Taken ill, spends several weeks in a hospital.
1886	Exhibits at last Impressionist Exhibition. Goes to Pont-Aven in Brittany for the first time. Returns to Paris and meets van Gogh.
1887	Goes to Panama, works as laborer on Panama Canal to earn money for passage to Martinique. As sailor, returns to France.
1888	Returns to Brittany. Has first one-man show in Paris. Paints *The Vision After the Sermon, Still Life With Puppies, Breton Peasant Women*. Goes to Arles to join Vincent. Théo van Gogh supplies money for both men. Returns to Paris after violent episodes with Vincent and paints *Le Christ Jaune, La Lutte de l'ange avec Jacob*.
1889	Exhibits at the Café Volpini. Returns to Brittany for the third time. Does lithographs.
1890	Paints *Portrait of a Woman*, which shows his strong admiration of Cézanne. Returns to Paris.
1891	Thirty of his paintings are auctioned for 9,860 francs at Hotel Drouôt to raise money for his Tahitian trip. Sails for Tahiti. Arrives at Papete after two months. Moves 25 miles south of Papeete to Mataieu area. Paints *Ia Orana Maria, Tahitian Landscape*. Lives with Tehura, a girl of about 13, his first Tahitian mistress.
1892	Does woodcut, *Women at the River*. Paints *Ta Matete, Words of the Devil, The Spirit of the Dead Watching*, etc.
1893	Becomes ill, spitting up blood. Is penniless. French Government brings him back to France, where he inherits a little money from an uncle. Lives with Annah la Javanaise in Paris. Has exhibition at Durand-Ruel.
1894	Meets his wife for last time in Copenhagen. Goes to Brittany with Annah. Returns to

1895	Paris after brawls in defense of Annah. She disappears. Second auction sale—an absolute failure. Returns to Tahiti, to west coast.
1896	Takes a new "wife," who gives Gauguin a son. Paints *Nativity*.
1897	His daughter Aline dies. Stops writing to his wife. Paints *Nevermore, Whence Come We?, Te Rerioa, Les Trois Tahitians*.
1898	Tries to kill himself by taking arsenic. Paints *Le Cheval Blanc*. Works in Public Works office.
1899	Publishes satirical broadsheet, *Le Sourire*,

GAUGUIN: Self-portrait. John Hay Whitney Collection, New York. Oil.

Journal Méchant. Paints *Tahitian Women With Mango Blossoms, On the Beach, Tahiti*.
1900	Moves to Dominiha, on the Marquesas Isles, where he is happy.
1902	Develops eczema and heart trouble. Knows he is dying.
1903	His hut is destroyed by a cyclone. Gets in trouble with the bishop and police for championing the natives. Is sentenced to three months' imprisonment and fined 1,000 francs. Does not have money to return to Tahiti. Paints *Breton Village Under Snow* (see text). Dies in the Marquesas Isles on May 8.

Suggested reading:
Intimate Journals, by Paul Gauguin (Heinemann).
Letters to His Wife and Friends, by Paul Gauguin (Saturn).
Gauguin, by Charles Estienne (Zwemmer).
Gauguin, by John Rewald (Heinemann).
See also Post-Impressionism in general reading list (page 163).

GIOTTO

Giotto di Bondome c.1266-1337
Florentine Early Renaissance Master

c.1266	Is born at Colle, north of Florence. Father may have been a blacksmith or farmer.
1276	Giotto is apprenticed to Cimabue. (There are two legends of his apprenticeship: 1— that his father apprentices him to a wool merchant whose store is near Cimabue's studio, and Giotto spends so much time in the

GIOTTO: Portrait, detail, by Uccello. Grand Palais, Paris. Oil.

studio that his father takes him from the merchant and asks Cimabue to accept him as a pupil; 2—that Giotto is tending sheep and drawing on a stone when Cimabue stops by; astonished by the boy's talent, he asks if Giotto would like to learn how to paint.

1296   Paints fresco scenes from the life of St. Francis, in the Upper Church of San Francesco at Assisi (see text).

1298-   Probably works in Rome. Is thought to have
1300   painted a fresco in San Giovanni Laterano, and created mosaics and an altarpiece for St. Peter's (now lost).

1303   Paints *The Crucifixion* and *The Madonna in Gloria*, perhaps the first painting in which the Madonna is shown smiling.

c.1305   Marries. (He will have eight children, about whom little is known except that they were considered quite unattractive.)

1305   Dante visits him in Padua. Giotto paints fresco cycle in the Arena Chapel at Padua—his greatest remaining work, comprising 38 scenes from the lives of Joachim and Anna, the Virgin and Christ, done in three rows on the side walls, with a *Last Judgment* on the entrance wall.

1312   Is inscribed in the guild of doctors and apothecaries, to which painters in Florence belong.

c.1317   Executes fresco scenes from the life of St. Francis and scenes from the lives of St. John the Baptist and St. John the Evangelist in the Bardi and Peruzzi chapels, respectively, in Santa Croce, Florence.

1329   Works for King Roberto in Naples.

1334   Is appointed chief architect of the Cathedral of Florence, one of the greatest honors bestowed upon him.

1337   Dies on January 8 and is buried with great honors in Florence.

Suggested reading:
Giotto, by Eugenio Battisti (Skira).
Giotto, by Carlo Carra (Zwemmer).
Giotto, by Emilio Cecchi (McGraw-Hill).
See also The Renaissance and National Surveys of Painting *(Italian Painting)* in the general reading list (page 163).

GOYA

Francisco José de Goya y Lucientes 1746-1828
Spanish Rococo Master

1746   Born on March 30 at Fuendetodos, near Saragossa. Father is a master guilder; mother is of noble descent. Attends *Escuela Pia*, a school run by monks.

1760   Is apprenticed to José Luzan, a local painter. Learns to draw by copying prints. Studies with Luzan for four years.

1763   Competes for scholarship at the Academy of San Fernando in Madrid. Fails to receive one vote.

1766   Fails to be elected to Academy again.

1770   Journeys to Italy. Remains in Rome for a time.

1771   Returns to Saragossa. Royal Academy at Parma, Italy, awards him second prize for painting entered in previous year's competition. Gets first commission, murals, for Cathedral at Saragossa and for Carthusian monastery.

1773   Marries Josefa Bayeu, sister of painter Francisco Bayeu. She will bear him five children, possibly many more (legend says twenty), but only one, Xavier, survives childhood.

1774-   Moves to Madrid. Commissioned to do tap-
1779   estry cartoons for the Royal Manufactury at Santa Barbara. Finishes about sixty. Begins etchings from works of Velázquez. Is presented to the Royal Family.

1780   Submits his *Christ on the Cross*; unanimously elected to the Academy of San Fernando.

1781   Is asked by the King to paint one of seven altar pictures for the Church of San Francisco el Grande. Goya, impatient with current trends in art, works unenthusiastically for three years with Bayeu, Velázquez, Castillo.

1782   Paints his first dated portrait.

1783-   Executes four altar paintings in church at
1785   Salamanca. Completes six portraits for the Bank of San Carlos. Becomes assistant director at Academy of San Fernando.

1786   Becomes official painter for the tapestry manufactury.

1789   Charles IV appoints him Court Painter.

1792   Seriously stricken while visiting Cadiz; right side of his body is paralyzed. Recovers, but the illness costs him his hearing.

1793-   Paints *The Procession of the Flagellants, The*
1794   *Village Bullfight, Scene From the Inquisition, The Madhouse*, etc.

1795   Succeeds Bayeu as Director of Painting for the Academy. Does portrait of the *Duchess of Alba*. Has love affair with the Duchess—only one of several for her.

1797   Lives with the Duchess of Alba (now a widow) on her estate in Andalucía. Paints second portrait of her (see text). Perhaps angered by her fickleness, begins *Caprices*, a series of etchings about the mores of Spanish society.

1798-   Becomes First Court Painter. Does portraits
1800   of *Queen Maria Luisa* and the *Countess of Chinchon*. Paints *The Maja Clothed* and *The Maja Nude*, identical poses of a young woman, probably inspired by the Duchess. Completes *The Family of Charles IV*.

1802-   Duchess of Alba dies in 1802. Portraits of

GOYA: Self-portrait, 1797. Metropolitan Museum of Art, New York, Dick Fund, 1935. Wash drawing.

1807   the *Count and Countess of Fernán-Núñez*. Xavier, Goya's son, presents him with a grandson, Mariano.

1808   Napoleon invades Spain; popular uprisings. Charles IV abdicates. Goya is commissioned to paint his successor, Ferdinand VII—who is driven into exile.

1810   Begins a series of etchings, *The Disasters of War*.

1812-   Wife dies in 1812. Ferdinand VII returns to the
1814   throne; persecution of liberals ensues. Many of Goya's friends driven into exile. Paints *The Charge of the Mamelukes* and *The Shootings of May Third*.

1815-   A revolt deposes Ferdinand. Goya's *Tauroma-*
1820   *chia*, a series on bullfighting, is published. Plagued by poor health, he moves into the *Quinta del Sordo* (Deaf Man's House). Paints *The Black Paintings*, fourteen somber works on the walls of his home. Begins etchings, *The Disparates*, or *Proverbs*.

1823-   After Napoleon's defeat, French army re-
1824   stores Ferdinand VII, who takes vengeance on the liberals who sympathized with Napoleon. Despite Goya's politics, he is not harmed—but the Inquisitor criticizes the "obscenity" of his two early *Majas*. Leaves Spain for Bordeaux, where friends are in exile. Lives with Leocadia Weiss and her two children.

1826   Visits Madrid briefly. His portrait is painted by the Court Painter, López, by King's order.

1827-   Visits Madrid again. His final work is por-
1828   trait of *Don José Pio de Molina*. Dies in Bordeaux on April 16.

Suggested reading:
Goya, by J. Lassaigne (Hyperion).
Goya, by Pierre Gassier (Skira).
Goya, by Frank Lambert (Institute of Hispanic Studies).
Goya, a Study of His Portraits, by Elizabeth Du Gué Trapier (Hispanic Society of America).
Francisco de Goya, by August L. Mayer (J. M. Dent).
See also National Surveys of Painting *(Spanish Painting)* and The Great Centuries of Painting in general reading list (page 163).

HALS

Frans Hals 1580/81-1666
Dutch Portraitist and Genre Painter

1580 or   Born in Antwerp. His father is a well-to-do
1581   draper from Malines, near Brussels.

1591   Family moves to Haarlem.

c.1591   Enters studio of Karel von Mander.

1615   First wife dies after a beating he gives her, leaving him with their two children and a house, which he is forced to sell.

1616   While he is visiting Antwerp, three legal actions are taken against him for debt. (He often pawns furniture or pictures to make ends meet.) Paints the earliest of his guild group portraits, *Officers of the Company of St. George*.

1617   Marries Lysbeth Reyniers, a simple, loyal, devoted woman who gives him at least ten children—some of whom cause great heartache. (A half-witted son and delinquent daughter are put into institutions.)

1620   Paints portraits of *Paulus von Beresteyn* and his wife *Catharina Both van der Eem*.

1622   Paints *Portrait of a Man*—thought to be a self-portrait.

1625-   Paints portraits of great vigor and zest:
1632   *Young Flute Player, The Gypsy Girl, Banquet of the Officers of St. George* and *Banquet of the Company of St. Adrian*, etc.

1633   Paints *Assembly of the Officers of St. Adrian*.

This work makes his reputation in the Netherlands. Is invited to Antwerp—Rubens's hometown—to paint a group portrait of one of the local Civic Guards. But he leaves after quarrels without finishing the work.

1641 Paints the impressively composed *Governors of St. Elizabeth's Hospital.*
1643 Paints *Portrait of a Man in a Black Cap.*
c.1650 Paints *Hille Bobbe,* a genre portrait.
1652 A baker to whom he owes money forces the sale of his possessions: three mattresses, an armoire, a table, five pictures. Hals is destitute.
1656 Paints *Portrait of Tyman Oosdorp,* a somber work, all in blacks and grays, which affirms his joyless plight.

HALS: Self-portrait. Clowes Fund Collection, Indianapolis, Ind. Oil.

1664 The Paupers' Fund of Haarlem allocates three cartloads of peat to him, to tide him over the winter. The municipality awards him an annuity of 200 florins. Paints two group portraits, *Male and Female Regents of the Haarlem Almshouse* (see text).
1666 Receives further assistance from the Paupers' Fund, including, at his death, a payment of four florins to the gravedigger "to open a tomb in the Groote Kerk for Meester Frans Hals."
Suggested reading:
Frans Hals, by G. S. Davies (Bell & Sons).
Frans Hals, by J. E. Edgecumbe (Stokes).
Paintings of Frans Hals, by N. S. Trivas (Phaidon).
Frans Hals Paintings in America, by Wilhelm R. Valentiner (Sherman).
See also Flemish and Dutch Painting in general reading list (page 163).

HOGARTH

William Hogarth 1697-1764
English Social Satirist

1697 Born in London, the son of a poor schoolmaster and literary hack.
1720 Ends his apprenticeship to an engraver of silver plate. Sets himself up on his own as an engraver. Begins to study painting with Sir James Thornhill, hoping to become a historical painter in the grand manner.

HOGARTH: Self-portrait, 1758, Hogarth Painting the Comic Muse. Brooklyn Museum, New York. Engraving.

1724 Publishes his first plate, *Masquerades and Operas.*
1726 Prepares twelve large engravings for Butler's *Hudibras,* considered the best of his book illustrations.
1729 Elopes with 20-year-old Jane Thornhill, the only daughter of Sir James Thornhill.
1731 Six paintings known as *A Harlot's Progress* bring him fame.
1732 Advertises his *A Harlot's Progress,* a series of six engravings, and meets with great public success.
1733 Begins engraving *The Rake's Progress,* a drama in eight scenes of the career of a spendthrift, young Tom Rakewell.
1735 Presents *The Rake's Progress.*
1738 Paints *Four Times of the Day,* a series depicting 18th-century London life.
1742 Paints *The Graham Children.*
1745 Auctions the original oil paintings of *The Harlot's Progress* and *The Rake's Progress, Four Times of the Day* and *Strolling Actresses* for £427. Issues *Marriage à la Mode* engravings. Paints *Self-Portrait With His Dog Trump.*
1749 Visits France and paints *Calais Gate,* a satire on French poverty and superstition, intended to avenge his arrest while sketching the gate.
1753 Publishes his book *Analysis of Beauty.*
1754 Paints *Chairing the Member* (see text) as part of an *Election Series.*
1764 Dies in London.
Suggested reading:
Hogarth and His Place in European Art, by Frederick Autal (Routledge & Kegan Paul).
William Hogarth, The Cockney's Mirror, by Marjorie Bowen (Methuen).
William Hogarth, by Austin Dobson (Heinemann).
The Drawings of William Hogarth, by A. P. Oppé (Phaidon).
Hogarth's Progress, by Peter Quennel (Collins).
See also National Surveys of Painting *(English Painting)* and Eighteenth Century in general reading list (page 163).

HOKUSAI

Katsushika Hokusai 1760-1849
Japanese Master (Tokugawa Period)

The artist known as Hokusai used some 30 different names. Artists in Japan would change their "art name" whenever they altered their style or the medium in which they worked. The artist's surname was the name associated with the school or style of a particular master.

1760 Born of an artisan named Nakajima Ise, in a shabby district of Edo (now Tokyo). (Some say he is adopted by Nakajima Ise.)
At an early age, is put to work in a book-

seller's shop, where he first becomes interested in prints and illustrations.
1774- Apprenticed to a wood engraver and learns
1777 the craft. (Wood engraving is not considered an art in Japan at this time.)
1778 Accepted as a pupil by Katsukawa Shunsho, one of the great popular artists and book illustrators of the time.
1779 Finishes his apprenticeship. Is given the art name of Shunro, with the right to use the art surname of Shunsho's school, Katsukawa.
1780 Illustrates the *Story of Gompachi and Murasaki,* a paperback, the first in a series for which he also writes the text. It is the first example of his mastery and astonishing knowledge of the history, legend, language and customs of Japan.
1790 His series of naturalistic prints called *Festivals of the Green Houses* is issued by one of the leading publishing houses, Tsutaya Jusaburo. Creates a series of prints with Chinese subjects, *Chinese Boys at Play* (now in the Boston Museum). The Chinese influence is strong at this time.

(Hokusai marries twice, but little is known about either of his wives, except that they were both separated from him, either by death or divorce. He has five children: two sons and three daughters. One son becomes a mirror maker and causes his father constant trouble. The youngest daughter, Oyei, an artist of some talent, divorces her husband and looks after her father in his old age.)

1796 Breaks with the Katsukawa School and changes name. Is frequently in difficult financial straits (as he will be for a decade). Often hawks red peppers and calendars to make ends meet. Studies the prints and paintings of the classical artist Korin, whose art exemplifies Japanese decoration. This style becomes a part of his amalgam.
1797 As Sori, begins a new activity, designing *surimono:* invitations, announcements, greeting cards, accompanied by verse and decorated with block prints. *Surimono* receives its definitive form from Hokusai.
1798 His prints appear in a number of albums of poetry. Now associates on an equal basis with the best artists. The copperplate engravings of Europe influence him. His new perspective, shading and realistic representation show Western influence.
1799- From this time on, Hokusai has pupils and a
1806 "school" of close followers. Has many name changes, each new one indicating a change of style in his work: Sori, Kako, Hokusai, Gwakyojin Hokusai, Hokusai Shinsei, Shinsai

HOKUSAI: Believed to be a self-portrait. Guimet Museum, Paris. Brush drawing.

—all are used. He masters the art form of figures with landscapes.

1812 Visits Nagaya. (From now to 1823, he travels extensively—to Osaka, Kyoto and other places in Japan.)

1814 Publishes his first book of sketches from life, *Mangwa*. (Fifteen more books are published in his lifetime.)

1820 Draws many landscapes and bird and flower prints.

1823 Produces the first of the famous *Thirty-Six Views of Fuji*.

1828 His work is interrupted by serious illness.

c.1830 Illustrates *The Imagery of the Pacts of China and Japan* (see text).

1833 Adopts his final name, Gaky-rajin (The Art-Crazy Old Man), after completing his last set of landscape designs: *Chiye no umi (The Ocean of One Thousand Pictures)*, which he signs "Zen (formerly) Hokusai-I-Itso."

1833-1836 Some of his finest books are published: *Toshisen*, an anthology of Chinese poems of the T'ang period, the immortal *Hundred Views of Fuji* (1834 and 1835) and *Warriors*.

1834 Hokusai is exiled to the distant town of Uraga because of the disgrace brought upon his family by a grandson.

1836 Returns to the capital, during a great famine. Survives by producing an incredible number of paintings and drawings.

1837 Loses his paintings and drawings in a fire—a calamity he has feared all his life. Is driven to produce more and more work.

1840 After he reaches 80, Hokusai always adds his age to his signature. The last decade of his life is dedicated to brush painting. He lives in "the squalor of a hovel," attended by his daughter.

1849 Dies at Hensho-in, a monastery at Seitencho, Asakusa, Tokyo, with his brush in hand—saying that, if he had only been given five more years, he might have become a great artist.

Suggested reading:
Hokusai, by J. Hillier (Phaidon).
Hokusai, by Elise Grilli (Charles Tuttle).
See also Oriental Art in general reading list (page 163).

HOLBEIN

Hans Holbein the Younger c.1497-1543
German Renaissance Master

c.1497 Born in Augsburg, the son of Hans Holbein the Elder, painter of religious pictures and portraits.

1515 After early training in art from his father, journeys to Basel, Switzerland, with brother

HOLBEIN: Self-portrait, 1543. Uffizi, Florence. Chalk.

Ambrosius. Works as assistant to Hans Herbst. Employed by a printer to design title pages. His first design is used for More's *Utopia*. Meets Erasmus; illustrates his *The Praise of Folly*.

1517 Goes to Lucerne to decorate the mansion of Jacob van Hertenstein.

1519 Returns to Basel. Becomes a member of the painters' guild. Acquires Swiss citizenship. Marries (?). Finishes *The Flagellation of Christ* and *The Last Supper*.

1521 Paints *The Dead Christ*.

1523 Paints *Erasmus of Rotterdam*, which is given to Archbishop Warham in England; designs glass windows and woodcuts.

1526 The Reformation, with its negative attitude to religious painting, depresses the market for art. Holbein travels to London, with letters of introduction from Erasmus to Sir Thomas More and Archbishop Warham; receives commissions for portraits of *Warham*, *Wyatt*, *Sir Henry Guildford*, *Lady Guildford*.

1528 Returns to Basel. Watches iconoclasts destroy every religious work in Basel in one day. Townspeople commission him to finish some frescoes in the town hall.

1530 Returns to England. Political changes deprive him of the patronage of Sir Thomas More and Archbishop Warham. The merchants of the Steelyard commission *The Triumphs of Wealth and Poverty*. Completes portrait of *George Gisze*.

1537 Wins favor in fashionable circles. Becomes Court Painter for Henry VIII. Completes portraits of *Jane Seymour*, *Henry VIII*.

1539 Paints *Anne of Cleves* and others (see text). Except for short official trips, ends his days at the English court.

1543 Dies of the plague.

Suggested reading:
Hans Holbein, the Younger, by A. B. Chamberlain (Dodd, Mead).
Holbein, by S. L. Bensusan (Stokes).
Hans Holbein the Younger, by G. S. Davies (Bell & Sons).
Holbein, by Beatrice Fortescue (Methuen).
Hans Holbein, by R. W. Nicholson (Chapman & Hall).
See also The Renaissance and National Surveys of Painting *(German Masters of Art)* in general reading list (page 163).

KLEE

Paul Klee 1879-1940
Swiss-German Expressionist and Fantasist

1879 Born December 18 at Munchenbuchsee, near Bern, Switzerland. His father is a German music teacher; his mother is Swiss.

1898 Graduates from *Literaturgymnasium* in Bern. Refers to himself as "a future painter." Goes to Munich to begin art studies.

1900 Studies at Munich Academy. Writes parents: "I shall make painting take steps forward."

1902 Travels to Italy. Though impressed by Leonardo, Pompeiian wall paintings, etc., writes: "Imitate nothing. I am suspicious of any attempt to try to do something not of one's own time." Returns to Bern. For almost four years, works at drawings, etchings, paintings on glass.

1905 On brief visit to Paris, sees the work of Cézanne, Renoir, Sisley. Writes: "I have nothing to learn from the French."

1906 Marries Lily Stumpf, a pianist. They settle in Munich. She gives piano lessons; Klee paints and keeps house.

1907 A son, Felix, is born.

1908 Is exhibited in Munich and Berlin. Sees work

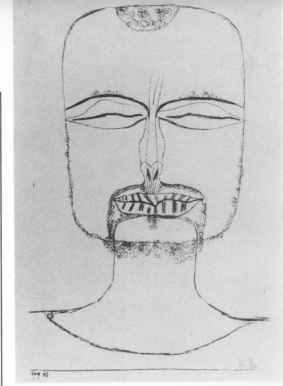

KLEE: Self-portrait, Lost in Thought, 1919. Felix Klee, Berne. Lithograph.

of van Gogh in Germany.

1910 Fifty-six of his works are shown at Zurich, Bern and Basel. He writes Lily that he can no longer spend so much time doing housework; asks for half days for his work.

1911 Meets Kandinsky, Jawlensky, Marc and joins their *Blaue Reiter* (Blue Rider) group. Begins illustrations for Voltaire's *Candide*.

1912 Exhibits in Second Exhibition of the Blue Riders. Visits Paris again. Influenced by Cubism, particularly work of Robert Delaunay. Meets Picasso and Braque.

1914 Visits Tunis and Kairouan in North Africa. Feels this is the decisive event of his career.

1916 Is called to serve in World War I; his closest friends, August Macke and Franz Marc, are killed. "The more horrifying this world becomes," he writes, "the more art becomes abstract."

1918 *Die Sturm*, a Berlin publication, publishes a special issue of fifteen of his drawings.

1919 Begins to work more in oils (rather than drawing or watercolors).

1920 Has major showing (362 works) in Munich. Receives appointment from Walter Gropius to the Bauhaus in Weimar. Kandinsky also teaches there.

1923 Is exhibited at Kronprinzen-Palais, Berlin.

1924 First shows in the United States.

1925 Paints *Fish Magic* (see text).

1926 Becomes professor at new Bauhaus in Dessau.

1928 Visits Egypt from December to January, 1929; again deeply impressed by North Africa.

1930 Is given show of "Divisionist" paintings at Museum of Modern Art, New York.

1931 Becomes professor of art at the Dusseldorf (Germany) Academy of Fine Arts.

1933 Is called a "culture Bolshevist" by Hitler, flees Germany for Bern. His parting words to students are: "Gentlemen, there is in Europe an ominous smell of blood."

1935 Is given retrospective exhibition in Bern, Basel and Lucerne. Begins to suffer from sclerodermia after an attack of measles.

1937 One hundred and two of his works are confiscated in Germany; seventeen of them appear in Nazi exhibition of "Degenerate Art." Braque and Picasso visit him in Bern.

1939 Begins his *Angel* series. Has premonitions of death.

1940 Dies at Muralto-Locarno on June 29.

Suggested reading:
Paul Klee, by Alfred Barr, Jr. (Museum of Modern Art, New York).

Paul Klee, by Will Grohmann (Harry N. Abrams, Inc.).
Paul Klee, by Nello Ponente (Skira).
Paul Klee, by Carola Giedion-Welcker (Viking).
Klee, by Herbert Read (Faber & Faber).
See also Modern Painting in general reading list (page 163).

LEONARDO

Leonardo da Vinci 1452-1519
Florentine Renaissance Master

1452 Born on April 15 in Anchiano, near the town of Vinci, the illegitimate son of a notary, Ser Piero da Vinci, and a peasant girl, Caterina di Piero del Vacca.
1457 His father legitimizes his birth by taking him into his household. His mother has married a peasant.

LEONARDO: Believed to be a self-portrait, detail, c.1515, Study of an Apostle. *Gemeente Museum, Amsterdam. Pen and ink.*

1469 Is apprenticed to the workshop of Verrocchio. Very early distinguishes himself by technical innovations in representing light and shade.
1470 Becomes a member of the Company of Florentine Painters.
1475 Is given a free hand by Verrocchio in depicting an angel kneeling on the left side of his *Baptism of Christ.* Part of the background landscape may also be Leonardo's.
1482 Despairing of the possibility of getting sufficient patronage from Lorenzo the Magnificent, Leonardo writes a letter to Lodovico Sforza, Duke of Milan, citing his talents as engineer, architect, designer of military equipment, etc., as well as his ability to "do in painting whatever may be done, as well as any other, be he who he may." Comes to Milan on Lodovico Sforza's invitation.
1483 Signs a contract on April 25 with the Fraternity of the Immaculate Conception in Milan, to paint the center panel of an altarpiece—his *The Madonna of the Rocks* (see text).
1487 Designs plans for the central dome of Milan Cathedral and builds a wooden model to illustrate his proposals.

1490 Does the settings and costumes for a spectacular pageant, the *Festa del Paradiso,* in the Sforza Castle. Goes to Pavia as consultant for the projected cathedral.
1495 Is called to Florence for consultations on the Great Council Hall of the Signoria Palace. Michelangelo is also consulted. Begins fresco, *The Last Supper,* in the refectory of the Convent Church of Santa Maria delle Grazie, Milan. His constant experimentation with application of fresco makes work go slowly.
1499 Returns to Florence; is now absorbed in study of physical geography.
1500 Works briefly in Mantua and Venice; does a chalk drawing of *Isabella d'Este.*
1502 Accepts appointment as Engineer General to Cesare Borgia. Inspects fortifications in Romagna.
1503 Is commissioned by the Signoria of Florence to do a painting of the *Battle of Anghiari,* for the Council Hall of the Palazzo Vecchio. Again experiments with technique; is thought to have abandoned the work before it is entirely completed.
1506 Returns to Milan, which is now under French rule. Does drawings for a funeral monument with equestrian statue. Devotes himself more to scientific studies and research than to painting.
1507 King Louis XII of France requests Florentine Signoria to extend Leonardo's leave.
c.1510 Begins to experiment with oils, a relatively new medium in Italy. Works on *St. Anne, the Virgin and Child.* Reaches new heights with the subtlety of his *sfumato*—treatment of light and shading.
1513 Leaves for Rome on invitation of Giuliano de' Medici, but Giuliano ignores him once he arrives. Lodges in the Belvedere of the Vatican.
1515 Is present at a meeting of Pope Leo X and King Francis I in Bologna.
1516 At year's end, visits France by invitation of Francis I. Takes along the *Mona Lisa, St. Anne, the Virgin and Child* and *John the Baptist,* possibly as gifts. Lives at Chateau of Cloux near Amboise.
1517 Is visited by Cardinal Louis of Aragon, to whom he shows his paintings and notebooks, written in "mirror writing"—i.e., in reverse. Paralysis strikes his right hand.
1519 Dictates a last will and testament in April. Dies at Cloux on May 2. Is buried in the cloister of Saint Florentin in Amboise.

Suggested reading:
The Notebooks of Leonardo da Vinci, edited by Robert Linscott (Modern Library).
Leonardo da Vinci, by Kenneth Clark (Cambridge University Press).
Leonardo, by Ludwig Goldscheider (Phaidon).
The Mind of Leonardo da Vinci, by E. McCurdy (Dodd, Mead).
Leonardo, the Florentine, by A. R. Taylor (Harper).
See also The Renaissance in general reading list (page 163).

MATISSE

Henri Matisse 1869-1954
Modern French Master

1869 Born on December 31 in Cateau, northern France. His mother is artistically inclined; his father is a grain merchant. Attends school in St. Quentin.
1889 Becomes interested in painting while convalescing from appendicitis attack.
1890 Obeys father's wish that he prepare for the law, by entering University of Paris.

MATISSE: Self-portrait, c.1903. Collection Carl Zigrosser, Philadelphia Museum of Art. Etching and drypoint.

1891 Returns to St. Quentin; works as law clerk; also studies art.
1892 Persuades father to send him back to Paris for further art study. Works under Bouguereau. Is especially interested in the late works of Goya.
1893 Studies under Moreau at École des Beaux-Arts.
1896 First shows his work at the Salon de la Nationale. Does landscapes and seascapes in Brittany.
1897 Becomes friendly with Pissarro, turns toward Impressionism and Pointillism.
1898 Marries Amelie Payayre, who will bear him three children. Works on decorations for 1900 World's Fair.
1900 Works in sculpture, is absorbed by problems of form.
1904 Exhibits at Ambroise Vollard's, but attracts little attention and makes few sales.
1905 Exhibits with Vlaminck, Derain, Rouault—to severe critical disapproval. The group is labeled *Les Fauves,* or "Wild Beasts." Matisse is the acknowledged leader. Paints *Calme et Volupté* and *Woman With a Hat,* posed for by his wife. Begins to sell. Paints *Interior at Collioure* (see text).
1906 Opens his own art school. Gertrude Stein introduces him to Picasso; a lifelong friendship is begun.
1907- Works on three bronze heads of *Jeanette.* Has
1910 first retrospective exhibition and is shown in New York. Completes sculpture *Reclining Nude.*
1911- Visits Morocco twice. Continues to work in
1913 sculpture. Receives more critical disapproval at New York's Armory Show.
1915- Paints *The Piano Lesson, Young Girl Bath-*
1917 *ing, Moroccans in Prayer, Interior With a Violin.* Moves to Nice; meets Renoir.
1918- Completes statue of *Venus.* Paints *The White*
1921 *Plumes* and *Self-portrait.* Does sets for Stravinsky-Diaghilev ballet *Le Chant du Rossignol.*
1927 Receives first prize (for *Le Compotier*) at the Carnegie International Exposition.
1930 Retrospective exhibition in Berlin.
1931 Extensive travels in Russia, Italy, Spain, Germany, Tahiti, the United States. Is commissioned to decorate Albert Barnes's museum at Merion, Pa.
1932- Retrospective exhibitions in Stockholm, Par-
1939 is, New York. Retires to Vence, near Cannes. Illustrates James Joyce's *Ulysses.*
1940- Undergoes serious operation, which leaves
1945 him a semi-invalid. Begins to make compositions with scissors from colored paper. Large exhibits at Salon d'Automne and the Victoria and Albert Museum in London.
1946- Begins what he later calls his masterpiece:
1948 designing a chapel at Vence—including altar, vestments, windows and religious paintings.
1952- The Matisse Museum is opened at Le Cateau.

149

1953 Matisse donates 100 paintings valued at up to $14,000,000.
1954 Dies of heart attack, November 3.
Suggested reading:
Matisse: His Art and His Public, by Alfred H. Barr, Jr. (Museum of Modern Art, New York).
The Art of Henri Matisse, by Albert Barnes and Violette DeMazia (Scribner).
Men and Monuments, by Janet Flanner (Harper).
Jazz, by Henri Matisse (Piper-Bücherei).
See also Modern Painting and Fauvism in general reading list (page 163).

MEMLING: *Self-portrait, c.1467, detail,* Donne Triptych. *National Gallery, London. Oil.*

MEMLING

Hans Memling or Memlinc c.1433-1494
Flemish Master

c.1433 Is born at Seligenstadt-on-the-Main, a small town in northwestern Germany. His parents are believed to have come from Memmelinck, in northeastern Holland—hence his name.
c.1455 Probably studies the craft of illuminating manuscripts at Cologne (since he later accurately draws city's architecture).
c.1460 Enters workshop of Rogier van der Weyden, in Brussels.
1465 Following van der Weyden's death (1464), Memling settles at Bruges. Becomes citizen.
1467 Receives commission for a *Last Judgment*, from an Italian patron, resident of Bruges.
c.1470 Receives the title of Town Painter. Is given a studio for his private use in the *Maison Dieu*, town property. Becomes a popular portraitist for the city's Italian merchant colony. Paints *Passion of Christ, Two Horses, Lady With a Pink* (see text).
1475 Begins work for the Hospital of St. John at Bruges, his perennial patron (which today houses his finest work: *Granada* diptych, the *Deposition* triptych, the *Adoration of the Magi* altar).
c.1497 Marries Anne de Valhenaere, by whom he has three sons.
1484 Is commissioned by the burgomaster of Bruges to execute the *St. Christopher* triptych.
1487 His wife dies.
1489 Works on the *Shrine of St. Ursula*, one of his most popular works, for the Hospital of St. John.

1494 Dies August 11, the leading master of Bruges, one of its wealthiest citizens and, according to a contemporary, "the most accomplished and excellent painter of the Christian world." Buried in the Church of St. Giles.
Suggested reading:
Flemish Painting, by Jacques Lassaignes and Robert Delevoy (Skira).
Early Netherlandish Painting, Vol. 1, by Erwin Panofsky (Harvard).
Early Flemish Painters, by Martin Conway (John Murray).
See also Flemish and Dutch Painting in general reading list (page 163).

MICHELANGELO

Michelagniolo di Lodovico Buonarroti-Simoni
1475-1564
Florentine High Renaissance Master

1475 Born on March 6, at Caprese, son of Lodovico di Lionardo Buonarroti-Simoni, a respected civil official, and Francesca di Neri di Miniato del Sera. When Michelangelo is not yet a month old, the Buonarroti return to Florence, where he is placed in the care of a foster-mother at Setignano.
1481- His mother dies. His father remarries. Michelangelo returns to Florence to live with his father, stepmother, four brothers and an uncle. At school, he refuses to do anything but draw.
1488 Enters the workshop of Domenico and David Ghirlandaio, where he makes sketches of frescoes by Giotto and Masaccio and copies drawings of the old masters.
1489 Enters Bertoldo's school for sculptors; makes clay figures and his first work in marble—the head of a *Faun* (now lost).
1490 Lorenzo de' Medici invites Michelangelo to live in his palace. Meets leading humanists—Angelo Poliziano, who inspires him to make the relief of the *Battle of Centaurs*; Marsilio Ficino, the interpreter of Plato; and Cristoforo Landino, scholar of Dante. Creates the relief of *The Madonna of the Stairs*.
1492 Lorenzo de' Medici dies. Piero de' Medici invites Michelangelo to remain in the palace, but gives him only one commission—to make a statue out of snow. Finishes large marble statue of *Hercules*, dedicated to Lorenzo, and a wooden crucifix. (Both are lost.)
1494 The French army threatens Florence; Michelangelo flees to Bologna, then Venice. His money runs out, and he returns to Bologna, where he makes three statuettes for the shrine of San Domenico.
1495 Returns to Florence, carves a statue of *St. John* in marble for Lorenzo di Pierfrancesco de' Medici (now lost).
1496 Does a marble statue, in the antique style, of *Cupid* (now lost), which is sold in Rome to Cesare Borgia as a genuine antique. Michelangelo tries to regain possession of the statue. Arrives in Rome.
1496- Jacopo Galli buys his life-sized marble statues of *Cupid* (or *Apollo?*) and *Bacchus*.
1501
1499 Gets commission to sculpt a *Pietà*.
1501 Returns to Florence; obtains contract for 15 figures for the Piccolomini altar in Siena. (Only a few are actually completed.)
1502 Does a bronze *David* (since lost), which is sent to France.
1503 Receives contract for twelve Apostles for the Duomo in Florence. (Only one, *Matthew*, was begun.)
1504 Begins *Madonna With the Christ Child* (not completed until 1506). Executes three *tondi*

(a painting, fresco or relief executed on a circular base) of the Madonna—two sculptures and a painting.
1505 Pope Julius II summons Michelangelo to Rome, where he completes first designs for the tomb of Julius.
1506 Unhappy, he returns to Florence, resumes work on his cartoon for the *Battle of Cascina*, a work for half of a wall in the Palazzo Vecchio (the other half to be a mural painting of the *Battle of Anghiari* by Leonardo da Vinci). In November, meets Pope Julius in Bologna, makes a large bronze likeness.
1508 Pope Julius again summons Michelangelo to Rome to paint the ceiling of the Sistine Chapel.
1512 Sistine Chapel is finally finished.
1513 Julius II dies. Michelangelo continues work on his tomb until 1516.
1516 Discusses the execution of the façade of San Lorenzo with Pope Leo X.
1518 Gives up his house in Rome. Many of his cartoons are burned. Begins building a house and workshop in Florence, on the Via Mozza.
1519 Begins the *Statue of Christ*, commissioned in 1514; work on the first version is stopped because of a flaw in the marble. (A second version is completed in 1520.)
1521 Begins work in the Medici Chapel.
1523 Giulio de' Medici becomes Pope Clement VII.
1525 Alteration of plans for the tomb of Julius—a wall tomb instead of one standing free.
1526 In October, sends a new design for the tomb to Rome.
1527 Rome is occupied by French imperial troops; the Pope is besieged; the Medici are driven from Florence.
1529 Employed as a military engineer, to fortify

MICHELANGELO: *Self-portrait, 1545, detail,* Conversion of St. Paul. *Pauline Chapel, Vatican. Fresco.*

Florence against the Medici's return. Lends the city a thousand *scudi*. Paints *Leda and the Swan* for the Duke of Ferrara.
1530 Florence is taken by troops of Pope Clement VII; Michelangelo, in hiding, is promised immunity if he will continue work on the Medici Chapel. Resumes work. Does *Apollo*. His father dies.
1532 Completes reliquary loggia in San Lorenzo.

Fourth contract for the tomb of Julius. From August, Michelangelo is in Rome.

1533 Forms lifelong friendship with Tommaso de' Cavalieri, a young painter and sculptor, to whom he dedicates many poems and drawings. Returns to Florence, then decides to settle in Rome.

1534 Receives papal commission for a *Last Judgment*. In Florence, completes benches and a wooden ceiling for the Biblioteca Laurenziana, designed in 1526. Assistants carry on the work, which is finished in 1559. Leaves the Medici Chapel unfinished, to be worked on by assistants. In September, moves to Rome (never to return to Florence for the remaining 30 years of his life). Pope Clement VII dies and is succeeded by Paul III. Michelangelo, still working on the tomb of Julius, is ordered to begin the *Last Judgment* for the Sistine Chapel.

1538 Forms friendship with Vittoria Colonna, for whom he makes a *Crucifixion* and other religious drawings.

1541 Completes fresco of the *Last Judgment*.

1542 Pope Paul III commissions *Conversion of St. Paul* (see text). The tomb of Julius, after 40 years of work, is finally completed.

1545 Attacked by Pietro Aretino in an open letter —for "godlessness" and the unseemliness of the many nudes in the *Last Judgment*.

1546 Takes over the construction of the Palazzo Farnese; makes the first designs for rebuilding of the Capitol; begins work on St. Peter's.

1546- Begins second fresco in the Capello Paoline,
1550 the *Crucifixion of St. Peter.* Plans reconstruction of San Giovanni dei Fiorentini, Rome, on which he works until 1560.

1555 Francesco Urbino, Michelangelo's faithful servant and assistant for 25 years, dies. Michelangelo damages the *Florentine Pietà* with a slip of his hammer. Begins the *Palestrina Pietà* and the *Rondanini Pietà*. Does important religious drawings, especially *Crucifixions*.

1558 Begins model for the dome of St. Peter's, which he finishes in 1561.

1561 Works on plans to transform the Baths of Diocletian into the Church of Santa Maria degli Angeli; the designs for the Porta Pia, and the Sforza Chapel in Santa Maria Maggiore. Pope Paul orders some nudes in the *Last Judgment* painted over.

1564 On February 14, Michelangelo falls ill, but wanders about the city. Dies on February 18, with Tommaso de' Cavalieri and a number of doctors and friends about him. His body is secretly removed to Florence, where it arrives on March 10. Buried in Santa Croce, according to his wishes. Solemn commemoration is held in San Lorenzo on July 14.

Suggested reading:
Michelangelo, a Record of His Life as Told in His Own Letters and Papers, edited by R. W. Carden (Constable).
Michelangelo Paintings, by Ludwig Goldscheider (Phaidon).
Youth of Michelangelo, by Charles de Tolnay (Princeton).
Late Years of Michel Angelo, by Wilhelm R. Valentiner (Sherman).
See also The Renaissance in general reading list (page 163).

MIRÓ

Joan Miró 1893-
Spanish Abstract Surrealist

1893 Born at Montroig, in Catalonia, on April 20.

MIRO: Portrait, detail, Joan Miró and Daughter Dolores, *1937-38, by Balthus. Museum of Modern Art, N. Y. Oil.*

His father is a jeweler.

1907 Enrolls in the School of Fine Arts in Barcelona.

1910 Is forced to withdraw from school because his parents object to his proposed art career. They later become resigned.

1912 Enrolls in the Academy Gali in Barcelona, studies poetry and music, as well as art.

1915 Leaves school to paint alone—in Barcelona and Montroig.

1918 First one-man show, in Barcelona, is a local success.

1919 Visits Paris for the first time. Meets Picasso.

1920 Returns to Montroig, paints *The Table*, or *Still Life With Rabbit*, then leaves again for Paris.

1921 Exhibits at Galerie La Licorne. Returns to Montroig and begins nine months' work on *The Farm*.

1922 Finishes *The Farm*, which he later sells to Ernest Hemingway for 2,000 francs.

1923 Paints *The Tilled Field* and *The Catalan Landscape* while experiencing self-induced hallucinations.

1924 The formal beginning of Surrealism: *Maternity, Landscape, Carnival of Harlequin* (see text).

1925- Exhibits at Galerie Pierre, in Paris. Does
1927 sets and costumes for the ballet *Romeo et Juliette*. Has paintings in the first Surrealist show at the Galerie Pierre. Paints *Dog Barking at the Moon, Fratellini, Nude*. Has his second one-man show. Begins to sell his paintings at moderate prices.

1928 Travels in the Netherlands. Admires early Dutch painters, notably Vermeer and Steen. The trip inspires a series of *Dutch Interiors*. Completes *The Potato* and *Spanish Dancer*, made of paper, string and metal.

1929- Works with collage; shows in the Exhibition
1932 of Collages in Paris. Creates *La Fornarina*, an oil on burlap; *Construction*, made of wood and metal. Does sets for *Jeux d'Enfants*, Massine's ballet. Works with wood, feathers, paper, metal, glass.

1937 Does a large mural for the Spanish exhibit at the Paris World's Fair.

1939- Begins a series of 23 gouaches, each of which
1942 takes a month to complete. Begins to make ceramics.

1945 Lives at Gallifa in home of artist friend and collaborator José Artigas. Works mainly with ceramics, but paints *The Harbor, Woman and Bird in the Night, Woman Listening to Music* and finishes *Bird*, a bronze sculpture.

1947 Travels to America to create a mural for the Terrace Hilton Hotel, Cincinnati. The completed work measures 7' x 32' and is shown at the Museum of Modern Art, New York. Returns to Barcelona.

1950- Illustrates *Parler seul*, by Tzara, with 75
1951 lithographs. Returns to the United States to do a 6' x 19' mural for the Harkness Commons at Harvard University.

1953- Works on about 200 ceramics with Artigas.
1956 These sharply break with the more traditional pottery forms of the 1945 work. Is commissioned to create two murals for the UNESCO Building in Paris.

1957 Publishes *La Bague d'Aurore*, a series of etchings, aquatints and drypoints, in Paris. Becomes dissatisfied with some of his earlier work and destroys nearly a hundred canvases.

1958 Completes colored woodcuts for Eluard's book of poetry, *À Toute Épreuve*. Receives the Guggenheim International Award of $10,000 for the UNESCO murals, *Night and Day*.

1959 Has his 107th exhibition, at the Galerie Berggruen in Paris.

1960 Works on wall ceramics with Artigas. Exhibits in Barcelona, Paris, New York.

1961 Paints *Blue I, II, III*. Has simultaneous exhibits in Paris and in New York. Visits the U.S. for the third time. Has an exhibit in Geneva.

Suggested reading:
Miró, by Walter Erben (Braziller).
Joan Miró, by Clement Greenberg (Quadrangle Press).
Joan Miró: His Graphic Work, by Sam Hunter (Abrams).
Joan Miró—Atmosphere, by James J. Sweeney (Wittenborn).
Joan Miró, by James Thrall Soby (Museum of Modern Art, New York).
See also Modern Painting and Surrealism in general reading list (page 163).

MODIGLIANI

Amedeo Modigliani 1884-1920
Italian-born, Modern French Painter

1884 Is born at Leghorn, Italy. His father fails as a banker, and his mother, reputedly a descendant of the great philosopher Spinoza, supports a family of six by teaching French and English.

1898 Seriously ill with typhoid fever; is forced to

MODIGLIANI: Self-portrait, 1919. Collection of Francisco Matarazzo Sobrinho, São Paulo, Brazil. Oil.

leave school. Begins to study art. Is impressed by Titian, Dürer, Murillo.

1900 Contracts tuberculosis. Convalesces in Rome, Venice, Florence. Studies art in galleries and museums.

1906 Goes to Paris after inheriting some money. Takes a studio in Montmartre. Meets *Les Fauves*, the rebellious young painters led by Matisse. Becomes friends with Picasso and Utrillo.

1908 Shows pictures at the Salon des Indépendants. In dire financial straits, moves to a cheaper studio in Montparnasse.

1909 Becomes interested in sculpture. Especially influenced by Brancusi and African sculpture. Lives a dissolute life, drinks heavily, becomes addicted to hashish. Paints *The Beggar of Leghorn* and *The Cellist*.

1913- Meets Kisling and Soutine. Has love affair
1914 with Beatrice Hastings, English poetess. Sculpts *Caryatid*.

1915 Exhibits at a private studio. Sells some work to Paul Guillaume. Paints *Bride and Groom, Leon Bakst, Rosa Porprina, Beatrice Hastings*.

1916 Attracts the attention of Leopold Zborowski, an art dealer, who undertakes to sell his paintings. Works for the dealer Cheron for 40 francs and a bottle of brandy per painting. Paints *Jacques Lipchitz and Wife*.

1917 Completes *Nude, Head* (sculpture). Meets Jeanne Hébuterne, who becomes his mistress. Paints *Nude on Cushion, Leopold Zborowski, Jean Cocteau, Kisling*.

1918 In poor health, spends the winter at Nice, on money from Zborowski. Paints *Chaime Soutine, Seated Nude*.

1919 Returns to Paris. Jeanne bears him a daughter, Gina. Becomes critically ill and is hospitalized. Paints *Jeanne Hébuterne* (see text).

1920 Dies of tuberculosis. Thousands attend his funeral. Jeanne, pregnant with their second child, commits suicide.

Suggested reading:
Modigliani: Man and Myth, by Jeanne Modigliani (Orion).
Modigliani, by James Thrall Soby (Simon & Schuster).
Modigliani, by Claude Roy (Skira).
Modigliani, by Jacques Lipchitz (Abrams).
See also Modern Painting in general reading list (page 163).

MONET

Claude Oscar Monet 1840-1926
French Impressionist

1840 Born in Paris on November 14. His parents run an unsuccessful grocery business.

1845 Family moves to Le Havre, where he attends school and acquires great, lifelong love of the sea.

1856 Sells his first caricatures in a painting-supplies shop.

1858 Meets Boudin, whose luminous landscapes lead him to realize that his true medium is color.

1859 Goes to Paris; works at the Académie Suisse, where he becomes friendly with Pissarro.

1860 Enters military service; chooses to go to Algiers.

1862 Becomes so ill that he is discharged. Returns to Le Havre; works with Boudin and Jongkind. In November, enters the studio of Gleyre in Paris. Because Gleyre demands an Old Masters style, Monet convinces Renoir, Sisley and Bazille to leave Gleyre's studio with him.

MONET: *Portrait*, Claude Monet in His Floating Studio, *1874, by Manet. Pinakothek, Munich. Oil.*

1865 Enjoys a success at the Salon with *Pointe de la Here* and *The Seine at Honfleur*. Meets Gustave Courbet, whose friendship and influence are lifelong.

1866 Paints *Camille* (or *The Lady in Green*) and *Le Déjeuner sur l'Herbe*. Sends *Camille* to the Salon; is praised by one critic. Meets Manet, who influences him greatly.

1867 His mistress, Camille, gives birth to a son, Jean. *Femmes au Jardin* is refused at the Salon. To meet great financial difficulties, his paintings are seized and sold in lots of 50—at 30 francs a lot.

1868 Attempts suicide, then continues to paint with bold style and original coloring.

1869 At Bougival, with Renoir, paints scenes of *La Grenouillère*, a bathing place—the first thoroughly Impressionist pictures.

1870 Is rejected at the Salon again. Marries Camille. Spends summer at Trouville and Le Havre. In September, embarks for England. In London, meets Durand-Ruel, who begins to buy his work and exhibits one painting.

1872 Settles at Argenteuil.

1873 Sets up a studio in a boat. Paints regattas and riverbank scenes.

1874 Is the acknowledged leader of Impressionism. (The word "Impressionism" derives from the phrase of a critic, vis-à-vis Monet's *Impression: Sunrise*). Lives in poverty and despair. Renoir often visits and brings him bread.

1875 First showing of Impressionist paintings at Durand-Ruel—a disastrous failure.

1876 Second Impressionist Exhibition at Durand-Ruel receives violent criticism ("dreadful spectacle of humanity turning into madness"). Writes to a patron, asking for help: "It is with a sad heart that I write you. . . . I cannot resolve my troubles, the creditors are adamant. . . . We will be thrown out of the little house where I could live simply and work so well. I don't know what will happen to us. . . ."

1877 Third Impressionist Exhibition; Monet exhibits 30 canvases. Inspector of the Academy of Fine Arts writes: "The canvases provoke laughter and are pitiful. They demonstrate the most profound ignorance of drawing, composition and coloring."

1878 Settles at Vetheuil, keeping a *pied à terre* in Paris. His second son, Michel, is born. He is in dire financial straits again.

1879 His wife Camille dies. "September 4, 1879: Alone in the world with two children, without means, without a penny ahead of me."

1880 One-man show at La Vie Moderne. Exhibits at the Salon. Refuses to join in the Fifth Impressionist Exhibition. The movement is disintegrating.

1881- Lives at Poissy with Mme. Hoschede, the
1883 widow of an art collector who had bought his paintings. Summers at the seaside. Mme. Hoschede becomes the second Mme. Monet. They settle at Giverny. One-man show in March, 1883. Goes with Renoir to the Riviera.

1884 Goes to Bordighera and Menton. Makes lavish use of strong color.

1886 Visits the Netherlands. Georges Geoffroy meets him: "Claude Monet works in front of the *Cathédrale* of Port Daumois, in the wind and under the rain [dressed in] high boots, covered with sweaters and a hooded slicker. The wind occasionally tears the palette or the brushes out of his hands. . . . [He] persists and goes on painting as though in a battle."

1888 Two-man show with Rodin.

1890 Begins studies of the effect of light on the same scene under changes of hour, season, atmospheric condition.

1891 Paints series of haystacks. Visits London. With success, he buys a house, lays out a flower garden, a water-lily pool, builds a boathouse.

1892 Paints the *Poplar* and *Rouen Cathedral* series.

1895 Visits Norway. Paints snowscapes and the effects of the Northern lights.

1898 Refuses the Legion of Honor because he is outraged by the behavior of France in the Dreyfus affair.

1902 Begins the first of more than 50 canvases which he calls *Les Nymphéas*—the famous water-lily series (see text).

1904 Exhibits London scenes, which show the influence of Turner.

1908 In Venice, as in London, tries to render luminous mists.

1911 Mme. Monet dies.

1914 Plans huge studio—70 feet long, 40 feet wide, 50 feet high—for the large *Nymphéas*. His son Jean dies.

1916 At the age of 76, starts the most ambitious project of his life: huge canvases, 7' x 15' long, for the *Nymphéas* series. His daughter-in-law comes to live with him, until his death.

1918 Premier Clemenceau selects paintings from the new *Nymphéas* that Monet agrees to give to France, on the occasion of the Armistice. He insists upon keeping canvases so that he can improve upon them until he dies.

1922 Regains eyesight after operation for cataract, which had been causing a slow progression toward blindness. Continues work on the *Nymphéas*.

1923 Official presentation to France of a set of *Nymphéas*. In accordance with his wishes, these will be installed in two oval-shaped rooms in the Orangerie in Paris.

1926 Dies at Giverny, December 5.

Suggested reading:

Claude Monet, by William C. Seitz (Museum of Modern Art, New York).

Claude Monet, by Raymond Cogniat (Abrams).

Claude Monet, by Margaretta Salinger (Abrams).

See also Impressionism in general reading list (page 163).

PICASSO

Pablo Ruiz Picasso 1881-
Spanish-born Modern French Master

1881 Born on October 25 in Malaga, Spain. His father, José Ruiz Blasco, teaches painting; his mother, María Picasso López, is perhaps descended from a family of goldsmiths.

1891 Moves to Corunna with family; is already drawing and painting in oils with skill.

1892 Follows strict academic apprenticeship in art under his father's watchful eye.

1895 Family moves to Barcelona; Picasso's father finds him a studio of his own.

1897 Begins to develop his own style. First exhibition in Barcelona. Goes to Madrid to enroll in the Royal Academy of San Fernando. Bored, spends his time in the Prado Museum.

1899 Returns to Barcelona. Joins anarchistic painters, poets and writers in Modernist movement. Meets Jaime Sabartés, who becomes his lifelong friend and, later, secretary.

1900 First trip to Paris. Sells three works to Berthe Weill, the owner of a small gallery. Influence of Toulouse-Lautrec evident.

1901 Becomes co-editor of *Arte Joven* (Young Art) in Madrid. On second trip to Paris, meets Ambroise Vollard and Max Jacob. Studies and is influenced by Impressionism. Exhibits at Vollard's. Is nicknamed "Little Goya."

1902 Returns to Barcelona. Enters his "Blue Period," producing works of intense mood and blue color. Is shown by both Vollard and Berthe Weill. Third Parisian trip. Leaves France, poverty-stricken.

1903 Last year in Barcelona; is influenced by the bold distortions and elongations of El Greco.

1904 Settles permanently in Paris. Prefers painting at night—by oil lamp. Becomes intrigued by circus life and acrobats *(saltimbanques)*.

1905 Enters his "Rose Period." Begins to attract a following, notably a wealthy Russian patron, Tschoukine.

1906 Meets Matisse and Gertrude Stein; does her portrait. First shows influence of primitive sculpture. Begins work on *Les Demoiselles d'Avignon*, the launching point of Cubism.

1907 Contracts with Daniel-Henry Kahnweiler, his lifelong dealer, for all his work.

1908 Gives a celebrated banquet for Henri Rousseau, in admiration of his Primitivism; falls under the influence of Cézanne's work.

1909 Summer in Spain; returns to launch Analytical Cubism, with Georges Braque—the attempt to render form by manipulating light; their works are largely monochromatic.

1912 Goes south, to recuperate from illness with Eva (Ma Jolie) Gouel. Productive period, with Braque, for Cubism. Returns to Paris and works in collage, a form he is credited with discovering for modern art. Shows thirteen paintings and three drawings in the Second Post-Impressionist Exhibition.

1913 Moves into Synthetic Cubism with Braque; they render objects simultaneously in various aspects. Color returns to his work. Paints *The Card Player*.

1915 Still immersed in Cubist style, begins precise, naturalistic drawings in the tradition of Ingres.

1917 Executes sets and costumes for Diaghilev's production of the ballet *Parade*, the first of a long collaboration.

1918 Marries Olga Koklova, a Russian ballerina.

1920 Enters Neo-Classical period—fulsome, monumental nudes.

1921 A son, Paul, is born. Still does Cubist works, notably *Three Musicians* and numerous still lifes.

1925 Experiments with Surrealism. Exhibits in First Surrealist Exhibition.

1926 Begins series of violently distorted heads with seemingly arbitrary arrangements of features.

1929 Begins his *Metamorphoses*, using primeval shapes, somewhat anticipating the work of Henry Moore.

1931 Illustrates Ovid's *Metamorphoses* in pure classical style. Turns to sculpture more and more.

1933 The bullfight engrosses him, as in his earliest work. Bullheaded men dominate his compositions. His marriage to Olga is ending.

1935 Has a daughter, Maia, by Marie-Thérèse Walter. Publishes some poetry.

1936 Becomes deeply involved in the politics of the Spanish Civil War; denounces German and Italian intervention.

1937 Does violent engraving, *Dream and Lie of Franco*; paints the great *Guernica*, depicting the horrors inflicted on the town by Fascist bombers.

1938 His work takes an Expressionist and decorative turn, with double-faced heads.

1939 Is given comprehensive show, *Picasso: Forty Years of His Art*, by Museum of Modern Art, New York, and Art Institute of Chicago.

1940 Spends war years in Paris, unmolested by the Germans, but forbidden to show his work publicly. Does innumerable portraits of Dora Maar, a close companion.

1944 Announces his adherence to communism, but does not alter painting style. Six weeks after the Liberation, 75 of his paintings and five sculptures are shown in the Salon d'Automne. Riots between his enthusiasts and deprecators.

1945 Is given large show at Victoria and Albert Museum, London. Turns to lithography. New model, Françoise Gilot, herself a painter.

1947 Offers ten paintings as a gift to the French Government. Has a son, Claude, and two years later a daughter, Paloma, by Françoise Gilot.

1948 Draws his famous *Dove*, in reality a white pigeon, for the Communist Peace Congress.

1949 Settles at Vallauris, in south of France. Devotes himself chiefly to ceramics.

1953 Françoise and Picasso separate.

1954 Moves into villa, *La Californie*, at Cannes with Jacqueline Roque and her daughter. Does lithographs, aquatints, ceramics, paintings.

PICASSO: Self-portrait, 1901. Private collection, N.Y. Oil.

1955 Paints *Portrait of Madame Z* (see text).

1957 Is given retrospective 75th Anniversary Exhibition by the Museum of Modern Art, New York, and Art Institute of Chicago.

1958 Works on series inspired by Velázquez's *Las Meninas*.

1959 Moves to the Chateau of Vauvenargues, northeast of Aix-en-Provence. Marries Jacqueline Roque.

1962 Nine New York galleries cooperate in unprecedented birthday salute to Picasso at 80, each showing one period of his long life's work.

Suggested reading:

Picasso, His Life and Work, by Roland Penrose (Harper).

Picasso, Fifty Years of His Art, by Alfred H. Barr, Jr. (Museum of Modern Art, New York).

The Private World of Pablo Picasso, by David Douglas Duncan (Ridge Press).

Pablo Picasso, by W. Boeck and J. Sabartés (Praeger).

Picasso: The Recent Years, by Sidney and Harriet Janis (Doubleday).

Picasso, by Christian Zervos, eight volumes (Cahiers d'Art).

Picasso's Picassos, by David Douglas Duncan (Harper).

See also Modern Painting and Cubism in general reading list (page 163).

RAPHAEL

Raphael Sanzio, Raphaello Santi 1483-1520
Italian High-Renaissance Master

1483 Born in Urbino, a flourishing cultural center, on April 6. His father, Giovanni de' Santi, is a painter and poet. His mother is Magia di Battista di Nocola Ciarla.

1491 His mother dies.

1494 His father dies. His stepmother and an uncle, Bartolmeo, a priest, become his guardians.

1499-1502 Studies under Perugino at Perugia. Helps decorate the Sala del Cambio at Perugia. Paints *The Three Graces* on panel.

1502 Paints *St. Michael*. When Perugino returns to Florence, Raphael fills the demand for religious paintings.

c.1503 Paints *The Coronation of the Virgin*.

c.1504 Goes to Siena as assistant to Pinturicchio.

1504 Paints *The Marriage of the Virgin*. Moves to Florence. Becomes good friend of Fra Bartolomeo. Begins to study the nude.

RAPHAEL: Self-portrait (figure on left), detail, The School of Athens. *Vatican. Fresco.*

1505-
1507　Paints the portraits of *Angelo Doni* and his wife *Maddalena Strozzi.* Executes two commissions in Perugia, then goes to Urbino. Paints a second *St. George, La Belle Jardinière, The Entombment of Christ.*

c.1508　Paints *Madonna del Baldacchino.* Goes to Rome, on invitation from Pope Julius II.

1509-
1513　Begins his great cycle of decorations in the *stanzas* (rooms) of the Vatican: *Desputa del Sacramento, School of Athens, Parnassus* and *Jurisprudence.*

1513　Pope Julius II dies. Pope Leo X keeps Raphael on.

1514　Pope Leo is so pleased that he makes Raphael director of all the architectural and artistic departments of St. Peter's and the Vatican. Lives in great splendor in a palace built by Bramante; dresses like an aristocrat; is surrounded by a court of pupils. Unwillingly consents to marry Maria Bibbiena, Cardinal Bibbiena's niece—a marriage that never takes place (see text).

1514-
1517　Decorates the Stanza dell' Incendio del Borgo in the Vatican.

1515　Pope Leo commissions Raphael to draw ten cartoons, describing scenes from the Acts of the Apostles, to be made into great tapestries. (Some of the cartoons are now in the Victoria and Albert Museum, London.)

1516　Adorns the bathroom of Cardinal Bibbiena with frescoes glorifying Venus and the triumphs of love. Paints *The Sistine Madonna.*

1517　Makes preliminary drawings for the Sala di Costantino in the Vatican. (These are painted by others after his death.)

1519　Seven of the tapestries from his drawings are hung on the walls of the Sistine Chapel.

1520　All ten tapestries are finished. Dies in Rome on April 6, after a ten-day fever. Is buried in the Pantheon. His epitaph reads: *"Ille hic est Raphael"* (He who is here is Raphael).

Suggested reading:
Raphael, by Oskar Fischel (Kegan Paul).
Raphael, by Felix Lavery (Stokes).
Raphael, by A. P. Oppe (Methuen).
Raphael, by Wilhelm E. Suida (Phaidon).

See also The Renaissance in general reading list (page 163).

REDON

Odilon Redon 1840-1916
French Symbolist and Post-Impressionist

1840　Born in Bordeaux, on April 20, to Bertrand and Marie Redon. His mother, called "Odile," is a Louisiana-born Creole; Odilon is named for her.

c.1844　Often sick, he is sent by his parents to live in the country at Peylerebade, a family estate managed by an old uncle. The bleak countryside, according to Gascon legends, has a "magical" atmosphere. It affects the lonely boy's imagination. He sees little of his parents, though they live in Bordeaux.

1855　Takes drawing lessons from a watercolorist and writes: "I would bring in . . . drawings of imaginary beings which haunted me . . . all in a world of despair." Admires Delacroix.

1857　Begins formal art studies in Bordeaux, in architecture—at his father's insistence. Meets Armand Clavaud, a botanist, who influences his future work, introduces him to Hindu

REDON: Self-portrait, 1867. Collection Ari Redon, Paris. Oil.

poetry, writings of Flaubert, Poe, Baudelaire.

1861　Takes brief trip to the Pyrenees. Is impressed by the "desolate solitudes" of the landscape.

1862　In Paris, fails the oral examinations for the architecture division of the École des Beaux-Arts. Returns to Bordeaux. Studies with a local sculptor.

1863　Meets Rodolphe Bresdin, a master engraver; black-and-white has strong influence on him.

1864　When his father urges that he study with a recognized master, returns to Paris to work with Gérôme, an academician. Finds him stifling ("The teaching I was given did not agree with my nature"). Soon leaves to study with Corot.

1867　An etching is accepted by the print section of the official Salon. It is signed *"O. Redon, élève de Bresdin."*

1870　Soldier in military campaign against Prussia; "My resolve dates from this moment . . . my vision was increased tenfold."

1871　Released from army for "general weakness, result of fever." Concentrates on working in charcoal and lithography.

1874　His father dies; the modest support he had received ends.

c.1875　Meets Fantin-Latour, from whom he learns a new technique of lithography.

1878　Goes to the Netherlands to study Rembrandt's work.

1879　*Dans le Rêve,* his first portfolio of lithographs, is published.

1880　Marries Camille Falte; born on the French island of Bourbon, near Madagascar.

1881　His first show of lithographs is held in the offices of *La Vie Moderne.* It is not advertised.

1885　First flower painting, *Flowers in a China Cup.*

1886　Invited to exhibit his drawings in the eighth group show of the Impressionists; though hung in a hallway, they attract many.

1887　First son, Jean, dies several months after birth. Redon publishes somber lithographs.

1889　Son, Ari, is born.

1891　Begins to use pastels: "These soft materials are restful and bring me joy."

1895　"It is true that I am abandoning black more and more. It exhausts me." Gauguin influences his color.

1899　Album of lithographs, *L'Apocalypse,* is published. Participates in painting exhibitions in Paris and the Netherlands. His work influences Vuillard, Bonnard, Matisse.

1900　Flower painting becomes "the bread on our table."

1906　Is voted president of the Salon des Indépendants; French Government purchases his work.

1908　Paints *Ophelia* (see text.)

1913　Forty Redons are shown at the International Exhibition of Modern Art, in New York.

1916　His son is called to the front. Dies in Paris, July 6.

Suggested reading:
Odilon Redon, Gustave Moreau, Rodolphe Bresdin, by John Rewald and others (Museum of Modern Art, New York).
Odilon Redon, by Walter Pach (Association of American Painters and Sculptors).

See also Post-Impressionism in general reading list (page 163).

REMBRANDT

Rembrandt Harmenszoon van Rijn 1606-1669
Dutch Master

1606　Born July 15, in Leyden, the Netherlands. His father is a relatively prosperous miller.

1620　Studies briefly at the Latin School of the University of Leyden. Becomes a student of a local architectural painter for three years, then studies under Pieter Latsman for six months in Amsterdam.

1625　Works at his studio in Leyden with Jan Lievens.

1628　Has several pupils, including Gerard Dou. Receives 100 florins per year from each student.

1629　Paints *Judas Returning the Thirty Pieces of Silver.*

1630　His father dies. Paints *The Raising of Lazarus.*

1631　Moves to Amsterdam and is soon in great demand in fashionable circles. *The Anatomy Lesson of Dr. Tulp* is his first major commission. His elder brother, Gerrit, dies. Meets Hendrik van Uylenburgh, an art dealer, and lives in his home.

1633　Paints *Christ in the Storm on the Lake of Gallilee.*

1634　Marries Saskia van Uylenburgh, cousin of the art dealer, who brings him a dowry of 40,000 guilders. Rembrandt, extremely popular, lives on a lavish scale. He collects art and often makes an opening bid for a picture

REMBRANDT: Self-portrait, 1652-53. Rembrandt House, Amsterdam. Pen and wash.

that is so high no one bids against him.

1635-1638 Paints *The Rape of Ganymede, The Blinding of Sampson, The Angel Leaving Tobias and His Family, Samson's Wedding Feast.*

1639 Buys an extremely expensive house in the Jodeen Breestraat.

1640 Death of his mother.

1641 Titus, the only one of four children to live beyond infancy, is born.

1642 Saskia dies. Rembrandt is commissioned to do a portrait for a company of the Civil Guard of Amsterdam. This picture, *The Black Watch,* does not please bourgeois Amsterdam's conception of beautiful art—and marks the beginning of a decline in his popularity. Paints *The Supper at Emmaus.*

1645 Hendrickje Stoffels moves into his house as housekeeper and nurse for Titus, to the horror of Calvinist Dutch society.

1652 Fewer and fewer commissions are offered. Paints *An Old Man in Thought.*

1654 Hendrickje is excommunicated for living in sin with Rembrandt. They have a daughter, Cornelia. Rembrandt is unable to marry Hendrickje, because Saskia's will requires an accounting of money left to Titus if Rembrandt should remarry—and he has already spent the money to satisfy his many creditors. Paints *Bathsheba, Woman Bathing,* posed by Hendrickje.

1655 Paints *The Polish Rider* and *The Flayed Ox,* which will inspire Delacroix and Daumier.

1656 Is declared bankrupt. An inventory of his goods is taken by the Insolvency Chamber.

1658 Most of his possessions are sold at public auction. Hendrickje and Titus become art dealers; they "employ" Rembrandt—in order to protect his earnings from being taken over by creditors. Paints *Portrait of Titus.*

1658-1662 Rembrandt moves to Rozengracht, a poorer section of town. He lives in poverty. Paints *Hendrickje Stoffels, Moses Showing the Tables of the Law, The Syndics.*

1664 Death of Hendrickje.

1668 Death of Titus, shortly after his marriage. Paints *Self-portrait* (see text).

1669 Rembrandt dies.

Suggested reading:
Rembrandt, by Otto Benesch (Skira).
Rembrandt, by Tancred Borenius (Phaidon).
Paintings of Rembrandt, by Abraham Bredius (Phaidon).
Drawings of Rembrandt, by Otto Benesch (Phaidon).
Rembrandt, by Ludwig Münz (Abrams).
See also Flemish and Dutch Painting in general reading list (page 163).

RENOIR

Pierre Auguste Renoir 1841-1919
French Impressionist

1841 Born on February 25 at Limoges, the son of working-class parents, who own a tailor shop.

1845 Family moves to Paris.

1854 Is apprenticed to a porcelain and earthenware factory, where he spends four years, becoming skilled in decorating porcelain. Begins to study paintings at the Louvre: Boucher's *Diana at the Bath* is his "first enthusiasm." Studies Ingres, especially the *Portrait of Mme. Rivière* and *La Source.* Studies the statues of Jean Goujon, a 16th century

RENOIR: Self-portrait, 1897. Sterling and Francine Clark Art Institute, Williamstown, Mass. Oil.

sculptor. (More than forty years later, the influence of Ingres and Goujon can be seen.)

1862 Enrolls at the École des Beaux-Arts; meets Bazille, Monet, Sisley.

1869 His poverty is such that he is grateful for a full meal at his father's table. Often takes food to Monet, who is destitute.

1870 Serves in regiment of cuirassiers during Franco-Prussian War. Two of his paintings are shown in the Salon. Paints *Moulin de la Galette, Mme. Charpentier and Her Children.*

1881-1882 Makes first trip to Italy, then Algeria, having become somewhat successful. Is excited by the art of Pompeii. Begins a great series of nudes, first in Naples, then in Paris, which will continue for a decade. Influenced by the color of the Venetian masters and Raphael. The influence of Michelangelo will show in

---

the heavy limbs and bodies of Renoir's paintings and sculpture, in the last years of his life. Algeria reawakens his love for Delacroix. Returns to Paris. Marries Aline Charigot, one of the people in *Luncheon of the Boating Party.* (Three sons are born of this marriage.)

1883 Enters upon his *period aigre* ("sour period"), so named by some of his critics, who feel that he has deserted Impressionism. "About 1883, I had wrung Impressionism dry. I finally came to the conclusion that I knew neither how to paint nor how to draw. In a word, Impressionism was a blind alley, as far as I was concerned...." Paints *The Bathers* (now in the Tyson Collection in Philadelphia), which he later declares his masterpiece. Paints several versions of *Mme. Renoir and Her Son Pierre.*

1886 After bickerings and dissension among the Impressionists, Renoir refuses to continue to participate in their shows. His reputation is now established.

1894 First serious attack of arthritis, which eventually cripples him. (Signs of arthritis had appeared in the '80's.)

1904-1907 Paints *Coco* (Claude Renoir) and *Lady With a Fan* and begins to work in sculpture.

1910 Paints *Gabrielle in a Red Blouse* and *Self-Portrait of the Artist.*

1911 Paints *Gabrielle With a Rose* (see text). Although he travels often to find a cure for his disease, his health worsens. But his fame grows, as do the honors accorded him.

1912 Despite a serious stroke, continues to paint—with brushes tied to his hands. His incapacitation becomes such that, in order to complete his sculptures, he sketches the figure on paper or canvas, has an assistant set up the mass of clay, then indicates what he wants done.

1915 Mme. Renoir dies, after nursing her two sons (who had been severely wounded in World War I). Her death is a terrible blow to Renoir, but he continues to work. "Don't ask me if painting should be objective or subjective —I don't give a damn about such things.... I just struggle with my figures until they are a harmonious unity with their landscape background. I want people to feel that neither the setting nor the figures are dull and lifeless."

1919 Taken to the Louvre in a wheelchair, on his last visit. Dies at Cagnes on December 3.

Suggested reading:
Pierre Auguste Renoir, by Rosamund Frost (Hyperion).
Renoir, by William Gaunt (Phaidon).
Renoir, by André Leclerc (Hyperion Miniatures).
Pierre Auguste Renoir, by Walter Pach (Abrams).
See also Impressionism in general reading list (page 163).

ROUAULT

Georges Rouault 1871-1958
French Expressionist

1871 Born on May 27 in Paris, in a cellar, during a bombing at the time of the Commune revolution. His father is a cabinetmaker.

1881 Receives his first art instruction from his grandfather, who admires Rembrandt, Daumier, Manet and Courbet.

1885 Is apprenticed to Hirsch, a stained-glass maker. Attends evening classes at the École des Arts Décoratifs.

1891 Studies at the École des Beaux-Arts, under Élie Delaunay.

1892 Delaunay dies; Gustave Moreau takes his

place. Rouault becomes Moreau's favorite pupil. Wins first prize at the École with a series of religious subjects. Meets Matisse, who is also studying there.

1894 Wins the *Prix Chénavard* with his *The Child Jesus Among the Doctors*.

1895 Wins the *Prix Fortin d'Ivry* with *Christ Mourned by the Holy Women*. Tries for the *Prix de Rome* for second time. Again fails. Paints and exhibits work on religious and mythological themes.

1898 Moreau's death profoundly affects him. Is appointed curator of the Gustave Moreau Museum. Breaks with style of the academicians. Has a nervous breakdown; convalesces in Savoie.

1901 Meets J. K. Huysmans, who wants to form a group of Catholic artists at a Trappist monastery. Thinks of taking monastic vows.

1902 Sick again. Convalesces in Haute-Savoie.

1903 Returns to Paris. Paints clowns, prostitutes, figures of the Commedia dell'Arte. Exhibits at the First Salon d'Automne.

1904 Meets Léon Bloy, a Catholic writer, who influences him tremendously. Exhibits eight

ROUAULT: *Self-portrait, 1929. Museum of Modern Art, N. Y., gift Mrs. John D. Rockefeller, Jr. Color lithograph.*

pictures, 32 watercolors and pastels at the Salon d'Automne.

1906- Occasionally works with a ceramist, Mettley.
1912 Meets the important art dealer Ambroise Vollard.

1906 Paints first *Odalisque*.

1908 Marries Marthe Le Sidaner. (They will have three daughters and a son.) Begins his series of *Tribunals* and *Judges*.

1909 First one-man show at the Drouet Gallery, Paris.

1911 Becomes friends with Jacques Maritain, the Catholic philosopher. Paints social themes, family life, workers, peasants.

1913 Returns to religious subjects. Vollard buys the contents of his studio.

1914 Publishes first poems, *Les Soirées de Paris*.

1916 Vollard fits out a studio in his own home for him.

1917- Painting in richer colors: clowns and reli-
1930 gious paintings. Illustrates Jarry's *Ubu Roi*

and Vollard's *Réincarnations du Père Ubu* and *Le Miserere*.

1922 Does series of lithographs, *Les Clowns*.

1924 Receives the Legion of Honor. Large retrospective exhibition. Does etchings and poems for *Paysages Légendaires*.

1926 Publishes his first book, *Souvenirs Intimes*.

1928 Paints *The Holy Face* (see text).

1929 Creates sets and costumes for a Diaghilev ballet.

1930 Publishes *Le Cirque de l'étoile Filante* with his own text and etchings. Has first foreign exhibitions. Colors become more varied and brilliant.

1932 No longer dates his works after 1932.

1938 The Museum of Modern Art, New York, presents his first comprehensive exhibition of prints.

1939 Ambroise Vollard dies.

1947 Wins lawsuit against Vollard's heirs. His unsold and unsigned pictures now belong to him.

1948 On November 5, burns 315 pictures returned from Vollard in presence of bailiff. Makes stained-glass windows for church in Haute-Savoie. Exhibits paintings and prints at the Venice Biennale. First trip to Italy.

1948- Changes his palette, painting in yellows, reds
1952 and greens.

1949 Visits the Netherlands and Belgium.

1951 Is named Commander of the Legion of Honor.

1952- Retrospective exhibitions at the Musée d'Art
1953 Moderne in Paris, Cleveland Museum of Art, the Museum of Modern Art, New York, County Museum, Los Angeles.

1958 Dies in Paris on February 13.

Suggested reading:

Georges Rouault, by Edward A. Jewell (Hyperion).
Georges Rouault, by Lionello Venturi (Weyhe).
Georges Rouault, by Marcel Brion (Braun).
See also Modern Painting and Fauvism in general reading list (page 163).

ROUSSEAU

Henri Julien Félix Rousseau, called *"Le Douanier"*
1844-1910
French Primitive

1844 Born May 21 in Laval, France. Father is a tinsmith.

1862 Enters the army. Is assigned to regimental band as a flute player.

1869 Marries Clémence Boitard. She bears him seven children during their 20-year marriage; only one survives infancy.

1870 Serves in the Franco-Prussian War as a sergeant.

1871 Goes to work for the customs service as a *gabelou* (minor inspector) at a toll station on the outskirts of Paris.

1884- Retires from the customs service. Begins to
1886 paint. Very poor, he copies documents for a lawyer and opens a stationery store, where his wife tries to sell his paintings. To add to a small pension, he gives music lessons. Begins to exhibit at the Salon des Indépendants.

1889 Wife dies. Writes a comedy, which is not produced.

1890 Paints *Myself, Portrait Landscape*. Meets Gauguin, Pissaro, Seurat and others.

1891 Paints *Storm in the Jungle*—claiming that the lush vegetation in the painting was inspired by the jungles he saw in Mexico while serving with the army. (No records show that Rousseau was ever in Mexico; frequent visits to the botanical gardens are, probably, the source of his inspiration.)

ROUSSEAU: *Self-portrait, 1890, Myself; Portrait Landscape. Prague Museum. Oil.*

1895 Paints *War* (later lost; not recovered until after World War II).

1898 Attempts to sell *The Sleeping Gypsy* to his hometown: "I will let it go for 2,000 to 1,800 francs because I would be happy that the city of Laval possess a remembrance of one of its children. . . ." The offer is refused.

1899 Marries Rosalie-Josephine Nourry. Collaborates on a five-act drama, *A Russian Orphan's Vengeance*, which is never produced.

1902- Paints *Adam and Eve, Path in the Woods at
1903 St. Cloud*.

1905 Paints *The Holy Family, The Hungry Lion*.

1906- Meets Max Weber and critic Wilhelm Uhde,
1907 who later publishes the first monograph on Rousseau. Picasso, always an admirer of Rousseau's work, gives a banquet in his honor. Paints *The Merry Jesters, Liberty Inviting the Artists, Football*.

1909 Paints *The Poet Inspired by His Muse*. In trouble with the law over an alleged check forgery. Rousseau, always gullible, had helped a friend "recover some money stolen from him by the Bank of France." Rousseau's paintings are introduced in his defense—to show the extent of his naïveté. He receives a two-year suspended sentence.

1910 Paints *The Dream* (see text), *Portrait of Joseph Brummer*. Dies. Later in the year, his first one-man show is presented by the Stieglitz Gallery, in New York.

Suggested reading:

Rousseau, by Douglas Cooper (Braun).
Five Primitive Masters, by Wilhelm Uhde (Quadrangle Press).
See also Post-Impressionism and Modern Painting in general reading list (page 163).

RUBENS

Peter Paul Rubens 1577-1640
Flemish Baroque Master

1577 Born in Siegen, Westphalia, of Flemish parents. Because his father, a lawyer, is an exiled official, the family lives in Cologne for most of the time until the father dies.

1589 Family returns to Antwerp. He receives a classical education. Is page to an eminent lady.

c.1592 Begins his painting apprenticeship, studying successively with Tobias Verhaecht, Adam van Noort and Otto van Veen.

1598 Is listed as master in the Antwerp painters' Guild of St. Luke.

1600 Travels to Italy. Works chiefly in Mantua, Rome and Genoa. Is influenced by Michelangelo, Raphael, the Venetians, Caravaggio.

c.1603 Visits Spain, probably for a year. Does a series of the *Twelve Apostles*.

1605 Returns to Italy, working chiefly for Vincenzo Gonzaga, Duke of Mantua. Completes an altarpiece for Church of Santa Trinità.

c.1609 Settles in Antwerp. Becomes Court Painter to Archduke Albert. Establishes large studio. Marries Isabella Brandt.

1610 Executes *The Erection of the Cross* for the Antwerp Cathedral.

1611 Begins work on his masterpiece of this era, *The Descent From the Cross*, also for the Antwerp Cathedral.

c.1614 Begins to be interested in battle, hunt and abduction scenes—largely from mythology.

RUBENS: Self-portrait, c.1639. Louvre, Paris. Chalk drawing.

Continues to fulfill church commissions.

c.1616 Begins first of his large decorative projects: a tapestry cycle, *Deens Mus*. Starts the decoration of his own large house.

c.1620 Finishes 39 paintings for the Church of the Jesuits, Antwerp.

1622 Begins first of his great international commissions, a *History of Marie de' Medici*, 21 gigantic compositions for the Luxembourg Palace in Paris.

1626 Wife dies, leaving two sons.

1628 Sent on diplomatic missions to Spain and England. Is knighted by Charles I. While in Spain, copies works of Titian.

1630 Marries Helene Fourment, 16. (She will bear him five children.)

1632-1635 Works on large decorations in London (the ceiling of Whitehall) and Antwerp.

1635 Wealthy, influential, universally esteemed, he buys the Château de Steen, outside Antwerp, for his home.

1636 Visits Spain again—to work on decoration of the Torre de la Parada, outside Madrid, and other commissions from King Philip IV.

c.1638 Paints *Helene Fourment* (see text).

1640 Dies at Antwerp on May 30.

Suggested reading:

Recollections of Rubens, by Jacob Burckhardt (Phaidon).

Peter Paul Rubens, by Hans Gerhard Evers (Bruckmann).

Peter Paul Rubens, by Julius S. Held (Abrams, Inc.).

See also Flemish and Dutch Painting in general reading list (page 163).

SEURAT

Georges-Pierre Seurat 1859-1891
French Pointillist and Neo-Impressionist

1859 Born on December 2, in Paris, to middle-class parents.

1875 Studies at Municipal School of Design under academic sculptor Justin Lequien, who perhaps influences him toward basic premise of his art: that "painting is the art of hollowing a surface."

1877 Enters École des Beaux Arts. For two years, studies under a pupil of Ingres, Henri Lehmann, an anti-Romantic, anti-Impressionist. Acquires lifelong interest in the theory of composition. Ranks 47th in class of 80.

1879 Spends year in military service at Brest, where he first sees the sea and beaches, giving him his love of seascapes.

1881 Continues studies in Paris, working in museums, copying works of Ingres, Poussin, Holbein. Discovers Delacroix. Becomes fascinated by scientific color theories of Helmholtz and Chevreuil.

1882 In his own studio, works on rigid schedule, but dines nightly with his mother. Draws chiefly in black and white.

1883 Develops his theory of painting. Begins work on *Une Baignade*, going daily for several months to a bathing spot on the Seine at Asnières, opposite the Ile de la Grande Jatte. Shows charcoal portrait of the painter Aman-Jean, in the Salon.

1884 *Une Baignade* is rejected by the official annual Salon. Joins a group of dissidents, including Redon and Signac, to create the Salon des Indépendants, where *Une Baignade* is exhibited. Begins work on *Sunday Afternoon at the Grande Jatte*.

1885 *Sunday Afternoon at the Grande Jatte*, still unfinished, becomes the "manifesto" of the new Pointillist movement. Friends join Seurat's color research: Signac, Henry-Edmond Cross, Émile Verhaeren. Is introduced to Pissarro, who becomes an enthusiast of his theories.

1886 *Grande Jatte* is exhibited in the eighth and final exhibition of the Impressionists: Monet, Renoir and Sisley protest and withdraw. Felix Feneon, a critic, greatly impressed, becomes spokesman for the new movement. Seurat summers at Honfleur "to wash the studio light from my eyes." *Grande Jatte* appears at the second exhibition of the Indépendants. *Une Baignade* is shown in New York.

1887 Exhibits in Brussels, with group known as "The Twenty." Starts *Poseuses* and *La Parade*. Is much influenced by the writings of Charles Henry, a scientist and aesthete, on

SEURAT: Self-portrait. Gallatin Collection, Philadelphia Museum of Art. Black conté crayon.

"the character of line" and its emotional effects on the spectator. Exhibits seven landscapes, some drawings and sketches at the Indépendants' salon.

1888 *Poseuses* and *La Parade* (see text) appear at the Indépendants. Spends summer working at landscapes in Port-en-Bessin.

1889 Begins his *Femme se poudrant* (a portrait of his mistress, Madelein Knobloch) and *Chahut*. *Poseuses* is shown at Brussels.

1890 *Femme se poudrant* and *Chahut* are shown at the Indépendants. Summers at Gravelines. Begins *Le Cirque*, his last major work.

1891 Sends incomplete *Le Cirque* to the Indépendants. Taken ill while hanging works for this show. Dies three days later, on March 29.

Suggested reading:

Seurat, by John Rewald (Les Editions Braun et Cie).

Seurat, by Daniel Catton Rich (Art Institute of Chicago).

See also Post-Impressionism in general reading list (page 163).

TITIAN

Tiziano Vecelli 1477/1487-1576
Venetian High Renaissance and Baroque Master

1477 or Born in Pieve di Cadare in northern Venetia.

1487 His father is a distinguished councilor and soldier. While still a child, Titian is sent to Venice to study under Gentile Bellini, then Giovanni Bellini at whose studio he works with Giorgione. (Later, is believed to enter a partnership with Giorgione.)

1507-1508 Decorates the Fondaco de' Tedeschi with Giorgione.

c.1510-1512 Paints *Sacred and Profane Love*. Flees from the plague that kills Giorgione. Goes to Padua, where he executes frescos of *The Life of St. Anthony*.

1512 Returns to Venice. Obtains a broker's patent. Becomes superintendent of the government works. Sets up a workshop on the Grand Canal. Paints *The Three Ages of Man*.

1513 Refuses Pope Leo X's offer to go to Rome.
c.1515 Paints *Flora*.
1516 Is appointed official painter of the Venetian state; gets an annuity. Begins to paint for Alfonso I of Ferrara.
1518- Completes *The Assumption of the Madonna*,
1522 *The Worship of Venus*, *Pesaro Madonna*, the *Bacchanal* (see text), *Bacchus and Ariadne*.
1523 Paints for the Marquis Federigo Gonzaga of Mantua. Works on the *Entombment of Christ*.

TITIAN: *Self-portrait, c.1550. Ehem. Staatliche Museen, Berlin-Dahlem. Oil.*

1525 Marries Cecilia (last name unknown) and legitimizes their first two children, one of whom, Orazio, becomes a painter.
1530 Paints his first portrait of Charles V. Paints *St. Peter Martyr*, which wins in competition against Palma Vecchio and others. His wife Cecilia dies.
1531 Settles in a large house in the north of Venice.
1532- Paints *Portrait of Charles V With his Dog*.
1533 Charles V makes Titian a Knight of the Golden Spur and Court Painter.
1534 Begins altarpiece, *Presentation of the Virgin*.
1535 Goes to Rome; is made Roman citizen. Paints Pope Paul III. Returns to Venice.
1538 Paints *Venus of Urbino*.
1545- Again visits Rome. Paints *Portrait of Pope*
1546 *Paul III With his Nephews Alessandro and Ottavio Farnese*. Lives at the Vatican, meets Michelangelo.
1547 Spends nine months at Charles V's court in Augsburg. Returns to Venice.
1548 Returns to Augsburg, paints another portrait of Charles V.
1550- Again goes to Augsburg. Meets the future
1552 Philip II of Spain. Paints several portraits of him and accepts commission for a religious work.
1554 His favorite daughter, Lavinia, marries. Finishes *The Holy Trinity*.
1555- Paints self-portraits and *The Entombment*.
1559
1560 Lavinia dies in childbirth.
c.1570 Paints *Christ Crowned With Thorns*.
1573 Begins work on a large *Pietà*.
1576 Dies of the plague on August 26.
Suggested reading:
Titian: His Life and Times, by J. A. Crowe and G. B. Cavalcaselle (John Murray).

Titian: The Paintings and Drawings, by Hans Tietze (Phaidon).
Titian, by René Huyghe (Braun).
Titian, by Georg Gronau (Duckworth).
Titian: His Life and Work, by Claude Phillips (Seeley & Co., Ltd.).
See also The Renaissance in general reading list (page 163).

TOULOUSE-LAUTREC

Henri Marie Raymond de Toulouse-Lautrec-Monfa
1864-1901
French Post-Impressionist

1864 Is born at Albi on November 24. His father, the Count Alphonese, and his mother, the Countess Adèle, are first cousins.
1872 Begins school in Paris. A delicate boy, he is often absent, and takes the baths at Amélie-les-Bains. He already shows a most precocious talent for drawing.
1878 Slips on drawing-room floor and breaks his leg. Fifteen months later, on a recuperative trip to Barèges with his mother, he breaks the other leg. Neither limb ever develops naturally. He is left grotesque and deformed.
1879 During his convalescence, his parents encourage his interest in art.
1880 Is taught by René Princeteau, a deaf-mute painter of martial and equestrian scenes.
1882 Passes his baccalaureate exams at Toulouse and moves to Paris. Studies briefly with two academic painters.
1884 Discovers the work of Manet, Degas and Berthe Morisot.
1885 Settles into a studio in Montmartre, in the center of the night life, the music halls, cafés and bordellos, which become his favorite subject matter.
1886 Meets van Gogh, Pissarro, Degas, Gauguin, Seurat. Is an enthusiastic purchaser and student of the inexpensive Japanese prints that have begun to appear in Paris. Learns particularly their design, economy of composition and coloring in broad, flat areas, which he later brilliantly adapts to his posters.

TOULOUSE-LAUTREC: *Self-portrait. Collection of M. Exteens, Paris.*

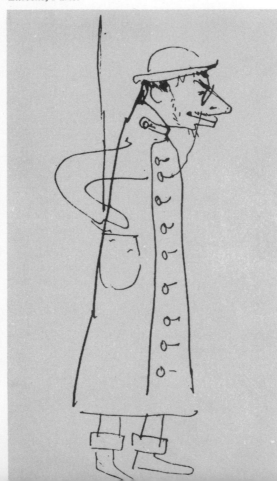

1889 First exhibits at the Salon des Indépendants. Shows *Au Bal du Moulin de la Galette*. Also does many portraits.
1891 First poster for the Moulin Rouge cabaret, inspired by "La Goulue," a dancer.
1892 Finishes his first lithographs; begins a series of scenes from the *maisons closes* (houses of prostitution) in Montmartre.
1893 Is included in an exhibition of paintings of Montmartre life, at Goupil's gallery. Degas visits the gallery and is impressed.
1894 Completes a large painting, *Au Salon de la rue des Moulins*, from his studies of houses of prostitution. Publishes his first album of lithographs of Yvette Guilbert, singer and cabaret entertainer. Paints *Gabriel Tapié de Céleyran in a Corridor at the Comédie Française* (see text). Visits Brussels.
1895 Does many portraits of theatre and music-hall figures. Visits London, where he paints Oscar Wilde, visits Whistler. Returns to Paris. Is introduced to the world of horse racing by Tristan Bernard.
1896 Travels widely—Spain, Portugal, the Netherlands. In Spain discovers El Greco. Exhibits in Brussels.
1897 Takes new studio. Gives up poster work for lithography.
1898 Visits London for his exhibition at Goupil's. His health is failing rapidly now—a result of constant dissipation and drink.
1899 Is committed to a sanatorium in Neuilly. Paints from memory his series *Le Cirque*, partly to prove his sanity. A press campaign by his friends results in his release.
1900 Visits Bordeaux and Le Havre. Does a series of paintings inspired by the opera *Messalina*, seen at Bordeaux.
1901 In rapidly deteriorating health, he returns to his mother at Malrômé. Dies of a stroke on September 9.
Suggested reading:
Toulouse-Lautrec, by Gerstle Mack (Knopf).
Lautrec, by Jacques Lassaigne (Skira).
Toulouse-Lautrec, by Douglas Cooper (Abrams).
Toulouse-Lautrec, by Sam Hunter (Pocket Library of Great Art).
See also Post-Impressionism in general reading list (page 163).

TURNER

Joseph Mallord William Turner 1775-1851
British Landscapist, Seascapist, Romantic Impressionist

1775 Born the son of a barber on April 23, near Covent Garden, London.
1784 *A View of Margate Church*, his earliest known drawing.
1788 Decides to be a painter; colors prints for engravers and architects, in return for free instruction.
1789 Enters the Royal Academy. Works briefly in studio of Sir Joshua Reynolds. Lives with his parents in Maiden Lane, using an attic as a studio.
1790 Exhibits first work at Royal Academy, *A View of the Archbishop's Palace, Lambeth*.
1792 Commissioned to make drawings for *Copper Plate Magazine*, he tours the countryside, sketching landscapes and harbor scenes. Begins to make a name through prints of his drawings.
c.1794 Travels through England and Wales executing topographical landscapes for *Pocket Magazine*.
1797 Shows seascape in Royal Academy exhibition.

1799 His drawing *Norham Castle* earns him the title Associate of the Royal Academy. (He later calls it the real beginning of his artistic career.)

1801 Moves from his father's house to a separate studio. His mother suffers a mental breakdown.

1802 Is elected a full member of the Royal Academy, a high honor and rarity for one so young. This assures him income and patronage. His father comes to live with him, man-

TURNER: Self-portrait, c.1798. Tate Gallery, London. Oil.

ages his household, stretches and varnishes his canvases.

1803 Travels in France and Switzerland, filling six sketchbooks. Draws at the Louvre, with particular interest in the work of Claude Lorrain and Titian. Shows *Calais Pier* at the National Gallery.

1804 Quarrels with the Royal Academy; builds his own gallery, in his Harley Street quarters, to exhibit his works.

c.1805 Exhibits *The Shipwreck* in his own gallery; sells it for 300 guineas, a very high price. Permits engravings to be made from the work, the first of a series of large engravings, after his paintings, which rapidly enhance his reputation.

1806 Executes a series of drawings for engravings (which eventually number 50) called *Liber Studiorum*, designed after the *Liber Veritas* of Claude Lorrain.

1807 Accepts appointment as Professor of Perspective at the Royal Academy. Is known to be miserly; dismisses his engraver when he tries to raise his price.

1808 Spends time at the country estate of Sir John Leicester, filling notebooks with his close observations on nature.

1809 Exhibits several paintings accompanied by poetic quotations. Is praised by Thomas Lawrence, Britain's outstanding portrait painter, as a landscapist "full of sentiment and certainly genius."

1810 Estimates his painting assets at £2,000 and his total assets at £12,000. Decides to buy a house in Twickenham and build a new gallery.

1813 The president of the Royal Academy attacks Turner and his followers, calling them "The

White Painters" because of the cloudiness and Impressionism of their work. Turner's work suffers temporary loss of popularity.

1817-1819 Visits Belgium, the Netherlands, the Rhine, Scotland, Italy.

c.1823 Opens new gallery and sells his first oil painting since 1818. Works on *The Battle of Trafalgar*, a commission from George IV.

1832 Goes to Scotland to make sketches for a publication of Sir Walter Scott's poems; stays with Scott.

1834 Again travels on the Continent, visiting Germany, Italy, France. Spends some time in Venice painting. His engravings of travels are highly popular.

1835 Enters his last period of painting—completely personal impressions of landscapes and experiences.

1840 Condemned by the academicians, he meets Ruskin for the first time. Ruskin writes: "Introduced today to the man who beyond all doubt is the greatest of the age."

1842 Exhibits *Snowstorm* at the Royal Academy. Its full title is: *Steamboat off a Harbor's Mouth Making Signals in Shallow Water, and Going by the Lead* (see text). He also added the note: "The author was in this storm on the night the *Ariel* left Harwich."

1843 Ruskin's *Modern Painters* appears, defending Turner's late style and challenging the critics for their obtuseness. Turner begins to sell large paintings again.

1845 Is invited to send work to a Congress of European Art in Munich.

1851 Dies on December 19, a death listed as "natural decay." Leaves the nation his paintings.

Suggested reading:
The Life of J. M. W. Turner, R.A., by A. J. Finberg (Clarendon).
Masters of British Painting, by Andrew Carnduff Ritchie (Museum of Modern Art, New York).
See also Nineteenth Century in general reading list (page 163).

UCCELLO

Paolo di Dono 1397-1475
Florentine Pre-Renaissance Master

1397 Is born in Florence, the son of a barber-surgeon.

1407 Barely 10, he enters the workshop of sculptor Ghiberti; his first job is to shine up one of the famous golden doors for the baptistry of the Duomo (cathedral).

1414 Joins St. Luke's Guild as painter.

1415 Is admitted to the guild of doctors and apothecaries, probably signifying his mastery of the art of the goldsmith.

c.1425 Leaves Florence for Venice, where he is employed as a master mosaicist at St. Mark's. Executes a figure of St. Peter on the façade. (This figure is no longer in existence.)

1431 Returns to Florence.

1432 With his reputation not yet made, the *Operaii* of Florence's Duomo make inquiries in Venice as to whether his work for St. Mark's "was satisfactory and how his reputation stood...."

1436 Is chosen to execute a commemorative fresco above the tomb of Sir John Hawkwood; it is intended as an economical substitute for a marble monument. Uccello's researches in perspective lead to a most effective illusion.

c.1440 Becomes a close friend of the sculptor Donatello and the mathematician Giovanni Manetti.

c.1443 Visits Padua and obtains commission, through Donatello, to paint some "giants in chiaro-

scuro" in the Casa dei Vitaliani. (Mantegna admires them greatly, later in the century.)

1446 Rents a house in the Via della Scala, in Florence, and a workshop in the Piazza San Giovanni; his tax return indicates a wife, Tommasa di Benedetto Malifici.

c.1450 Executes frescoes in Santa Maria Novella on the subject of *The Flood* and *The Life of Noah*, works of extraordinary virtuosity in the rendering of perspective—then not entirely mastered by artists.

UCCELLO: Self-portrait, detail. Grand Palais, Paris. Oil.

1453 His wife gives birth to a son.

c.1456 Is commissioned to paint three panels of *The Battle of San Romano* for the bedchamber of Lorenzo the Magnificent, in the Medici's Riccardi Palace (see text). Daughter is born.

1465-1468 Is called to Urbino, where he begins a *Profanation of the Host* series for the Cathedral; the work is not finished because Uccello is accused of having more interest in perspective than in the holy figures.

1469 Writes at end of his tax return: "I am old and without means of livelihood, my wife is ill, and I can no longer work."

1475 Dies penniless. Is buried in his father's grave at Santo Spirito, Florence.

Suggested reading:
Uccello, by John Pope-Hennessy (Phaidon).
Lives of the Artists, by Giorgio Vasari (Simon & Schuster).
See also The Renaissance in general reading list (page 163).

VAN EYCK

Jan van Eyck 1380/1390-1441
Early Flemish Master

1380-1390 Born in Maeseyck, in province of Limburg. Studies art with his brother, Hubert. Both are employed at the court of French princes. After the French are defeated at Agincourt, the brothers seek employment at the court of the Duke of Burgundy.

1412-1417 Perhaps contributes certain pages to the Turin-Milan *Book of Hours*, executed for William IV, Duke of Bavaria. Executes several large miniatures for William IV of Holland;

VAN EYCK: Self-portrait, 1434, detail, Giovanni Arnolfini and His Wife. National Gallery, London. Oil.

his brother assists him.

1417   William IV dies; Jan van Eyck continues to live at the court under Jean de Bavière.

1425   Is appointed Court Painter to Philip the Good, Count of Flanders and Duke of Burgundy. Settles in Lille.

1426-   Makes distant and secret journeys to paint
1427   the portraits of various princesses whom Philip the Good is considering marrying.

1427   Begins his earliest dated work, the Ghent altar, with Hubert, on commission for Jodicus Vydt.

1432   Completes the Ghent altar. Paints Tymotheas.

1433   Paints Man With Turban and Madonna.

1434   Paints Arnolfini portrait (see text).

1435   Does the "coloring" of six of the statues on the façade of the Town Hall in Bruges.

1436   Paints van der Paele altar in Bruges.

1437   Style becomes increasingly austere: paints Saint Barbara.

1439   Paints Madonna of the Fountain, portrait of his wife Margaret, unsigned Madonna With Carthusian, perhaps completed by Petrus Christus.

1441   On July 9, the death of Jan van Eyck is inscribed in the records of the Church of Saint Donatianus in Bruges.

Suggested reading:
Hubert and Jan van Eyck, by Leo van Puyvelde (Scribner).
Jan Van Eyck, by Ludwig Baldoss (Phaidon).
The Van Eycks and Their Followers, by Martin Conway (Murray).
See also Flemish and Dutch Painting in general reading list (page 163).

VAN GOGH

Vincent van Gogh 1853-1890
Dutch-born Post-Impressionist

1853   Born March 30 in Groot-Zundert, the Netherlands, oldest child of Anna and Theodorus, a Calvinist country parson.

1857   His brother Théo is born.

1869   Enters employ of Goupil & Co. in The Hague, a firm of art dealers in which his uncle, also named Vincent, is a retired partner.

1872   The voluminous correspondence between Théo and Vincent begins.

1873   Is transferred to the London office of Goupil & Co. Begins drawing in his free time. Théo enters Goupil branch in Brussels.

1874   Depressed over rejection of his marriage proposal to the daughter of his landlady, returns to the Netherlands. His uncle arranges his

transfer to the Paris office.

1876   Is dismissed from Goupil's. Teaches and sells books—enjoying neither.

1877   Studies for admission to theological seminaries in Amsterdam and Brussels; fails entrance examinations; calls this period "the worst time of my life."

1879   Becomes a lay evangelist in the Borinage, Belgium's coal-mining area; is dismissed for his curious conduct and unreasonable zeal.

1880   Returns to Borinage, this time chiefly to draw the miners and their families. Decides to become a painter. Théo supports his art studies in Brussels, where he visits museum, studies anatomy and perpective.

1881   Spends summer in Etten with his family. Falls in love with a widowed cousin. Is again refused. Suffers deeply and renounces all worldly ambition. Determines to dedicate himself to art.

1882-   Paints at The Hague, studying under his cou-
1883   sin Anton Mauve, a well-known artist. Meets a poverty-stricken woman who is approaching the end of pregnancy. He lives with her and makes her family his own. When she returns to prostitution, he writes Théo: "She has never seen what is good, how can she be good." Moves to Drenthe to be closer to peasant life, which he determines to paint, in the tradition of Millet. Is in poor health.

1884-   Returns to his father's new vicarage at Nue-
1885   nen, where he completes some memorable studies of the local weavers. Family quarrels hasten his departure to Antwerp, where he almost starves. Visits the Rijksmuseum in Amsterdam. Deeply moved by the Rembrandts. His Potato Eaters is completed; he considers it a summation of his work and study to that time. Becomes increasingly interested in color; starves himself to buy paints.

1886   Arrives in Paris in February to live with Théo. During two years, studies and meets Pissarro, Seurat, Toulouse-Lautrec, Gauguin. Is influenced by the Impressionists' use of color and the design of Japanese prints. Paints landscapes outside Paris; increasingly interested in portraits; meets Pére Tanguy, who shows a few of his works.

1888   Leaves in February for Arles, tired of city life and the cold, gray climate. Is overwhelmed by the South, writing Théo: "I have never had such a chance, nature here being so extraordinarily beautiful. . . . Life is almost enchanted after all." Reaches his peak work here (The Sower, The Sunflowers, Starry Night, etc.). Also does best portrait work: The Postman, Roulin, The Arlésienne, etc. Invites Gauguin to join him in a cooperative "studio of the future." They quarrel continually. Finally, in a viclent frenzy the day be-

VAN GOGH: Self-portrait, c.1888, Study by Candlelight. Collection William Goetz, Hollywood. Oil.

fore Christmas, van Gogh cuts off part of his ear. Is hospitalized at Arles.

1889   Voluntarily commits himself to the asylum at Saint-Rémy in May. Spends a year working feverishly between attacks. Paints cheerless landscapes around the asylum; makes copies of works of Delacroix, Rembrandt and Millet from memory; does self-portraits (see text) and The Reaper, a premonition of his impending doom. Exhibits work at Salon des Indépendants.

1890   Théo arranges for him to stay with a Dr. Gachet at Auvers, an hour from Paris. A landscape is sold at Brussels (the only painting sale of his life). Is praised in Mercure de France. Leaves for Auvers on May 21. Is enthusiastic over new surroundings, but despairs of his own condition. Shoots himself in a field on July 27. Dies on July 29. Théo writes home: ". . . Oh, Mother! he was so my own, own brother." Is buried in a wheat field. Théo dies six months later, to be buried beside Vincent.

Suggested reading:
The Complete Letters of Vincent van Gogh, three volumes (New York Graphic Society).
Van Gogh, by Meyer Schapiro (Abrams).
Van Gogh, by Robert Goldwater (Pocket Library of Great Art).
See also Post-Impressionism in general reading list (page 163).

VELÁZQUEZ

Diego Rodríguez de Silva y Velázquez 1599-1660
Spanish Baroque Master

1599   Born in Seville of Portuguese ancestry, baptized on June 6. His father, Juan Rodríguez de Silva, is a lawyer.

1610   Begins apprenticeship to Francisco Pacheco.

VELÁZQUEZ: Self-portrait, detail, 1656, The Maids of Honor. Prado, Madrid, Oil.

1617   Applies for admission to the painters' Guild of St. Luke in Seville.

1618   Marries Pacheco's daughter, Juana de Miranda.

1619   Completes first dated painting, The Adoration of the Magi; is influenced by Caravaggio.

1622   Makes first trip to Madrid; is appointed Painter to King Philip IV and moves into the palace. This early fame is decisive, supplying steady royal patronage.

1628   Rubens visits the Spanish court and persuades Velázquez to visit Italy.

1629 Makes his first Italian trip; copies Renaissance masterpieces and is greatly influenced by the Venetians. Paints profusely, but makes no reputation in Italy. Sends home a completed work, *The Forge of Vulcan*.

1631 Returns to Spain; executes countless portraits and decorative projects of the court, as well as studies of dwarfs and buffoons.

1635 Paints *Surrender of Breda*—one of the best-known historical scenes in art—depicting the capture of a Netherlands town by the Spanish; work shows unequaled unity of composition, despite his making every figure a portrait.

1644 Accompanies Philip IV to Aragon, painting one of many portraits of him.

1648 Leaves on a second trip to Italy, where he paints a portrait of *Juan de Pareja* (see text) and one of Pope Innocent X, based on a work of El Greco. Purchases old Italian masters for Philip, does landscape studies of Medici gardens and returns to Madrid in June, 1651.

1651 Official duties as palace marshal take time away from his painting.

1656 Paints *The Maids of Honor*, in which he himself appears with brush and palette—the only authentic self-portrait of Velázquez.

1657 Paints *The Spinners*, widely regarded as the climax of his work. Shows unusual Impressionistic technique, transforming objects into phantoms of light.

1660 Attends the marriage of Maria-Theresa to Louis XIV on the Isle of Pheasants. Dies on August 6, reputedly from overfatigue after nuptial preparations.

Suggested reading:

Velázquez, by Aureliano de Beruete (Methuen).
Velázquez, by Elizabeth du Gué Trapier (Hispanic Society of America).
Velázquez, by José Ortega y Gasset (Random House).
Velázquez, by Margaretta Salinger (Pocket Library of Great Art).
See also National Surveys of Painting *(Spanish Painting)* in general reading list (page 163).

VERMEER

Johannes van der Meer, known as Jan Vermeer.
1632-1675
Dutch Genre Painter

Art experts and historians find it extremely difficult to determine the order of Vermeer's paintings. He himself dated only two pictures, *The Procuress*, 1656, and *The Astronomer*, 1668. His work is generally divided into three periods: EARLY WORK; of which *Christ in the House of Martha and Mary, Diana and Her Companions* and *The Procuress* are notable; GENRE SCENES: *Little Street, Girl Asleep, Woman Weighing Gold, View of Delft, Young Woman at the Casement*; FINAL PERIOD: *Love Letter, The Geographer* and a companion piece, *The Astronomer, Allegory of the New Testament* and two different versions of *Lady at the Virginal*.

1632 Born in Delft, Holland, to Reynier Janssoon, a silk weaver, picture dealer and innkeeper, and Dingnum Balthasars. Baptized on October 31.

1653 Marries Catharina Bolenes on April 5, at the age of 21. (Of this marriage, there are 11 children.) Enters the artists' guild of Delft. It is speculated that the test picture for admission to the guild is a large work on a Biblical theme: *Christ in the House of Martha and Mary* (now in Edinburgh). This is one of three large early paintings, distinctly different from the rest of his work; a mythological subject, *Diana and Her Companions*, and a genre painting, *The Procuress*, are the others. At some time in his early life, it is speculated, Vermeer goes to Italy; believed to have been influenced by Italian art, especially Caravag-

gio; otherwise, he never leaves Delft, except for one trip to Geoda in 1675, the year of his death.

1654 Powder magazine in Delft blows up, killing Carel Fabritius, a disciple of Rembrandt, with whom Vermeer studied.

1656 Paints *The Procuress*, one of only two paintings Vermeer dates.

1663 Balthasar de Monconys goes to see Vermeer in Delft, hoping to buy some paintings; but the artist has none to show him. He works very slowly, and his small output is quickly bought by a small group of collectors, mostly in Delft.

1668 Paints *The Astronomer*, second and last picture on which he paints the date.

1672 The art business, which Vermeer was forced to enter because of continual financial troubles, comes to an abrupt end.

1675 Dies at the age of 43, leaving his widow and 11 children with nothing but debts. Has appointed the famous scientist Anthony van Leeuwenhoeck, inventor of the microscope, as his executor; his friendship with Leeuwenhoeck shows his interest in optical research, reflected in his painting. Wife is forced to

VERMEER: *Believed to be a self-portrait (left)*, detail, The Procuress. *Picture Gallery, Dresden. Oil.*

give his paintings as payment for debts.

1866 Etienne Thoré-Bürger, French journalist, publishes three articles on Vermeer—and "discovers" him for the world.

Suggested reading:

Vermeer, by Lawrence Gowing (Faber & Faber).
Jan Vermeer, by Ludwig Goldscheider (Phaidon).
Vermeer of Delft, by Edward V. Lucas (Methuen).
Johannes Vermeer, Painter of Delft, by P. Swillens (Spectrum).
See also Flemish and Dutch Painting in general reading list (page 163).

VERONESE

Paolo Caliari, known as Veronese
1528-1588
Venetian Renaissance and Baroque Master

1528 Born in Verona (to which "Veronese" refers).

c.1538 First learns sculpture under his father Gabriele, a stone breaker (one who quarries marble).

1541 Begins to study painting with Antonio Badile, whose daughter he later marries. His early

VERONESE: *Self-portrait, 1573, detail*, Feast in the House of Levi. *Academy of Fine Arts, Venice. Oil.*

works show the influence of the Venetian-Veronese tradition, with a developed decorative sense.

1548 Does *Bevilacqua Lazise* altarpiece in Verona.

1551 Decorates the Sacristy of San Liberale, Castelfranco.

1553 Decorates the Villa Emo, Fanzalo.

1555 Settles in Venice, where he remains until his death, except for brief journeys. The *Transfiguration*, completed after two years, shows the influence of Raphael and Titian. Paints for the sacristy at San Sebastiano.

1560 Francesco Sansovino writes: "Paolo is beginning to make a name for himself as an excellent painter, an agreeable talker, a young man pleasant to consort with." Veronese becomes close friends with the architects, Palladio Sansovino and Scamozzi. His approach to life is that of an aristocrat born to the purple—as is evidenced throughout his work—although he is the son of a stone breaker.

c.1560 Works on famous feast scenes: *Supper at Emmaus* and *Wedding at Cana*.

c.1562 Does later versions of the above subjects.

1570 Paints mythological and allegorical subjects: *Venus and Mars, Wisdom and Strength* and *Vice and Virtue*.

1573 *Last Supper*, also called *Feast in the House of Levi*, shows maturity and richness of style. Is arraigned by the Inquisition for "having introduced such ludicrous figures as dwarfs, people dressed like Germans" into *Last Supper* (see text).

c.1575- Redecorates the Doges' Palace, Venice, after
1585 the fires of 1574 and 1577. Executes decorations for the Sala del Collegio, including the *Venice Enthroned With Justice and Peace*, and does the *Triumph of Venice*, for a palace ceiling. His decorative work leads to Italian Rococo style.

1588 Dies in Venice.

Suggested reading:

Paulo Veronese: His Career and Work, by Percy H. Osmond (Sheldon).
Paulo Veronese, by Nancy D. Bell (Newnes).
See also The Renaissance and National Surveys of Painting *(History of Italian Painting)* in general reading list (page 163).

100 BOOKS: SUGGESTED READINGS IN ART

This list of 100 books, arranged by periods and schools of art, is designed to help the reader who may be interested in widening his knowledge of painting and painters. It is limited to books available in English.

Books about specific painters will be found at the end of each painter's biography, on the preceding pages.

POPULAR REFERENCE WORKS AND ENCYCLOPEDIAS
Art in East and West, by Benjamin Rowland, Jr. (Harvard).
Art in the Western World, by David Robb and J. J. Garrison (Harper).
Art Through the Ages, by Helen Gardner (Harcourt, Brace).
A History of Western Art, by Erwin O. Christiansen (New American Press).
Men of Art, by Thomas Craven (Simon & Schuster).
Principles of Art History, by Heinrich Wölfflin (Dover).
The Story of Art, by E. H. Gombrich (Phaidon).
A Treasury of Art Masterpieces, by Thomas Craven (Simon & Schuster).
The Encyclopedia of Painting, edited by Bernard S. Myers (Crown).
The Picture History of Painting, by H. W. and D. J. Janson (Abrams).

ON ART AND AESTHETICS
Aesthetics and History, by Bernard Berenson (Doubleday).
Art, by Clive Bell (Putnam).
Art and Connoisseurship, by Max J. Friedländer (Beacon).
The Art in Painting, by Albert C. Barnes (Harcourt, Brace).
Artists on Art, by Robert Goldwater and Marco Treves (Pantheon).
Ideas and Images in World Art, by René Huyghe (Abrams).
The Language of Drawing and Painting, by Arthur Pope (Harvard).
Looking at Pictures, by Kenneth Clark (Holt).
Meaning in the Visual Arts, by Erwin Panofsky (Anchor).
A Social History of Art, by Arnold Hauser (Knopf).
The Taste of Angels: A History of Art Collecting from Ramses to Napoleon, by F. H. Taylor (Little, Brown).
Voices of Silence, by André Malraux (Doubleday).

NATIONAL SURVEYS OF PAINTING
Art and Life in America, by Oliver W. Larkin (Holt).
English Painting, by R. H. Wilenski (Branford).
French Painting, by R. H. Wilenski (Branford).
German Masters of Art, by Helen Dickinson (Stokes).
History of Italian Painting, by F. J. Mather, Jr. (Holt).
Spanish Painting, by E. Harris (Hyperion).

ORIENTAL ART
A Short History of Chinese Art, by Ludwig Backhofer (Pantheon).
Chinese Painting, by William Cohn (Phaidon).
The Enduring Art of Japan, by Langdon Warner (Harvard).
Japanese Colour Prints, by Wilfred Blunt (Pitman).
The Art of Indian Asia, by H. R. Zimmer and Joseph Campbell (Pantheon).
A Handbook of Muhammedan Art, by M. S. Dimand (Harvard).
Persian Painting, by Basil Gray (Skira).

THE GREAT CENTURIES OF PAINTING (A Skira Series)
(Highly readable surveys of the great epochs of Western painting. A more scholarly and detailed series—*The Pelican History of Art*, in 50 projected volumes—is currently being issued by Penguin Books.)
Lescaux, or the Birth of Art, by Georges Bataille.
Egyptian Painting, by Arpag Mekhitarian.
Greek Painting, by Martin C. Robertson.
Etruscan Painting, by Massimo Pallottino.
Roman Painting, by Amedeo Maiuri.
Byzantine Painting, by André Grabar.
Romanesque Painting, by Carl Nordenfalk and André Grabar.
Gothic Painting, by Jacques Dupont and Cesare Gnudi.
From Van Eyck to Botticelli, by Jacques Lassaigne and Giulio Argan.
From Leonardo to El Greco, by Lionello Venturi.
From Caravaggio to Vermeer, by Jacques Dupont and François Mathey.
From Watteau to Tiepolo, by François Fosca.
From Goya to Gauguin, by Maurice Raynal.

PICTURES FROM THE GREAT MUSEUMS (An Abrams Series)
Art Treasures of the Louvre, by René Huyghe.
Art Treasures of the Metropolitan, by the Curatorial Staff.
Art Treasures of the Pinakotek, by Ernst Buchner.
Art Treasures of the Prado, by Harry B. White.
Art Treasures of the Uffizi and Pitti, by Filippo Rossi.
Art Treasures of the National Gallery, London, by Sir Philip Hendy.
Great French Paintings in the Hermitage, by Charles Sterling.

MEDIEVAL ART
Art in the Early Church, by Walter Lowrie (Pantheon).
Art in Medieval France, by Joan Evans (Oxford).
Illuminated Manuscripts, by J. A. Herbert (Franklin).
Medieval Art, by C. R. Morey (Norton).

FLEMISH AND DUTCH PAINTING
Early Netherlandish Painting, by Erwin Panofsky (Harvard).
The Van Eycks and Their Followers, by Martin Conway (Murray).
From Van Eyck to Bruegel, by Max J. Friedländer (Phaidon).
Flemish Painting, by Jacques Lassaigne and Robert Delevoy (Skira).
Great Masters of Dutch and Flemish Painting, by Wilhelm Bode (Scribner).
Dutch Painting, by Jean Leymarie (Skira).

THE RENAISSANCE
The Creators of the Renaissance, by Lionello Venturi (Skira).
The Art of the Italian Renaissance, by Heinrich Wölfflin (Putnam).
The Art of the Renaissance in Northern Europe, by Otto Benesch (Harvard).
The Civilization of the Renaissance in Italy, by J. C. Burkhardt (Phaidon).
The Horizon Book of the Renaissance (Horizon Magazine and Doubleday).
Italian Painters of the Renaissance, by Bernard Berenson (Oxford).
Lives of the Artists, by Giorgio Vasari (Simon & Schuster).
The Medici, by G. F. Young (Modern Library).

EIGHTEENTH AND NINETEENTH CENTURIES
Rococo Age, by A. Schonberger and H. Soener (McGraw-Hill).
The Earthly Paradise, by Werner Hofmann (Braziller).
Landmarks in 19th Century Painting, by Clive Bell (Harcourt, Brace).
Nineteenth Century Painting, by John Rothenstein (Lane).
David to Delacroix, by Walter Friedländer (Harvard).

MODERN PAINTING
Modern Painting, by Maurice Raynal (Skira).
Masters of Modern Art, by Alfred H. Barr, Jr. (Doubleday).
Modern Art and the New Past, by James Thrall Soby (University of Oklahoma).
Since Cézanne, by Clive Bell (Harcourt, Brace).
What Is Modern Painting?, by Alfred H. Barr, Jr. (Museum of Modern Art).

IMPRESSIONISM AND POST-IMPRESSIONISM
The Century of the Impressionists, by Raymond Cogniat (Crown).
The History of Impressionism, by John Rewald (Museum of Modern Art).
French Impressionists, by Clive Bell (Phaidon).
Post-Impressionism: From Van Gogh to Gauguin, by John Rewald (Museum of Modern Art).

SURREALISM AND DADA
Dada and Surrealism, by Georges Hugnet (Museum of Modern Art).
History of Surrealist Painting, by Marcel Jean (Grove).
Dada Painters and Poets, edited by Robert Motherwell (Wittenborn).

ABSTRACT ART
Abstract Painting: Background and American Phase, by Thomas B. Hess (Viking).
The Tradition of the New, by Harold Rosenberg (Grove).

FAUVISM AND CUBISM
Fauvism, by Jean Leymarie (Skira).
The Rise of Cubism, by D. H. Kahnweiler (Wittenborn).
Cubism: A History of the Movement, by John Golding (Wittenborn).
Cubism and Abstract Art, by Alfred H. Barr, Jr. (Museum of Modern Art).

DRAWINGS
A Treasury of Drawings from Pre-History to Present, by Louis Lozowich (Lear).
One Hundred Master Drawings, by Agnes Mongan (Harvard).
Drawings Old and New, by Carl O. Schniewind (Art Institute of Chicago).
Great Draughtsmen from Pisanello to Picasso, by Jakob Rosenberg (Harvard).

ACKNOWLEDGMENTS

PERSONS

The material in this book was collected from a vast variety of sources and people, over a period of five years, and depended in no small measure upon the diligence of the following persons:

Leemarie Burrows Bernstein, who administered all arrangements for the photographing or reproduction of paintings, obtained technical data on each painting, negotiated permissions from museums, galleries and private owners throughout the world; *Charlotte Willard,* who conscientiously explored story possibilities for several dozen artists; *Selma Gordon Lanes,* who expertly conducted research, supervised the biographical chronologies in the appendix and compiled the recommended readings; *Phyllis Bernstein Kalb, Denise Aymonier, Doreen Kellams* and *Nancy Kiggins,* who researched many features; *David Maxey,* who helped organize the appendix.

Simonne Gauthier Finn-Bogasson, LOOK's representative in Paris, provided invaluable assistance by drawing upon her acquaintanceship with living painters, such as Braque and Chagall. *Mrs. Margaret Silberman* of New York, a frequent guest of Pablo Picasso at *La Californie,* interviewed Jacqueline Roque Picasso and provided material for the story behind *The Portrait of Madame Z.*

Jerry Burke, director of LOOK's research division, provided extra researchers in countless emergencies; *Frank Latham* and *Katharine R. O'Hare* applied their judgment and expertise as copy editors to innumerable questions of fact and interpretation.

William Rosivach was a tower of strength throughout the harassing vicissitudes of production; *William Townsend* supervised the many technicians in LOOK's art department during the usual crises of makeup, scheduling and remakes to which magazine publication is forever subjected.

TECHNICAL SOURCES

We are especially grateful for the invaluable cooperation and assistance, over a period of five years, by the staffs of: the Frick Art Reference Library, New York; the Art Reference Division of the New York Public Library; the Print Division of the New York Public Library; the division heads and information personnel of the Metropolitan Museum of Art, New York, and the Museum of Modern Art, New York; the curators and information officers of those museums and galleries in the United States, Europe, South America and Japan from whose collections we photographed paintings or arranged for reproduction permissions and rights (see below).

PHOTOGRAPHERS

The following photographers exercised their considerable technical skills, often under most trying conditions of lighting, space and physical discomfort, to provide us with color transparencies of the highest quality for paintings around the world: Ivor Ashmore, Frank Bauman, Pierre Belzeaux, Henry Beville, Richard Brittain, Robert Doisneau, Louis-Frederic, Hans Hinz, Laurent Jaulmes, Mike Lavelle, Erich Lessing, Erwin Meyer, Allen Mandelbaum, Ettore Naldoni, Arthur Rothstein, Savage Studio, Earl Theisen, Towne Studio, Heinz Zinram.

REPRODUCTION RIGHTS

We are most grateful to the following museums, galleries and individuals for granting us permission to photograph and/or reproduce paintings in their collections: Albright-Knox Art Gallery, Buffalo, N. Y.; Mr. and Mrs. Sidney F. Brody, Beverly Hills, Calif.; Chicago Art Institute; Church of Santo Tomé, Toledo, Spain; Department of Fine Arts, Carnegie Institute, Pittsburgh, Pa.; Earl of Radnor, Longford Castle, Salisbury, England; Frans Hals Museum, Haarlem, the Netherlands; Gallery Umeda, Osaka, Japan; Church of San Francesco, Assisi, Italy; Hermitage Museum, Leningrad; Hill-Stead Museum, Farmington, Conn.; British Museum, London; Hispanic Society of America, New York; Kunsthistorisches Museum, Vienna; the Louvre, Paris; Museum of Modern Art, New York; Mrs. Albert D. Lasker, New York; Musée du Petit Palais, Paris; Museum Toulouse-Lautrec, Albi, France; Museum Boymans/Vanbeuningen, Rotterdam; Metropolitan Museum of Art, New York; National Gallery, Washington, D. C.; National Gallery, Rome; National Gallery, London; Pablo Picasso; Philadelphia Museum of Art; John Work Garrett Library, Johns Hopkins University, Baltimore; Prado Museum, Madrid; San Marco Museum, Florence; Sir John Soane's Museum, London; Uffizi Gallery, Florence; the Vatican, Rome; Academy of Fine Arts, Venice; Wallraf-Richartz Museum, Cologne.

INDEX